One Step Ahead

Raising 3–12 year olds

MICHAEL GROSE

Newleaf

For Sue, Sam,
Emma and Sarah – my family

Home is where one starts from.
T. S. Eliot

Newleaf
an imprint of
Gill & Macmillan Ltd
Hume Avenue, Park West
Dublin 12
with associated companies throughout the world
www.gillmacmillan.ie

0 7171 3363 X
Printed by ColourBooks Ltd, Dublin

Published by arrangement with Random House Australia

The paper used in this book comes from the wood pulp of managed forests. For every tree felled, at least one tree is planted, thereby renewing natural resources.

A CIP catalogue record for this book is available from the British Library.

3 5 4 2

CONTENTS

INTRODUCTION

Increasingly children are discovering their voices and want to be heard. Many parents confuse this new voice with lack of respect and want to return to the good old days when children presumably knew their place. Or go back to a time when co-operation meant obedience and children hardly ever questioned the authority of their parents.

The democratic principles and practices outlined in *One Step Ahead* are as timely today as they were when the book was first released eight years ago. They provide parents with the framework to manage and lead children, and ultimately to help them take their place in a pluralistic society. Many parents confuse the notion of democratic parenting with a permissive approach where children are able to do as they please. Or they believe that to follow such an approach parents must offer children a smorgasbord of choices or they must discuss every little decision with their children. This is taking things too far. Children need effective and experienced leaders who have the wisdom to make decisions for the family but who also know when to involve their children. They also need parents who can set limits and resist children's attempts to change their minds. Democratic parenting is about wise leadership and effective behaviour management rather than about coercion and control or allowing children to do as they wish.

Two new sections have been added for this revised edition. A much needed chapter on bullying has been included to give parents advice on dealing with this problem that is still prevalent in schools. I have also included a chapter on puberty and adolescence so parents can prepare themselves and their children for this challenging stage of development.

The number of people who have told me that they like this book's down-to-earth, common sense approach has been flattering. It also means that I achieved my aim of giving practical advice about a range of problems and difficult behaviours that parents commonly face raising children in the three to twelve age group. I have used ideas that I have tried as a parent raising three lovely but lively children as well as ideas accumulated as a parent educator and seminar leader over the past twelve years.

I have resisted the temptation to write in terms of different family types such as sole parents, step-parents and dual parent families. The approach to family and child management outlined in this book is applicable to all family types.

Finally, parents tend to be a self-critical, anxious group so it is essential to be kind to yourself and resist the temptation to talk yourself down. Most of us are doing the very best job we can to raise our kids, and are trying to have a personal, and for many, a working life of our own. Children are not born holding a set of instructions or a glossy owner's manual for you to use. Much of our knowledge and skills come from trial and error. It is a hard job that we have volunteered for! Take pride in your accomplishments and gain pleasure from your children. I hope this book will help you do this.

Good luck and happy parenting.

Michael Grose
Spring, 2000

THE PRINCIPLES OF DEMOCRATIC PARENTING

1
DEMOCRATIC PARENTING

There's a monster in the house

A daily newspaper once ran this sensational headline over an article on the problems that parents face today. While the purpose of the headline was to grab attention, the content of the article was hardly startling. It repeated a message that we are hearing all too often – many parents need help raising their children.

The problems that many parents are experiencing relate to family living. There appears to be a common thread in the difficulties faced by parents – lack of co-operation between family members. This lack of co-operation is apparent when children refuse to eat, don't go to bed on time, fight and argue over every little issue, make constant demands on parents' time and through many common misbehaviours. Many parents appear to be in constant conflict with their children from breakfast to bedtime.

Conflict is not confined to the family home. Children find a host of public places, such as supermarkets and restaurants, to carry the good fight up to their parents. The temper tantrum, exhibited in many ways and in many public places, is a common occurrence. It is an effective form of emotional blackmail by children, usually ensuring that they have their own way.

Parents, at present, are in a dilemma. They are constantly made aware of the crucial role that they play in their children's development; society places high expectations on them to do their job adequately. They wear the mantle of blame for their children's inadequacies and misbehaviours. Yet, the traditional ways of influencing children clearly are inadequate in the present social climate. Even young children no longer accept their parents' judgement as absolute.

Why is there a problem?

It is clear that the traditional methods of raising children have become ineffective in recent decades. What has happened to render useless these methods of rearing children?

Many prominent theorists consider that rapid social and technological changes are the causes of parenting difficulties. Parents have reared their children since the dawn of time, often in conditions of great hardship. However, they have never had to do so in a time of such rapid economic, social and technological change as we are experiencing at present.

Today we are witnessing the emergence of democracy as a way of life rather than merely an abstract political principle. Persistent cries go up from parents and teachers for a return to the good old days, when kids knew their place and did as they were told. This is understandable. Many parents are experiencing great frustration as children increasingly fight against well intentioned demands. But it is futile to yearn for the good old days. Society as we know it has changed.

Social groups everywhere refuse to be dominated by other groups. Children, too, are no longer willing to accept an inferior status. Now that parents have begun to reject the autocratic family relationships of the past, children sense their equality and want to express it. The challenge for parents today is to find a replacement for the old autocratic model which is effective in developing co-operation in the family while still recognising the equal status of their children.

The traditional model of parenting, in which mother or father control their children, is being firmly challenged and rejected, even by very young children. The harder parents try to coerce and badger their children in the mistaken belief that they are doing what is best for them, the harder the youngsters fight back in the bid for recognition of equal status.

So what approach should parents take?

The principles of child raising developed by Austrian psychiatrist Alfred Adler early this century and refined by psychologist Rudolph Dreikurs in the United States in the 1960s are appropriate for use in the present social climate. The foundations of Adler's work are rooted in the principles of democratic living. He maintained that children are active decision makers who wish to control their own behaviours. This is not to say they can do as they want, regardless of the effect their behaviour has on others – that is permissive parenting, characterised by absolute freedom and no imposed order.

In a democratic family, children choose their own behaviour but must be allowed to experience the consequences of their decisions. Six-year-old Emma can choose not to eat dinner but she can expect no other food until breakfast is served. She is given the simple choice – to eat or not to eat – and she experiences the consequences of her decision. If she declines to eat she will probably feel hungry by bedtime and will learn that eating at mealtime has substantial benefits. She also learns that refusing to eat harms no one except herself. A permissive parenting approach would allow Emma not to eat her meal but a snack would be provided when the hunger pains begin. In the latter case the message is clear to Emma – she can do as she likes. An autocratic parent would force Emma to eat her meal. Each mouthful would take on the proportions of an epic movie: 'One more bite?' 'No!' Emma learns that her mother is more concerned about her eating than she herself is, and one more weapon is placed in her armoury.

Many parents have difficulty allowing children to choose their actions because they feel responsible for their children's behaviour. They therefore demand obedience, which inevitably leads to conflict. It is essential to remember that each person is responsible for his or her own behaviour. Parents are accountable for their own actions and it is wise to allow children to be responsible for theirs. It thus makes sense to free rather than control children so they may learn by the application of natural and logical consequences.

The parenting approach presented in this book is one that promotes democratic relationships, offers children realistic choices and encourages them to participate in family decision-making processes. Conflicts are resolved through sharing, discussion and trial and error rather than through arbitrary decision making by parents.

Features of democratic parenting

The following chapters outline the characteristics of the democratic approach to raising children. There are five principles that form the foundations of this exciting approach.

Social equality

The dominant democratic value is social equality. This means that, regardless of age, gender, race or religion, all people have the right to determine their own behaviours. Although children are not as experienced or skilled as their parents, they share the same right to decide their own behaviours. They do, however, require parental guidance to choose socially acceptable behaviours. Guidance, stimulation and influence rather than direct control are a parent's best strategies in our democratic climate.

Mutual respect

An essential basis for equality within adult–child relationships is mutual respect. This implies that parents and children respect each other's rights and dignity while maintaining respect for themselves. To gain respect from children it is essential that you treat them fairly and also that you respect yourself. For instance, when children are persistently noisy and boisterous in the family room, a respectful parent would withdraw permission to use that area for a reasonable period of time. This demonstrates self-respect – the parent is unwilling to put up with disturbing behaviour. It is respectful to children – it teaches them in a reasonable yet effective manner that the behaviour is unacceptable. A parent who smacks the offenders and locks them in their bedrooms shows little regard for the children's self-respect. This is also an impractical approach, as it invites the children to retaliate against such action.

Mutual respect is developed through the use of firmness and kindness. Kindness expresses respect for children and firmness gains their respect.

Shared responsibility

In a democratic family, parents and children share the responsibility for the maintenance of the family unit. Decisions regarding the family are made by all its members. The everyday routine of maintaining a household is shared according to age, ability and time available to each member to contribute to the running of the household.

Self-discipline

In a democratic family, children are able to decide their own behaviours but they must experience the consequences of any behaviour that violates natural or social order. A three-year-old who throws a temper tantrum will soon learn such a behaviour is futile if her mother leaves the scene each time the howls begin. Children generally modify their own behaviour if the consequences of their actions are unpleasant or of little benefit to them.

Co-operation

This term is often misunderstood by parents and teachers. In many cases a child who behaves exactly as his parents require is deemed to be co-operative. Co-operation is often confused with obedience. Co-operation is a group-oriented notion. In a co-operative family, children and parents work together to accomplish what is best for all. A co-operative person is concerned about the welfare of other people. Eight-year-old Thomas is being co-operative when he turns the television down because his father is taking a business phone call in the next room. Thomas recognises that his father needs a little silence and responds accordingly.

The benefits of democratic parenting

At a recent seminar I posed this question: 'What is your greatest concern as parents?' Almost unanimously the participants expressed the fear of raising children during the time of adolescence. Teenagers are exposed to many situations that require balanced judgement and the ability to make decisions. The stakes are high with this age group, the decisions involving issues such as alcohol, sex and drugs.

Clearly, parents need to provide children with a solid grounding in decision making if they are to steer successfully through the minefield of adolescence. Parents must also establish healthy relationships with their children so that they will make reasoned decisions about their behaviour rather

Features of democratic parenting

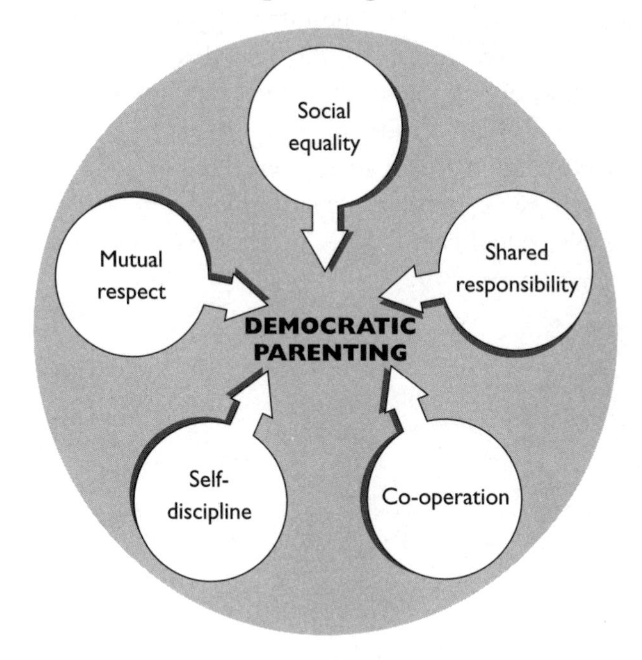

than make decisions just to spite their parents.

Democratic parents are more likely to raise responsible children who learn self-reliance at an early age. I asked a group of parents: 'At what age do we give responsibility to our children?' The participants were stunned at this and fumbled for appropriate responses. As soon as a child is able to walk he is able to assume some responsibility and become a contributing member of the family. When a toddler is undressed he should be handed the soiled clothing, and pointed in the direction of the laundry. The youngster learns that he must begin to contribute to his own welfare.

The ultimate aim of parents is to rear self-reliant individuals who are able to be autonomous adults. This self-reliance does not magically occur at the age of eighteen. The seeds are sown at infancy and continue to be nurtured throughout childhood. Responsible children are generally happy youngsters, secure in the knowledge that they are valued, contributing members of their families. They are less likely to misbehave, as they have no need to gain parental approval through constant attention seeking or power plays to prove their sense of worth. Harmonious relationships and responsible children are features of democratic families.

2
UNDERSTANDING CHILDREN'S BEHAVIOUR

Many parents are puzzled by the behaviour of their children. One minute youngsters can be co-operative little angels and the next minute absolute monsters. Such inconsistency can be baffling to parents trying to understand their children's behavioural changes. It is a constant source of amazement to most parents too that their children can all have different personalities, behaviour patterns and interests. One child may be an extrovert, another an introvert. One rough, the other kind and gentle. One child may be successful at school, while the other may prefer to concentrate on sport. Why do siblings differ so greatly when they have been raised using similar methods? It is a common assumption of many parents that children's differences can be accounted for by the fact that they inherit different traits. However, although heredity factors certainly play a part in children's personality make-up, to assume that children are victims of their parents' genes or even of their environment is to exclude a vital factor: children are thinking, social human beings who are able to determine their own behaviour.

To understand children we need to be aware of the motivating factors that influence the way they behave. The following ideas, based on Alfred Adler's research, provide an excellent framework for understanding children's behaviour.

The need to belong

We are all social beings. The basic motivation for all people is the desire to feel that they belong to a variety of social groups. The family is the first and most significant group that a child wishes to belong to. The initial task for youngsters is to find a place within the family – all their behaviour is directed to achieving a feeling of belonging within their families. From infancy children explore ways that will provide them with a sense of significance within the family group. Much of children's behaviour in the formative years is experimental. They explore behaviours that will gain parental recognition and acceptance. A baby soon learns that the best way to please her father is by smiling, whereas her mother can be summoned quickly with a blood-curdling wail. Young children will develop a repertoire of behaviours that gain recognition from parents and will eradicate those behaviours that have little effect. The behaviours that satisfy a child's need to belong do not have to be constructive or positive. Whingeing may seem senseless to a parent but it may be very useful to a child, gaining the desired attention. The essential criterion for any behaviour is that it satisfies a child's need to belong.

The message for parents is obvious. It is vital that feedback be given for behaviour that is useful and withheld for misbehaviour. A child can gain a sense of belonging either through co-operative behaviour that contributes to the family's well-being or through misbehaviour. How many families have a child who is a pest or a 'problem child'? These children find that misbehaviour works extremely effectively in terms of belonging.

Parents need to provide opportunities for children to contribute to family life in positive ways. As soon as children are physically able they should be encouraged to perform simple personal and group chores. When children believe that they can be functioning members of their family, they will employ positive ways of belonging to their most significant social group. A youngster who is discouraged from contributing to family life in constructive ways will soon learn that it is easier to belong to his family through misbehaviour.

A child's uniqueness

Each person views the world differently and reacts to daily situations in a variety of ways. Adults have developed established patterns of relating to people and encountering situations which reflect their personalities or psychological lives. These patterns remove the trial and error from our responses to various events that occur daily in our lives. This blueprint for living is formed in the first five or six years of life.

A child's unique personality characteristics are influenced by environmental and heredity factors but the most significant factor is a child's family position. As children are social beings, they are influenced by others around them. Within a family the development of a child's personality is influenced by parents and siblings. Each child is born into a different social environment, which is determined by those born before and those children who may follow.

Birth order

There are five recognised positions within a family. Each position has a corresponding set of characteristics.

First-born

For a year, at least, first-born children receive undivided attention from parents and grandparents. This position is almost regal and definitely worth preserving. The arrival of a second child alters this idyllic situation. A rival for attention is now in the family. Subsequently, eldest children spend a great deal of time and energy continuing to be first. They try hard to regain the honoured position of number one that has been removed by the arrival of the second-born. Eldest children frequently develop the notion that they belong in their family by being first or being the best. They will often take on tasks that will demonstrate their ascendancy over others. First-born children, in an effort to demonstrate their superiority, will often put down the second-born at every opportunity. First-borns often value power as a way of demonstrating their superiority over their younger siblings. It is no coincidence that many eldest children can be extremely bossy when young and argumentative when they are older.

Second-born

The second child is often born into a competitive atmosphere, due to the pressure exerted by the elder sibling. He or she is born in an inferior position and attempts to catch up with the older child. Second-born children tend to live life on the run. They often walk, talk and leave the nappies behind far earlier than their older siblings. Due to the competitive nature of this relationship, second-born children frequently adopt behaviours and characteristics that are the exact opposite of the first-born child's. In their search for significance within their family, first- and second-born children frequently excel in different areas and develop different personalities. Often, when the eldest child is responsible and pleasant, the second will gain a place in the family by being the troublemaker. The eldest child will delight in this situation and will make sure that parents are aware of any misdemeanours. The eldest will often block efforts for the second-born to contribute constructively to the family.

Youngest child

The position of last-born children places them at the foot of the family. They have older siblings who are both more capable and generally keen to help take care of them. They tend to be less competitive than their older brothers and sisters. Often youngest children develop cuteness as a characteristic and become experts at pleasing people and gaining attention. These children often have difficulty developing independence, surrounded as they are by older and more able siblings who are willing to provide assistance when called upon. It frequently takes these children a long time to shake off the 'baby of the family' tag.

Middle child

The middle child in a family of three is often in an extremely difficult position. This child has neither the advantages of the first nor the youngest. Often the eldest and the youngest child form an alliance against the middle child, who competes against both of them. Middle children often feel that life is unfair and frequently present the most difficulty to parents.

Only child

Only children spend much of their early years in the company of adults, so it is not surprising that they tend to develop characteristics that please their elders. Only children often have difficulty forming relationships with other children, which is understandable – they have had no experience with children in their family. Only children often either develop precocity due to their constant exposure to adult company or become spoilt and pampered individuals.

Children in families form alliances or compete with each other according to birth order and age differences. An alliance is evident when children develop similar behavioural and character traits. Competition between siblings is indicated by differences in interests and personality.

Purposeful behaviour

Parents are often confused about their children's behaviour. They cannot understand why a child may be lazy, stubborn or have an eating problem. It is better to look for the purpose behind a child's misbehaviour rather than ask 'Why?' The key to understanding behaviour lies in the purpose of children's activities. Children are lazy only when someone is willing to do things for them. A child will be stubborn if his parents are intent on controlling him. A child will develop an eating problem if her parents are concerned about the quantity and nature of the food she eats. All misbehaviour has the purpose of involving parents either directly or indirectly. Look at children who constantly fight and argue with each other. Parents usually become involved at some point in the dispute, whether it is to separate the combatants or to come to the aid of the 'victim'.

By focusing on the end result of misbehaviour, parents can react in ways that prevent it from achieving its purpose. Parents must change their ways of reacting to misbehaviour if they are to change their children's behaviour.

Goals of misbehaviour

Misbehaviour generally achieves one of four goals. When children feel that they cannot belong to their family through contribution or that their efforts are not valued, they will seek to belong through misbehaviour.

Attention

The most common goal of misbehaviour is attention. If a child wants to keep people busy with him and be noticed all the time, he is pursuing the goal of attention. This child reasons, 'I know I belong when I can keep others in my family busy with me.' Attention-seeking behaviour takes a multitude of forms including untidiness, showing off, nagging and crying. This goal is easy to identify, as parents feel annoyed or irritated by the activity.

Power

Children who pursue the goal of power want to assert their authority over their parents. The aim of power-seekers is to defeat their parents or to demonstrate that they can't make them do anything that they do not want to do. Power-drunk children frequently argue, throw temper tantrums and procrastinate in an effort to assert their authority over parents. Parents generally feel angry and challenged when confronted by power-seeking behaviour.

Retaliation

A less common but more difficult goal to deal with is retaliation. Some children who feel hurt or that they have been treated unjustly by family members will exhibit behaviour that hurts those around them. To hurt people, the revenge-seeker may hit, steal, refuse to co-operate, say spiteful things, or argue with others. The behaviour varies but the goal is the same. Parents when confronted with retaliatory behaviour feel hurt inside. They usually feel that they wish to get even with their children for wanting to hurt them.

Withdrawal

Children who are extremely discouraged or who possess a low self-esteem often try to lower others' expectations of them. These children feel that they are not worth much and may have been subject to humiliation in the past. They demonstrate behaviour that lowers other people's expectations of them in order to avoid further humiliation or hurt. Children who pursue the goal of withdrawal try to avoid feelings of failure by impressing others with their hopelessness. Parents feel helpless when confronted with behaviour that achieves this goal. 'I just don't know what to do with her any more' is a typical parental response to this goal.

As difficult as it may seem, parents should not respond to children in ways that satisfy the goal or purpose of their misbehaviour. They must stop giving undue service to attention-seekers, cease fighting with power-seekers, avoid showing hurt when confronted with retaliatory behaviour and not give up on or lower expectations of children who try to escape situations by withdrawing. By continually reacting to behaviour in predictable ways, parents maintain the misbehaviour of children – their goals are being satisfied. To change children, parents must first change themselves.

3
DEVELOPING RESPONSIBILITY IN CHILDREN

The most effective way of teaching children to be responsible is to give them responsibility. Children need to feel that they are accountable for their own behaviour and that they can make a significant contribution to the well-being of their family.

Towards independence

A major objective of parents is to raise responsible, independent children. Many parents make the mistake of leaving the development of independence to the teenage years. They ignore this important aspect in the children's formative years. If children have been given little responsibility as youngsters, they often find it hard to cope with the difficulties of adolescence. Many parents thrust enormous responsibilities on the shoulders of adolescents in an effort to develop independence. This type of training needs to start at a young age and continue into the teenage years.

Children like to feel useful by playing a significant role in the organisation and maintenance of the household. They like to help but they are often discouraged from contributing – they are considered too small for certain tasks or they can't do them as well as their older siblings. Often, in the mistaken belief that they are acting in their children's best interests, parents perform tasks for children that children are capable of doing themselves. The desire to be good parents needs to be replaced by the desire to be *responsible* parents.

Well-meaning parents don't always act in children's best interests. Consider the following two mothers' approaches to a similar situation. One is a 'good' parent who does not wish her daughter to experience hardship or discomfort and the other is a parent who wants her daughter to take responsibility for her actions.

Nine-year-old Megan left her lunch in the refrigerator when she left for school. Her mother noticed the lunch when she put away the milk from Megan's breakfast. She did not want her daughter to be hungry at lunchtime, so she drove to school and ducked into class to deliver it. Megan's mother blamed herself for not reminding her daughter to pack her lunch, although she noticed with interest that Megan remembered to put a packet of chips and a chocolate in her bag for a snack at recess.

Ten-year-old Litza left her lunch on the bench at home. Her mother noticed this and put it in the refrigerator so that it would remain fresh until she came home. Litza's mother believed that it was her daughter's responsibility to pack the lunchbox. If she became hungry at lunchtime then she would be more likely to remember to take it to school than if her mother brought it to her. Litza's mother realised that being hungry was her daughter's problem and seized on this as a valuable opportunity to promote a sense of responsibility in Litza for her own well-being. This mother also displayed confidence in her daughter's ability to handle some of life's smaller inconveniences without assistance.

Giving responsibilities to children is a great form of encouragement. It demonstrates our belief in their abilities to perform tasks. A parent who allows a four-year-old to choose her own clothes with guidance but not interference displays tremendous faith. The message is clear to the child: 'Mum thinks I am OK.' This is great for a child's self-esteem.

Children can help themselves

Children are very capable human beings if we allow them to be. They are able to do a vast array of tasks, although not always with the same skill as adults. Many parents feed toddlers themselves rather than put up with the mess that learner feeders usually make. Children will soon become proficient feeders if they are allowed to feed themselves. The inevitable mess will decrease with practice.

Parents need to be alert to children's readiness and willingness to do things for themselves. When a young child begins to use the soap in the bath, an astute parent will teach the child where to wash and gradually give this task to the child. Often a child may need to repeat the washing procedure if he is still caked in grime. This is all part of the learning process.

Similarly, children should be encouraged to be responsible for their own morning routines. When they can tell the time, they should be given an alarm clock and shown how to use it. The experience of regulating the morning routine teaches children a great deal about responsibility. They may miss breakfast or be late for school sometimes but the consequences will be unpleasant and they will regulate their routine accordingly.

When children are assigned tasks, parents should assume the role of teacher, providing positive guidance. For instance, a six-year-old child who makes her own bed may need considerable assistance. Her efforts, however imperfect, should be encouraged and accepted as genuine attempts to contribute. A parent using a commonsense approach may make the bed once a week and allow the youngster to be responsible for its maintenance on the other six days.

Family chores

A basic premise of democratic parenting is that children need to feel that they are useful members of their family. Parents should ensure that children have the opportunity to contribute to the well-being of their family. This is not merely good training for later years. It ensures that they are functioning members whose contribution to family life is valued.

Family chores can be shared among all members according to age, skill and availability of time. Toddlers are generally enthusiastic and able helpers around the house. Simple tasks such as setting the table, collecting mail, washing eating utensils and answering telephones are generally eagerly performed by most preschoolers. They provide ideal learning experiences for children who are developing new motor and language skills.

Primary-school children are able to assist with a wide range of useful tasks too numerous to mention. However, parents often have difficulty making children help around the house. To avoid conflict, parents often stop asking reluctant children to help. 'It is easier to do it myself' is the lament of many parents.

Children need to learn that co-operation within a family means that all pull their weight. With a little planning parents can allow children to experience the consequences of non-co-operation and effectively impress upon them the importance of doing chores (see page 120).

4
TEACHING AND TRAINING

Children's first teachers are their parents and their first classroom is the family home. As a child begins school, the importance of parents' teaching roles doesn't diminish – they are merely supplemented by a more formal approach to learning.

Children develop a wide range of abilities in their formative years. They need to develop social and physical skills, a set of values and language abilities that will enable them to communicate effectively with adults and peers. The role of parents in the development of these skills and values is extremely important.

Social skills

Young children challenge the view that the sun is the centre of the universe. They believe that everything revolves around them. As they grow older they learn that other people are just as significant as they are. When they begin to mix with other children and adults they learn that not everything goes their way. Children develop skills that enable them to socialise effectively with others.

Sharing

The ability to share time, space and toys should be encouraged from the earliest possible age. The ability to share is essential for success at school and is a prerequisite for the formation of friendships. Parents can teach the skills of sharing by encouraging siblings to play group games, swap toys and play co-operatively together in the house or in the backyard.

Children must learn that life is full of give and take. The earlier that they learn this concept, the happier they will be and the more able they will be to form friendships with adults and peers.

Behaviour in public

Many parents dread taking their children to shopping centres, on train rides and to friends' houses for fear of being embarrassed by the behaviour of their children in public. However, it is part of life for children to accompany parents to public places and they should be expected to behave according to the demands of the situation. When shopping at the supermarket, for example, it is reasonable to expect children to behave in a way that allows their parents to complete the task quickly and effectively without interference. Before venturing into public, parents need to clearly explain to children the behaviour that is expected of them. If the behaviour falls below the acceptable level, then the trip should be abandoned if possible. When children behave well in public, they should be encouraged for helping to make the visit or shopping trip a pleasant experience.

The development of good manners is often overlooked by parents. Good manners are an essential social skill and need to be constantly encouraged. Recently I witnessed a terrific example of a parent teaching this important social skill. A seven-year-old girl yelled at her father, 'Get my bike out of the shed!' Her father continued his conversation with his visitor, ignoring the demand. Incensed, the child persisted. 'Dad, I can't get my bike out of the shed. Can you get it?' Her father ignored the request. Realising that she had taken the wrong approach, she tried again. 'Excuse me Dad, could you please get my bike out of the shed? It is too hard for me to do.' 'Certainly, Alyssa,' her father replied. He was only to happy to assist his daughter when a polite approach was used.

Alyssa's father controlled his own behaviour in order to influence his daughter. He was able to elicit a reasonable response from her by failing to respond to her inappropriate demands. He did not harangue her or remind her to ask him properly. He showed through his actions that he was willing to assist her only when manners were used.

Physical skills

Seven-year-old Theo was unable to tie his shoelaces. He was physically capable of the task but he had not been taught the correct procedure. He refused to have swimming lessons at school because he feared that his friends would find out that he couldn't tie his shoelaces. His teacher, upon investigation, discovered the reason for his reluctance to participate in the swimming program. At lunchtime, away from the other children, the teacher showed Theo how to tie his shoelaces. The child learned the skill in no time.

Coping with shoelaces is one of the more basic physical skills that parents can teach children. It is part of a parent's role to ensure that children are able to perform the variety of physical skills required of them. Careful explanation, assistance, demonstration and practice are generally required to teach children these physical skills.

Values

As human beings we have a system of values that governs our behaviour, including the way we treat others. Many values, such as 'All people should be treated in a fair and equal manner', are part of our culture. Other values, such as 'Sport is a useful pursuit', are peculiar to individuals or specific groups such as families.

Children gain their values from a variety of sources. Family, friends and school are common sources of values. Sometimes children will value ideas that are different from those of their parents although, generally, young children's beliefs and ideas about the world align fairly closely with those of their parents. As parents provide models for children, it is important for them to be clear about the types of attitudes and beliefs that they display. Recently, a mother complained that her nine-year-old son refused to wash the dishes, claiming that it was women's work. I asked her if her husband shared this belief. The answer was an adamant 'Yes!' In this case the child's belief about gender roles was strongly influenced by the values of his father, with whom he strongly identified.

A father expressed his concern over his son's lack of competitiveness in sport and at school. The father, a successful businessman, believed that a competitive spirit should be a necessary ingredient in his son's make-up. This was a great source of conflict between the two, as the child did not share the same belief. He enjoyed Little Athletics but couldn't see the point of winning all the time. He enjoyed participating rather than competing. This difference in values should have been tolerated by the father and seen as an important step toward independence by his son.

Language

Language skills develop from the cradle. Children hear their parents talk and they respond to simple commands. As infants grow they begin to make simple sounds, which are first attempts at words. Toddlers begin to use single words, groups of words, then finally simple sentences. Language is a developmental process but children must hear language in order to speak.

Children learn to speak when they are spoken to, so parents need to speak to children at every opportunity. There is little need to correct grammar constantly if parents provide good models of speech. It is more beneficial if parents provide opportunities for children to talk, listen to what they have to say and give them feedback.

Similarly, reading and writing skills can be encouraged by parents who share stories with children, show an interest in their efforts at school and provide good role models for them to copy.

Parents as teachers

The training role of parents should be an enjoyable process rather than a chore. An effective teacher generally makes learning tasks fun and enjoys sharing time with children. A father recently stated that he spent a great deal of his recent holiday teaching his six-year-old son how to swim. The boy had improved only marginally but they both had fun together at the beach. The swimming had improved but the relationship was the big winner.

Guidance

Children respond better when they are guided and directed rather than have their faults constantly pointed out. Learning any skill can be a protracted process which requires encouragement rather than negative comments. A mother who taught her five-year-old son to set the table, giving brief instructions before the task, ignored the knife and fork which he misplaced. She commented only on the fact that he had been a great help to her. The next time the boy performed the task she reminded him about the knife and fork. He again mixed them up but he was happy to try again. With further practice and encouragement he completed this simple task correctly. This mother taught her child a skill without pointing out any errors. She avoided negative comments, which could easily have discouraged him.

Building on skills

An effective teacher or coach assesses a child's level of skill and builds from that base. It is pointless trying to teach a young child how to make a bed if she can't smooth out the sheets or tuck in a blanket. A three-year-old is capable of arranging her pillow on a bed, so this is a good place to start when teaching her to make a bed. The task can be extended as the necessary skills are developed.

A good teacher breaks complex skills into smaller tasks which are easy to master. A four-year-old can be taught how to wash himself by breaking the activity into small tasks: first the face, then the tummy, hands and so on.

Daily routine

Parents have a daily routine which may include such activities as cooking, washing, ironing, eating, showering and the like. Teaching and training should be part of that routine. It takes some thought, time and effort but these are justified by the results as children learn a variety of skills that develop responsibility and independence.

5
ENCOURAGING CHILDREN

Children who constantly misbehave generally feel discouraged and have a fragile sense of self. They find it easier to feel significant at home or at school by misbehaving. Remember your school days? No one ever took much notice of that quiet little girl who sat at the back of the room in the third grade: What was her name? But everybody knew about the loud-mouth who loved to tease the girls and annoy the teachers. He wasn't much good at his school work; he had given up trying. He was an expert at being a pest, however. He worked hard at that task with great success.

What about the quiet girl at the back of the class? She didn't have to attract unnecessary attention to feel worthwhile. She worked hard in school and reaped the benefits. Her self-image was positive. She was a girl who received plenty of encouragement both at home and at school.

Many children feel discouraged from succeeding at school and in the home, so they behave in unacceptable ways in order to feel significant and boost their flagging egos. A parent's prime purpose is to raise independent, self-reliant, happy people. The key to this is encouragement. Parents must explore ways which enable children to develop an 'I'm OK' feeling. Children with positive self-images are not deterred by failure. They are willing to take risks. An error is seen as a chance to try again, whether it is reading a book, tying shoelaces or throwing goals in a basketball game.

Build self-esteem

Children gain their self-esteem from those around them. Parents act as their mirrors. If you let a child know through your words and behaviour that she is stupid then she will grow up believing that she isn't worth much. It is so important for children to have someone they value believe in them. Parents are in an ideal position to influence a child's self-esteem. Encouraging parents have a positive outlook on life and believe in children's abilities. They believe that children can make correct decisions and can learn from their errors. They are undeterred by children's misbehaviour and focus on worthwhile behaviours. They see a glass of water as half full rather than half empty.

Realistic expectations

Encouraging parents have realistic expectations of their children. If you expect too much of children they will become discouraged when they can't reach your aspirations. Recently, I encountered a father who was experiencing great difficulty with his eleven-year-old son. The father was a doctor with high aspirations for his boy. He wished that the child would follow in his footsteps. The son had been struggling at school since his early years. As he completed each grade, the task of following in his father's footsteps grew harder and harder. By Year 6 the boy had decided that he couldn't succeed in the way his father wished, so he gave up trying and developed a 'behaviour problem'. His father, in the belief that he was acting in his son's best interests, badgered, bullied and criticised him. Unfortunately, it was all to no avail. The father did not realise that the standard he had set for his son to reach was beyond his capabilities, which was why the child gave up trying. It was far easier to misbehave than to strive for unrealistic goals. Parents' expectations should be aimed just above children's current abilities rather than where adults want them to be. It is reasonable to expect a five-year-old to make a bed by smoothing a doona and straightening the pillow. It is probably unrealistic to ask him to smooth out every crease in the sheets and fold hospital corners.

Give children responsibility

Believe it or not, children love being given responsibility. They readily respond to being given tasks which allow them to feel important. When you give children responsibility you send a message: 'I believe that you can do this.' Unfortunately, parents and teachers often give important tasks to the children who do not really need encouragement – the achievers. They do this because they know the responsibility will be accepted and the task performed successfully. Think back to the last time you had an important job to be done. Did you give the task to the eldest or most skilled child? Or was the youngest child or a less confident child given the chance to take the responsibility? Chores and responsibilities need to be shared between all members of a family.

Value risk-taking

Children are often afraid to take risks because they do not wish to make mistakes. They may believe that if they cannot do a task well they are failures or will be ridiculed. As a result children avoid participating in many activities that are threatening or offer the potential for failure. 'No way, I'm not going in the school play. I am not going to make an idiot of myself in front of the whole school!' declared Phillip. One wonders if Phillip will spend a lifetime avoiding new or threatening situations in an effort to protect his fragile ego.

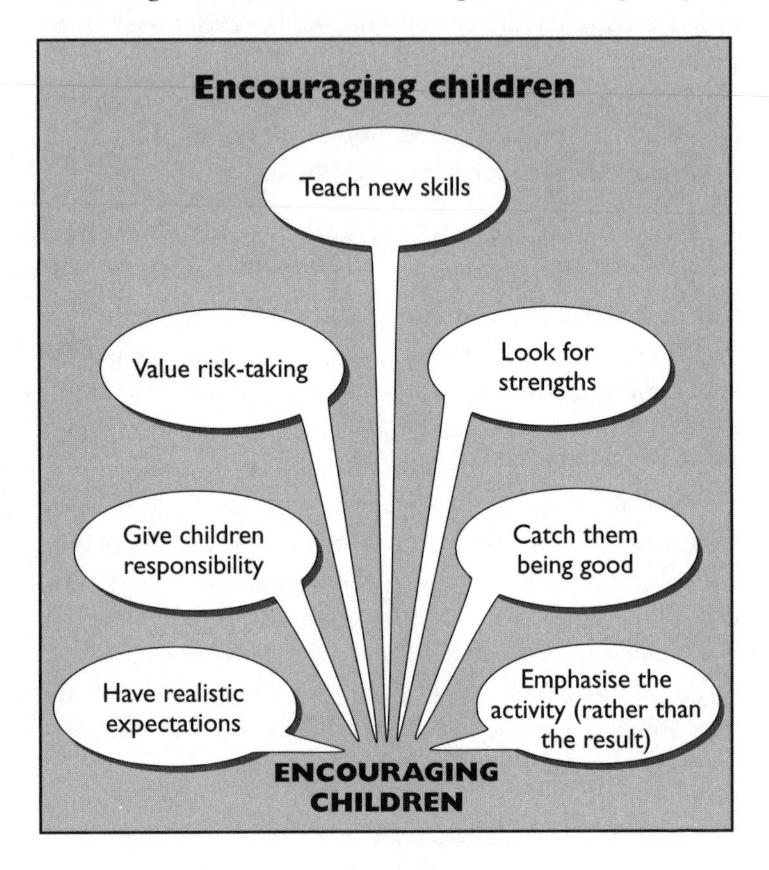

Parents need to show children that errors are acceptable. Mistakes are part of learning – ask any sportsperson. It is vital that we encourage children to take sensible risks so that they may extend themselves. Children need to be given the chance to 'mess up' so that they see errors as part of learning and developing new skills. It is important that children realise that their efforts do not always have to measure up to lofty adult standards.

Recently I encountered a mother who encouraged her five-year-old daughter to accept challenges and take risks. The child announced to her mother that she wanted to unpack the dishwasher. Her mother took a deep breath, looked at the contents of the wash and nodded her head in agreement. Wisely, she removed a couple of valuable items and made a hasty retreat from the kitchen. To her relief, the child completed the task successfully. From that day, the girl has taken complete charge of the dishwasher. She breaks the odd item but this is a minor consideration compared to the pride that she gains from her accomplishment.

Another parent, sensing her eleven-year-old daughter's interest in shopping, asked the child to compile the weekly buying list. The girl accepted the challenge with enthusiasm. Her keenness did not diminish when they both returned from the shopping trip, restocked the shelves and noticed that breakfast cereal had been left off the list. They both laughed at the omission and hastily checked that there was enough bread for toast. The wise parent ignored the error and focused on her daughter's achievement. The next week, when the girl compiled the shopping list, her mother noticed that cereal was the first item written.

It is important to allow children to take sensible risks and learn that mistakes are a part of growing up. Mistakes are to be expected if challenges are to be accepted.

Teach new skills

The art of encouragement takes many forms. Consider the concerned father who was placed in a dilemma by his ten-year-old daughter, Francesca. She wanted to ride her bike to school, but he thought it out of the question, given the dangerous nature of the route and her inexperience as a bicycle rider. He had great faith in her common sense, however, and he did not wish to discourage her. He devised a plan which would give her the skills and experience required to ride to school. He broke the journey into a series of small trips, each ride building on the previous trip. As Francesca completed each stage successfully her father extended the journey. After four months she was able to ride her bike safely to school. Her father was positive in his approach to her request and creative in his response. She appreciated the faith her father showed in her and was diligent in her application to the tasks set.

Look for strengths

Some years ago I enlisted a tennis coach to improve my flagging game. At the conclusion of the first lesson he told me about my weak backhand. He pinpointed all my flaws and didn't mention one strength. I left the first lesson feeling more discouraged than when I arrived. I decided that he could keep my money and I looked for another coach. I eventually found a suitable instructor. During the first hit-up he praised my forehand drives and drew attention to the crispness of my volleys. He then suggested we needed to work on my backhand, which was extremely fragile, to say the least. This coach had the wisdom to identify my strengths before trying to improve my obvious weaknesses. Generally, we only improve when we feel a measure of confidence.

Similarly, parents need to focus on what children can do rather than their deficiencies. Children will only improve in any behaviour or skill if they are confident that they can succeed. Criticism or continual exposure to deficiencies will only erode confidence, which is an essential element for success.

Eight-year-old Donna was having difficulty learning to

embroider. She presented her work to her mother, who ignored the misplaced stitches and drew attention to the work as a whole. She commented on Donna's choice of colours and attention to detail. Donna left her mother with renewed enthusiasm to complete her work, determined to try a more complicated pattern. Parents should stay positive in their attitude and focus on children's strengths.

Catch them being good

In the mistaken belief that they are acting in children's best interests, many parents constantly point out their children's misbehaviours. They do so because they believe that by pointing out the inappropriate behaviour children will change. Many parents are experts at 'catching children being bad'. It is far more useful to focus attention on children's appropriate behaviour. Children are more likely to adopt behaviours that meet approval if they gain positive attention for these actions.

Consider the father who transformed mealtime from a battlefield to a relatively civilised activity by drawing attention to his tribe's desirable behaviours and ignoring the misbehaviours. At mealtime he commented only on acceptable behaviour:

'I enjoyed hearing about your day at school, Helen.'

'It is good to see you use your knife and fork, Mart.'

'Alison, thanks for putting your dishes in the sink.'

'Great to see you join in our conversation, Beau.'

He showed enormous self-control to refrain from criticisms such as:

'Don't talk with your mouth full, Helen.'

'Beau, don't interrupt when others are talking.'

The children responded to his positive attitude and began

to behave within his guidelines whenever they shared a meal as a family.

Emphasise the activity

Many parents emphasise the results of an activity, top marks in school, winning races and creating wonderful works of art all receive extensive praise. What about the struggling student, the child who finishes at the rear in a race and the budding artist who is all thumbs? It is difficult to praise their results. Encouragement emphasises the activity rather than the result of an action. Parents can always encourage children's efforts but they can't always praise their results.

Consider these statements:

'You really tried hard during this term to improve in maths.'

'It is great to see that you're participating in Little Athletics.'

'You really enjoy art. Keep up the good efforts.'

They all focus on participation rather than on the result. They show that you are interested in their efforts without placing any pressure on them to excel. Children are usually aware of their own success and don't always need to be reassured by adults. Success is its own reward.

Encouragement is a potent change agent but many parents do not know how to begin. As with all new endeavours, it is best to start small. It is helpful to build the encouragement process into the daily routine, linking it with normal activities. For instance, when you kiss children goodnight, thank them for their assistance during the day or mention their improvement in a particular behaviour or skill. We can all be encouraging parents; it merely takes practice and a positive approach to children. Try to keep misbehaviour in perspective – don't take it too seriously.

Encouragement has a snowball effect: the more you give, the greater the benefits. It has a magical effect on anyone who receives it. It stimulates change in children, reinforcing the positive behaviour while gently discouraging the bad.

6
MANAGING BEHAVIOUR THROUGH SELF-DISCIPLINE

Children feel most secure in an environment where there are clearly defined rules and consistent methods of dealing with misbehaviours. Parents need to know how to react to misbehaviour in ways that are both effective and that allow children to maintain their dignity while learning socially acceptable behaviours.

Too often parents respond to children's misdemeanours with knee-jerk reactions. A child misbehaves and they respond with the first comment or response that they think of. It is little wonder that discipline is often haphazard and ineffective. Parents need to plan their approach to child discipline in much the same way as they plan a route to a holiday destination. They should know where they want to go and how to get there.

There are three approaches to the management of children's behaviour – punishment, laissez-faire and self-discipline.

Punishment

The traditional way of managing children's behaviour is by the use of rewards and punishment. 'A lolly when they are good and a stick when they are bad' is a colourful description of this approach. This method was adequate in its time but the reality is that it is largely ineffective today. Parents and teachers may rue this fact but it is true.

Punishment is the infliction of a hurtful experience for

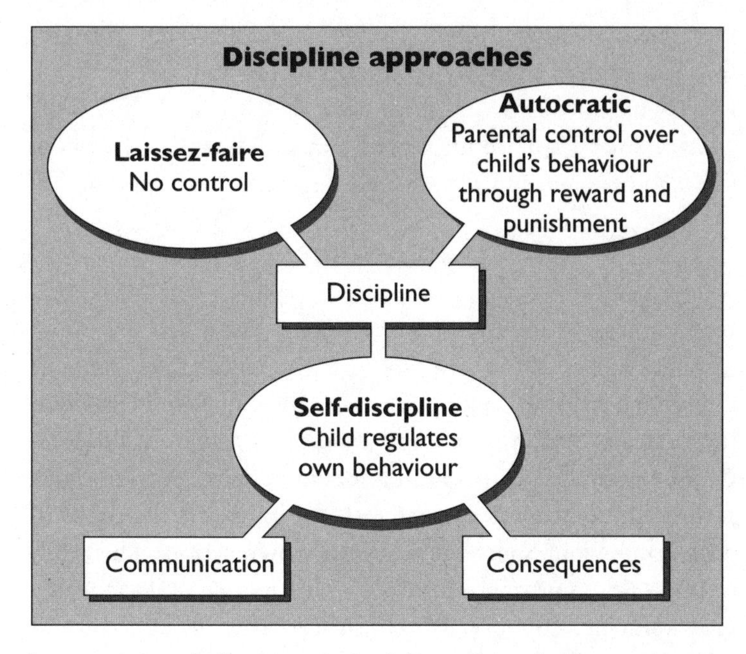

inappropriate behaviour. It is delivered in the hope that the misbehaviour will not occur again. It may take the form of a smack, a yell, an embarrassing remark, a loss of privileges or a deduction in pocket money. Whatever the form, its intent is to deter the person from misbehaving in the same way again.

The effect of punishment is to change behaviour temporarily but it will not necessarily eliminate it. The misbehaviour will be suppressed as long as the veiled threat of punishment is there. Punishment invites resistance and retaliation from children, particularly those who seek the goal of power. The use of punishment implies that parents are responsible for their children's misbehaviours. Children need to be given the opportunity to feel the consequences of inappropriate behaviour so they can adjust their way of acting accordingly. Often constant nagging and 'telling off' (a frequently used form of punishment) encourage the misbehaviour to continue. Children are receiving constant feedback and, in the absence of encouragement, any feedback is acceptable to some children, even if it is negative. 'At least Mum knows I am around,' stated one child, when asked how she felt about her mother's constant nagging and criticism.

Laissez-faire

One approach to child development, promoted by some 'experts' in the 1960s and 1970s, is the laissez-faire method. Children are not disciplined for misdemeanours and learn that they can do as they wish. This method is totally inadequate. Children must learn to live in a society where there are rights and responsibilities. They need to learn to respect the rights of others and take responsibility for their own actions. The result of using this approach is a totally undisciplined child who has great difficulty coping with school and other social situations.

Self-discipline

The most desirable form of behaviour management is self-discipline or self-control. As adults we are able to govern our own behaviours without anyone punishing us. In extreme circumstances adults may have a brush with the law and receive a punishment but in normal day-to-day circumstances we are able to regulate our own behaviour with minimal interference from others. This self-discipline can be developed in children from an early age. Using a combination of communication strategies and behavioural consequences, parents can instil in children a respect for order, offer them the freedom to regulate their own behaviour within limits and help them develop an appreciation for the rights of other people.

Communication strategies

Parents spend a great deal of time trying to tell children what to do. Generally, this is wasted energy, as some children are often very keen to let their parents know that they can't make them do anything. The children have it right. Parents should stop telling children how to behave and start informing them how they will react to children's misbehaviour. When children fight in the car they can be told: 'If you fight in the car I am going to return home, as I am unwilling to drive with that noise.' The children are not being told what to do; they are being informed of their parents' reaction to their fighting. If the children continue fighting, then the appropriate action should be taken or it will be seen as a useless threat.

Parents have considerable power over children's behaviour when they are able to control and alter their own behaviour. Instead of trying to change children's behaviour, the initial focus should be on changing their own actions.

Verbal directions

A simple verbal direction, stated quietly and calmly, can be a most effective counter to minor misbehaviour.

'Penny, please be quiet while I'm reading. You are too noisy.'

'Play in the lounge room, not in my bedroom please, Patrick.'

Verbal directions are informative and preventative. They let the child know the required form of action while stating the inappropriate behaviour. They are best used to prevent misbehaviour. If the directions are not followed, then an action in the form of a consequence should occur. If Patrick continues to play in the bed-room, then he should lose the privilege of using that room for a while.

There are two traps to be avoided when giving verbal directions. First, parents need to resist the temptation to yell or shout directions. The message to be delivered does not change when the decibels increase – merely parental blood pressure. Raised voices help to make children 'parent-deaf'. During a recent counselling session a mother conceded that her daughter would not respond to her requests. She had to tell the child three times to do everything. On the third attempt the mother admitted that she generally roared at her daughter, which usually achieved the desired response. When questioned about this later, the knowing daughter claimed: 'I hear Mum the other times she speaks but when she yells I know that she really means it.' This young girl is conveniently 'mother-deaf'. Her mother had raised her voice so often that the only way to gain any action was to shriek or shout.

Second, parents should try not to give directions in a totally negative manner.

'Don't play with your food, Justin.'

'Never throw your clothes on the floor.'

It is far more useful to give positive comments that inform children about preferred behaviour than to bombard them with negative statements.

Ignoring misbehaviour – tactical ignoring

Some misbehaviour that has the purpose of gaining a parent's attention is best ignored. Many parents feel compelled to make a response of some type when children are naughty. Ignoring misbehaviour is a passive response. It is acceptable to observe a misbehaviour and decide to ignore it, thus depriving the child of the feedback he is trying to gain.

Seven-year-old Felicity was flicking the ear of the family

cat while it was sitting on her mother's knee. Felicity was annoyed because her mother was reading rather than playing with her. The child thought that teasing the cat was a sure-fire way of gaining her mother's attention. Her mother recognised the game that Felicity was playing and continued to read rather than reprimand her daughter. Eventually, Felicity grew tired of the game and went to her room.

Behaviour statements

Sometimes it is sufficient to make children aware that they are behaving in an undesirable way to achieve a behavioral change.

'Philippa, you are making a noise while I am talking on the telephone.'

'You are running inside the house, Maria.'

When children are made aware of misbehaviour they have the opportunity to alter their actions. If the misbehaviour continues, then a consequence is appropriate.

Eye messages

The use of an eye message is an immediate, efficient way of conveying disapproval. When combined with a verbal message, direct eye contact can effectively inform a child that you disagree with his behaviour and you expect him to make a change. Often a stern look is enough to remind a child that his behaviour is unacceptable.

Distraction

An often overlooked but most useful way of temporarily changing a child's behaviour is by the art of distraction. Grandmothers are experts at diverting young children from mischief and directing their energies into more useful behaviours. Parents, often because they are overwhelmed by the day-to-day responsibilities of family and work schedules, can forget this effective method of maintaining order.

Distraction can take many forms – suggesting a game, giving a job, asking a question, beginning a conversation, inviting a child to assist and telling a joke all serve the purpose of diverting a child's attention away from irritating behaviour.

Procedural reminders

Sometimes children forget the rules and procedures of the family. They need to be reminded that their behaviour disturbs others, places them in danger or is about to cause damage. Appealing to reason and fairness will often lead to co-operation.

The broken record

Many children gain great pleasure from engaging their parents in arguments. Many children are consummate bush lawyers who will argue about every command or suggestion made. These children love to differ with parents over minor details. They are experts at diverting attention away from the main issues at hand. Consider this conversation between ten-year-old Tula and her mother:

Mum: Tula, I want you to come straight home from school tonight because we are going shopping.

Tula: Oh, I came straight home from school last night.

Mum: I must go shopping.

Tula: I hate shopping. Besides, you are so slow in the supermarket.

Mum: I'm slow in the supermarket because you keep fighting with your sister.

Tula: But I should be allowed some time to relax after school. I want to go to Bobbie's place.

It is often difficult to avoid these petty arguments that wear parents down and make them feel defeated. It is best to simply state your intention and then demonstrate that no further correspondence will be entered into. If children wish to continue to pursue a point of law, it can be done at another time, preferably at a family meeting or discussion.

A more effective approach by Tula's mother would be:

Mum: Tula, please come straight home from school tonight as I wish to go shopping.

Tula: Oh, I came home early last night.

Mum: That's true.

Tula: I hate shopping. Besides, you are so slow in the supermarket.

Mum: Tula, please come straight home from school tonight.

At this point Tula's mother leaves the room, signalling her unwillingness to argue. A clear statement of intention asserts her original position; she is not sidetracked down a path of her daughter's making. She remains in control of herself and the situation.

Behavioural consequences

As adults we learn to regulate our own behaviour because we experience the consequences of our actions. When we are rude to a shopkeeper we receive poor service; if we leave the windows down in the car during a storm the seats become saturated; when we don't pay our electricity bill we are left in the dark. When we feel the consequences of our actions (or lack of action) we generally respond accordingly and take the necessary steps to avoid an unpleasant experience in future. Similarly, children need to feel the consequences of their actions so that they can take the necessary steps to achieve behavioural change. Children, like adults, will not behave in ways that cause discomfort or lead to unwanted experiences. By experiencing consequences, children learn that there is a relationship between their actions and the outcomes. They learn to respect order, not for fear of punishment but to avoid negative experiences and to function effectively.

There are two types of behavioural consequences – natural and logical.

Natural consequences

If a child teases the neighbour's dog he may be bitten, if he leaves his raincoat at home he may get wet, if he spends all his pocket-money on the first day of the week he will have none left for the weekend. These are all natural consequences. No one needs to intervene for these to take effect. There is no need for adult interference, as each action leads to an undesirable experience that will prompt the child, if concerned, to act differently on the next occasion.

Logical consequences

Logical consequences are more frequently used in the family situation. They require parental intervention, as they are used when behaviour disturbs other people. A child who makes a noise in the family room is asked to leave. Children who fight over television programs lose the right to watch television until the argument is resolved. Similarly, children who refuse to clean up their toys lose use of them for a period of time. The consequence of each action is logically related to the child's behaviour. It is the situation itself rather than the authority of an adult that influences a child's behaviour.

The application of logical consequences requires thought, practice and faith in children's ability to regulate their own behaviour. When using consequences it is helpful to remember the three Rs – related, respectful and reasonable.

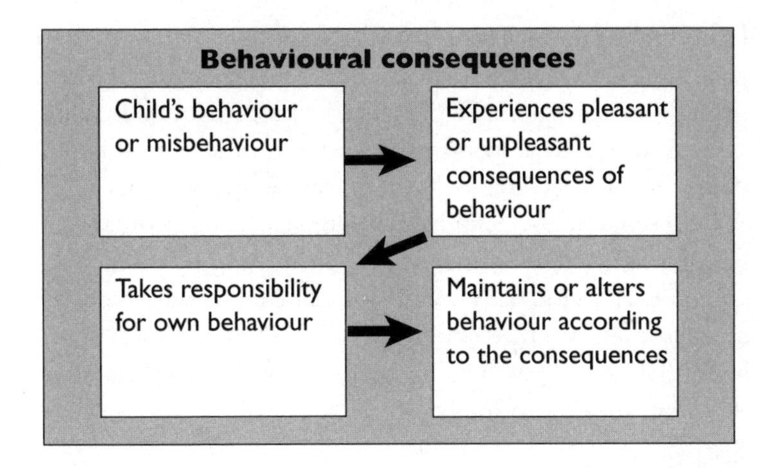

The consequences need to be related to behaviour so that children clearly associate a misbehaviour with its outcome. For instance, a four-year-old who repeatedly thumps other children while playing should be removed temporarily from her peers. The relationship between inappropriate play and removal is logical and should become apparent to the offender, although it may take a while for the message to sink in with some hardened cases.

Children often resent adults for trying to impose discipline which can be seen as unnecessary meddling. Ensuring consequences are *reasonable* and *respectful* minimises resentment and helps maintain the relationship between parent and child. The removal of the four-year-old thumper from her friends for a short period of time is reasonable. A seven-day ban on meeting her playmates, while perhaps bringing sighs of relief from her peers, is both unreasonable and shows little respect for her wellbeing. Similarly, a child who makes a mess at the dinner table will resent his parents if, in an effort to teach him to be tidier in the future, they insist that he cleans the entire kitchen.

IMPLEMENTING LOGICAL CONSEQUENCES

It is useful to discuss logical consequences with children prior to their implementation. This ensures that children are fully aware of what will occur if they misbehave. Children then choose to either behave appropriately or experience the consequences. A child who whinges at her mother can be told: 'When you whinge at me I shall leave the room.' The choice is clear for the child. If she chooses to whine at her mother, then a quick exit is in order. The child will soon learn that whining will bring no response and the behaviour should change accordingly.

Thought before action: As your first response to a child's misbehaviour that is directed to you is usually the one that the child is trying to provoke, it is important to think before reacting. When seven-year-old Danny shouts at his mother 'You stupid cow!', he is issuing an invitation to fight. Instead of reacting instantly with a verbal tirade or a smack, it is more effective if his mother responds in an unexpected way. She could take the wind out of his sails by agreeing with his summary of her or she could simply ignore him.

Of course, it is often difficult to avoid reacting to such provocation. It is futile to engage in games of a child's making. When children misbehave it is more effective to stop, take a deep breath and react in an unexpected way. This does not mean that you stand on your head in the corner of the room humming nursery rhymes when children are naughty. That is outrageous, rather than unexpected. It is essential that you side-step children's provocative attempts to gain attention or involve you in unwanted arguments. In short, provide children with a minimum of feedback when they misbehave.

Action not talk: 'How many times have I told you to turn that television down. You always have it so loud. Turn it down now!' shouts an exasperated mother.

The fact that this mother must keep reminding her children to turn the television down indicates that she is doing something wrong – talking too much. One reminder should be enough to indicate that a behaviour is inappropriate. If children do not respond, then appropriate action needs to be taken. This mother should turn the television off and indicate her willingness to allow her children to watch it the next day with the volume at a reasonable level. It is her actions rather than her words that will cause the desired change.

Nine-year-old Jenny always needed to be reminded to feed the family cat. Her father grew tired of constantly nagging her to do the chore. He decided to stop talking and to take action; after all, it was his daughter's responsibility to feed her pet. He discussed the matter with Jenny. He told her that he was unwilling to let the cat starve but he was not going to remind her to feed it any more. He told her that he would not serve her meal until the cat had been fed. Next evening Jenny watched television until mealtime. When the family was called to the table Jenny found that her meal had not been served. 'Dad, this isn't fair. Where is my dinner?' complained an indignant Jenny. He replied: 'You know what to do about it, Jenny'.

Through his behaviour this parent shifted the responsibility of feeding the cat to his daughter. It was his action rather than his talk that achieved the change in behaviour.

Tone of voice: Logical consequences are most effective if they are implemented calmly. When children leave their toys lying around the living room, they need to be reminded once to pick them up. If this does not occur, then the toys should be collected and placed out of children's reach for a few days.

It is not necessary to rant and rave at the children as well. The action of removing the toys is a strong reminder that they need to be cleared away when required. While an accompanying verbal blast may serve as a convenient release valve for an angry parent, it will only undo the effectiveness of a good consequence. The children will interpret the anger as a punishment and will probably be angry in return. Consequences don't need to be accompanied by angry words.

The use of behavioural consequences is a common-sense approach to discipline. Consequences help parents to maintain order with a minimum of conflict and teach children to be responsible for their own behaviour.

7
RESOLVING CONFLICTS

A certain amount of conflict is normal, in fact healthy, in families. Whenever four or five people live under the same roof there are bound to be disagreements. This notion is complicated, however, by the fact that a number of these cohabitants are children, who are less likely to see a situation from another person's point of view. They tend to see only their side when confronted with a problem or situation with a conflict of interests. Adults are often guilty of this as well. In any conflict, whether it is an industrial dispute or an argument over bedtime within a family, all parties involved must view the situation from the other side of the fence. They also need to be willing to shift ground and compromise with the warring faction. By adapting a few simple principles and adding a liberal dose of common sense, parents can help their families to resolve disputes with a minimum of bloodshed.

In the old autocratic days when Father was the undisputed head of the family, conflicts were dealt with swiftly and decisively. Father would decide the outcome of any argument and the other family members would abide by his decision. If the issue was bedtime he would determine the times that all children would go to bed. If the children were fortunate, he may have listened to their pleas before handing down his judgement, which was almost always in his favour. But for good or for bad, those autocratic days are gone. This traditional method of resolving disputes is no longer applicable. It is necessary to use new ways of resolving conflicts to the satisfaction of everyone.

It is important to realise that what parents and children

argue about is rarely the real issue. Parents often fight with children over any number of matters – bedtime, bathtime, choice of clothes, tidiness, use of money and completing meals are all disputes common to modern households. The underlying issues in all these disputes are power and prestige. When parents argue with children over such issues as the tidiness of the living room, the mess that children make often becomes secondary. The real issue becomes one of winning and losing. One mother complained: 'Peter always leaves the lounge room like a pigsty whenever he uses it. He leaves food scraps on the floor, his toys lying around and he is forever rearranging the furniture. When I ask him to clean it up he always moans that his sister made most of the mess and she doesn't have to clean it at all. If I am lucky he will clean some of it up but at a snail's pace, which makes my blood boil. I usually end up yelling at him to get moving, as I haven't got all day. This makes him go more slowly. Honestly, I could strangle him sometimes.'

Peter and his mother are locked in a battle about power and prestige. The concern about the state of the living room has become secondary – both sides have locked horns in a fight to the death. It appears Peter is winning handsomely. His mother feels that her prestige as a parent is being undermined because she can't make Peter clean the room to her liking. If she was merely concerned about the state of the room, she could try alternative measures such as collecting the toys and hiding them, placing a ban on food in the room or making the room itself off-limits until he shows a more responsible approach to its use. However, she is determined to win the fight and make her son do the right thing. Peter, on the other hand, is equally determined to show his mother that she can't make him do anything that he doesn't want to do. The living room is merely a convenient battlefield. Incidentally, Peter fights with his mother about many seemingly mundane issues. Peter's main concern is about power and his mother is worried about her prestige as a good parent, which takes a battering every time they argue or fight.

Resolving conflicts in the democratic way

Disputes in families wear parents out. There is little doubt that conflict causes more stress to parents than it does to children. Children don't seem to mind messy rooms, dirty clothes, noisy mealtimes and blaring music. They need to learn that their behaviour affects others in the house and that parents have a right to live in a sane environment. Sometimes it seems that this notion is at odds with having children! In a democratic family all members need to shift position in a dispute. This is particularly important if the concept of social equality is valued. Parents do not wish to be slaves to their children, just as children wish to have a degree of autonomy over their own lives.

Family conflicts can be resolved by following four basic steps. First, it is essential to abandon the idea of winning a dispute. It is better to try to find a solution to the problem. This is different from winning. It is necessary to *stop fighting and clearly identify the nature of the conflict.* In the case of the messy living room, Peter and his mother tried to solve their dispute democratically. They sat down when they were both calm and clarified the problem. The mother stated her desire for a clean room and spelt out her specific concerns about tidiness. She allowed Peter to give his viewpoint, as he also had some valid concerns. She discovered that his concept of tidiness differed markedly from hers. She also found it helpful at this point to identify the goals of Peter's behaviour. She realised that she became very angry about Peter's response to her requests, which indicated that Peter was pursuing the goal of power. She decided that she should side-step the struggle for dominance and together search for a solution to what had become a constant battle.

Once the problem has been identified and clearly defined to the satisfaction of everyone then alternative solutions need to be generated. It is wise to invite all members of the family to participate, as the solution is likely to affect everyone, at least indirectly. Often a brainstorming session, in which everyone provides suggestions or ideas, can be extremely effective. In the case of our untidy living room Peter's mother invited her daughter and husband to join them in exploring alternatives. They suggested solutions such as:

- Place a toy box in the living room for ease of storage.
- Clean toys away before getting a new one out.
- Children may play with toys in the living room before dinner.
- The room is to be cleaned before dinner and toys returned to the child's bedroom.
- The living room is not the place to eat food.

The suggestions can be endless and may seem quite simple. The important aspect is that those who are involved in the dispute are also involved in solving it.

The third step in resolving conflicts is to *evaluate the suggested solutions and adopt one or more of them*. This often means that both parents and children must give way to some degree. In the case of Peter's family, both Peter and his mother made concessions. Peter agreed not to eat food in the living room but he wasn't too happy about putting away his toys immediately after its use – he liked to come back and continue playing after a break and he found it annoying to get his toys out again. He thought that he would spend more time packing and unpacking toys than he would playing with them. His mother saw his point of view and they agreed that he should ensure that the room was tidied before dinner. She said that she didn't intend to remind any of her children to tidy the room before dinner and that she would confiscate for a week any items remaining after the agreed time. She also pointed out that she was unhappy about the room being constantly rearranged. If this occurred then the room would be off-limits for playing. The children agreed to the proposals.

The final step in this conflict resolution process is to *evaluate the effectiveness of the solutions.* Peter and his family agreed to put the new measures in place for a week before discussing their success or failure. When they met, some interesting points were raised. Peter claimed that he found it difficult to have the room tidied in time for dinner. Twice he found he ate a cold dinner, as his mother served the meal before he had cleaned his toys away. He asked if she would serve his dinner a little later than the others so he could have sufficient time to do his tidying. She was unwilling to do this, as she ate with the rest of the family and she did not wish to disturb her meal. So Peter decided to pack his toys away at five o'clock instead of leaving it until the last minute. His mother conceded that she found it difficult putting up with an untidy living room during the day but she complimented Peter on the responsible manner in which he was using the room. Secretly, she was extremely relieved that the fighting had stopped and she noted that Peter was generally more co-operative when requests were made at home.

Conflicts are resolved most effectively in families when parents involve children in the process. Children generally respond readily to a conciliatory approach and are capable of suggesting creative alternatives. They are more likely to abide by decisions made when they have been directly involved in the decision-making process, as they feel a degree of ownership of the shared decision.

8
DECISION MAKING IN FAMILIES

'It's time to go bed, darling!' Nine-year-old Emma remained glued to the television. 'Emma, time for bed!' 'Ah Mum, it is only eight o'clock. Sarah Thompson is allowed to stay up until at least nine o'clock.' 'Yes dear, but Sarah doesn't live here – we have different rules in this house,' remarked her mother, preparing for another battle. 'Mum, you treat me like a baby. I'm sick of you always telling me what I should do!' 'Emma!' her mother shouted in exasperation. 'Oh, all right, I'll go to bed. Will that make you happy? It's not fair! Good night!' yelled Emma as she slammed the bedroom door. Her mother shrugged her shoulders and wondered where she was going wrong with her daughter.

In this case the mother is bearing the brunt of her daughter's increasing feeling of powerlessness. Emma's resentful response is not aimed purely at her bedtime. It is directed at her mother who always makes decisions for her daughter. Her mother has not involved Emma in the matter of her bedtime. She decided what was best for her daughter without consultation. This parent would find she received a more co-operative response if she were to discuss the matter of bedtime with her daughter. Emma would be more likely to adhere to any rules or guidelines if she had a say in making the rules. Her mother needs to state the bedtime she is able to tolerate and listen to Emma's point of view. Together they can reach a time that is satisfactory to both of them. Children, like adults, are likely to abide by a rule or decision that they helped make rather than one that is imposed on them.

The question of who makes decisions in families is often the cause of a great deal of conflict. Parents, with the benefit of greater wisdom and experience, often believe that they are in the ideal position to decide what is in the best interest of children. Children do not always agree with this notion, particularly if the decision is about an issue that they believe only affects them, such as cleanliness. It is strange how children think that no one else can smell the stench of an unwashed body! It is indisputable that adults are able to make very good decisions for their children. However, it is also evident that many children resent constant intrusion by parents. 'It is none of their business' is a complaint I hear often from children.

Children want to participate in the decisions that affect them. Increasingly our schools are exploring ways in which children can be involved in formulating school and class rules and procedures. There is more flexibility in curriculum choices, even in the early primary years. Children are often allowed to choose the most appropriate method of learning. It is now becoming common procedure in a growing number of schools for children to choose the order of the learning activities that they will be involved in throughout the day. Children are encouraged to make decisions and accept a greater degree of responsibility for their learning at school than ever before. It is little wonder that many children become frustrated when their parents tell them what they should be doing most of the time.

Parents need to free themselves from the belief that they are responsible for their children's behaviour. Children, within limits, are able to assume responsibility for their actions. They also have a great influence on the behaviour of their siblings. The role of parents is to integrate the family, developing a sense of unity by sharing the decisions and the responsibilities between all the members. Family decisions and duties can be shared according to the age, maturity and ability of all members.

Family meetings

The family meeting is an effective way of unifying a family and developing a shared approach to its organisation. Through regular meetings, the responsibility of running a family can be shared equally between all its members. It is mutual responsibility in action. It is best seen as the decision-making body for the family, an excellent way of promoting a co-operative spirit between parents and children. Basic to the concept of family meetings is the principle that children like to live in an orderly atmosphere but they also wish to participate in the formulation of the procedures that govern their lives. They are more likely to stick to rules if they help formulate them.

Issues

There are four basic issues that can be discussed at family meetings. The important and often vexing task of allocating chores is best handled at a meeting of the family. A good strategy for parents to use is to provide a realistic list of duties. The children choose their chores and a roster is promptly drawn up. It may be someone's duty to make and display the roster. Children often grow tired of performing the same chores, so a new roster can be made each meeting.

The *resolution of conflicts and assistance with individual problems* are important issues for any family. These can be dealt with in a conciliatory manner by the family council. The concerns and difficulties of one member can be best addressed by the family as a whole. Consider the case of the Campbell family when seven-year-old Stephanie was having difficulty with her reading. At a recent interview Stephanie's teacher had stressed the fact that the child had to practise her reading constantly. This was mentioned at a meeting of the Campbell family. Both Stephanie's older brothers volunteered to hear her read each night. They also agreed to keep the television (a source of great distraction) off until Stephanie had completed her reading task. The entire family co-operated to help Stephanie overcome her reading difficulty. Her chances of success were very good with everyone pulling together to give her assistance.

Every family has its own routines, rules and procedures. But these often change as family circumstances change. As children grow older their interests vary, they pursue different activities and routines are interrupted. Ask any parent who now adds the role of chauffeur to his list of duties! The *establishment of a host of procedures and routines* is best left to a family meeting when all participants can be involved in fashioning workable arrangements that can suit everyone.

An item that should be high on any agenda for a family is *planning for enjoyment.* It sounds strange that we should actually plan for fun but often in our busy lives we forget all about the basic ingredient of family unity. Family meetings provide a great opportunity to focus on this essential element. If parents need any ideas in this area they can ask the children for guidance.

FORMAT

Family meetings are most successful when they are held on a weekly or fortnightly basis. They are doomed to failure if they are called by a parent on a needs basis. Children quickly get the idea that something must be wrong because their parents have called a meeting again. Family meetings will not work if children believe that they are merely a tool for parents to control them.

The most effective meetings are those which follow an agenda. Meetings which meander along are frustrating for the participants and rarely achieve their purpose. Family meetings work best when they follow a simple agenda which begins with some encouraging comments to each family member, covers two or three items of business and concludes with an enjoyable activity such as a game or a story. Initially, parents can lead the encouragement at the opening of the meeting. Comments such as 'Thank you, Sam, for cleaning the kitchen floor during the week' set a positive tone for the forthcoming discussion. They also provide an excellent model for children – encouragement is catching!

It is a good idea not to load the agenda with too many items. Children quickly become turned off if meetings turn into long-winded sagas. A time limit of twenty minutes provides ample opportunity to deal with important issues, although some families I have worked with conduct very long meetings which are very effective. The length of a meeting will vary according to different families. When starting out, short meetings are generally more successful.

Family meetings should not be gripe sessions. This will quickly turn children away. Parents, as leaders of the meetings, need to be positive in their outlook and in their approach to dealing with problems. Issues are best presented using non-accusatory language. Instead of 'You children are always leaving your bikes in the driveway', it is better to approach the situation in a manner that doesn't immediately place children on the defensive. For instance: 'We have a problem that I need your help with. When I come home from work I always have to park the car in the street as there are bikes in the driveway.

What can you do to help the situation?' Such an approach invites children to co-operate to find a solution.

As with all meetings, there needs to be a chairperson and a set of rules. At first parents will need to act as chairpersons but as the children gain in experience this role may be shared around. Simple rules regarding participation should be established early on to provide clear behavioural guidelines for children.

Children must realise that while meetings can be enjoyable, they are not to be treated as a game. A meeting is a forum for the family to participate in making decisions and resolving conflicts. For instance, at a family meeting I heard about, in an attempt to watch a certain television show the children banded together to try to put back the evening meal an hour. The mother stated that she was not willing to be a chef for anybody. She intended to serve the meal at six o'clock. If anyone wished to start dinner at seven o'clock they would be eating a cold meal.

STARTING OUT

Children are often suspicious of anything that disturbs the status quo at home. This is not because they are conservative by nature, but rather because they perceive that they have the most to lose by a change. As much as parents hate to admit it, children usually have the house running the way they want. Parents often sidestep issues to keep the peace, particularly if they have had a busy day. So children sometimes baulk at the idea of sharing responsibilities at a meeting of all the family.

Consider how a family I encountered began the process of conducting regular meetings. Michael, the father, announced that he wished to explore some ideas for an outing with the whole family the following weekend. He chose to hold the meeting in the lounge room with the television turned off.

He began by encouraging each of his children as well as his wife. This surprised everyone, as Michael was not known for displaying his feelings. He led the discussion about how they would spend the following weekend. The children were pleasantly surprised when he agreed to their suggestion of a trip to the zoo. He then invited them to meet again in a week's time to discuss the allocation of chores. They all reluctantly agreed to meet again. This time there was some heated discussion about the type of chores that they had to do. Michael allowed them to choose two chores each from a list that he had prepared. The next meeting concentrated on chores again. The children's enthusiasm grew as they saw that Michael was really willing to allow them to participate in the decision-making process, albeit in a small way.

Michael was wise – he started small and allowed the children's keenness to build. As time went by he widened the agenda to include family concerns and he provided the children with the chance to air their grievances. Michael also kept simple minutes as a record of decisions. He was also unperturbed when his twelve-year-old son Aaron claimed the meetings were a 'load of garbage' and that he wasn't participating any more. The meetings went on without him, yet he still felt the consequences of the decisions that were made. Eventually Aaron realised that if he was to have any influence on proceedings it was in his best interests to participate.

Regular family meetings are a powerful way of improving relationships and building co-operation between parents and children. They provide the means for children to share and accept responsibility, participate fully in family life and work co-operatively for the benefit of the group – their family.

But family meetings are not for me ...

The formality of family meetings is not for everyone.

Many Australian parents tell me that they don't hold formal meetings but they do take their children's ideas on board when making decisions. It is important to remember that the basic democratic principles discussed above can be applied through discussions in less formal settings. By listening to children, accepting and acting on their ideas and negotiating workable solutions to a whole range of family issues, parents can be authoritative leaders and still involve their children in the family enterprise. Meetings work for some but they don't work for every family. It is the principles rather than the processes that are important.

9
COMMUNICATING EFFECTIVELY WITH CHILDREN

Communication based on mutual respect is the key to our relationships with children. Mutual respect implies that we respect each other as well as ourselves. Parents are not respectful to their children if they spend most of their time nagging or criticising them. Neither are they showing respect for themselves if they capitulate when their children whinge and whine.

Communication is usually something we do without much effort or thought. It is an area that requires exploring, as we are constantly sending messages to those around us by the way we speak, listen and act.

Effective communication takes time and effort. Many parents lead such busy lives that they leave little time for real communication with their loved ones. A solution for busy people is to build a communication component into their daily routines. They should set aside a certain time each day when they sit down to talk and listen to their children. One busy mother told me how she greets her children on their arrival from school with a drink and a snack to be consumed at the kitchen table. While they are eating she joins them for a discussion about their day at school. This ritual takes precedence over any other activity she may have been involved in before the children came home from school. It provides both mother and children with the chance to talk in a quiet, calm atmosphere.

Listening

The ability to listen to children is perhaps the most difficult skill that a parent has to acquire. We are generally good at talking to them, as we get a great deal of practice doing this. To really listen to a child takes a good deal of effort and skill.

Effective listeners are people whom we want to talk to about our concerns and share our joys with. They are people we want to return to again and again to share our experiences with. Such people usually listen to us without judgement. They may not agree with our point of view or our behaviour but they accept us and understand how we feel. Children need to talk to adults who will not constantly judge their actions, but merely listen to them.

Consider eleven-year-old Jake who had a rotten day at school. His father, noticing him moping about the house, asked what was wrong. Jake sat down and told his father about the difficult time he was having with his teacher at school. His father, who was well-meaning, proceeded to advise Jake on the importance of trying to get along with his teacher. Jake felt despondent, as he didn't need advice; rather, he wanted a little understanding. He would be less likely to go to his father next time he needed an ear. His father effectively blocked communication by offering unsolicited advice. One of the skills of listening is knowing when to talk and when to keep quiet.

A good listener provides feedback during a conversation. Often this feedback takes the form of personal disclosure. It is reassuring when the person we are talking with shares something of themself with us. Nine-year-old Natasha was appearing in her first school play one evening. She confided to her mother how nervous she felt. Her mother told Natasha that she felt the same way about singing in front of audiences when she was young. She told her daughter of similar feelings at other times in her life. Natasha was still nervous but she felt better in the knowledge that her mother shared and understood her apprehension.

Many parents feel uncomfortable when their children develop opposing views from their own. Primary-school children are exposed to a variety of social issues and they are encouraged to develop their own opinions. It can be annoying when your seven-year-old son comes home from school and announces that from now on he is only drinking milk from ecologically sound bottles! However, the development of opposing viewpoints is a healthy sign. While it does not always mean that the child is thinking for himself, it does indicate that he is being exposed to influences other than your own. It is a sign of independence. This can be scary for some parents. It is essential that you tolerate different points of view in children if you wish them to continue meaningful communication with you. It is essential to keep the lines of communications open when children are treading the minefield of adolescence. The lines of communication are easier to establish during a child's early years than during the years of adolescence.

Speaking

Children enjoy holding conversations with adults. A conversation with a parent is a sign of acceptance. 'Mum thinks I am worthwhile because she talks with me about all sorts of things' revealed a nine-year-old girl to me during a counselling session. Children do not respond to being talked to in a condescending manner. A lecturer during my teacher-training years used to say: 'If we continually talk down to children they will spend the rest of their lives looking up to people.' It is best to talk to children of all ages openly and honestly. Encourage them to discuss ideas and accept their willingness to defend their actions or oppose your ideas. That is the basis of a respectful conversation.

A colleague told the story of a single father who had ceased conversing with his two teenage children. The family operated just like any other family, except for the fact that they did not speak to each other. During a series of counselling sessions my colleague discovered that the father had nagged, criticised and lectured his children so much that they avoided verbal contact with him at any cost. This is a tragic tale which highlights the fact that children do not want to be constantly lectured and nagged by well-meaning parents. Children generally want to find things out for themselves and so will often ignore parental advice. While this can be infuriating to parents and at times quite dangerous, there are times when experience is the best teacher. Talk should be saved for conversations, discussions and encouragement; it should not be used in ways that turn children off.

Some parents tell me that they do not know how to talk to children. These parents often use closed responses rather than open responses when they talk with children. A closed response promptly finishes a conversation, while an open response invites further dialogue. If Mark came home from school and said 'Someone stole my new pen. It's gone!', his father could end the conversation quickly with a closed answer: 'I bet you left it on your table. It probably lay there just begging to be stolen.' This would indicate to Mark that his father was not really interested in helping him with his problem. Besides, he had all the answers.

On the other hand, an open response such as 'Oh no! What do you think might have happened to it?' would indicate that he was interested in what Mark was saying and that he wished to assist him to explore the possibilities. Open responses usually take the form of questions and place the onus back on the speaker to talk. They do not smack of authority, only concern.

One of the hardest things for parents to do is to stop telling children what they should or should not be doing. We constantly send 'you-messages'. Are these phrases familiar? – 'You are being too noisy. Stop that racket, David!' 'You should be eating with your mouth closed.' 'Clean up the mess in the bathroom, Sharon.' 'Don't shout at me, young lady!'

Instead of telling children what they should be doing you can use 'I-messages' that communicate in a respectful way your feelings or displeasure about a certain behaviour. An 'I-message' has three steps:

When you ...

I feel ...

Because ...

'John, when you come home late from school I feel worried because I don't know where you are.'

'Anna, when you talk to me while I am using the telephone I feel annoyed because I can't concentrate.'

'When you fight with your brother I feel angry because you make so much noise.'

The use of I-messages places the responsibility on the children to change their behaviour. I-messages outline the inappropriate behaviour and your attitude clearly and simply. Of course, stating your concern is no guarantee that children will change their behaviour. It is a good idea to use an I-message once and, if the children do not respond, implement a behavioural consequence to achieve the desired change.

At times children do not wish to talk to parents. Consider the times that you have had a hectic day and your spouse or a loved one wants to have a conversation. All you want is a little space, a little time to yourself. The last thing you need is to talk to anyone. Children after a long day at school often feel that they need some private time. Like adults, they need to relax and distance themselves from the day's events. This can be upsetting to mothers who, wishing to find out about their child's day at school, are greeted with grunts and monosyllabic answers. It is best not to push your child; set aside a more appropriate time to talk about the day's events.

'Parent-deafness' is an ailment that afflicts many children. It is a relatively modern phenomenon that occurs in households where parents shout at children or are willing to issue instructions more than once. Youngsters sometimes only listen to what they want to hear. Try whispering 'Anyone for ice-cream?' They will run in from the backyard knocking you down in the rush. If you ask for the room to be tidied up they will pretend that you don't even exist. It is not necessary to shout at children to be heard. Shouting produces loud children and teaches them to respond only to shrieked instructions. Instructions or requests need be given only once. If they are ignored, then parents should act. When it is mealtime children need to be told only once that dinner is being served. If they choose to continue with their activity, that is their choice. However, dinner can be placed on the table and allowed to go cold. When mealtime is completed, any uneaten meals can be removed from the table and stored for tomorrow night's meal, if appropriate. Such action is an effective cure for parent-deafness.

Effective communication needs to be fostered. It is an essential element in relationships and vital for the functioning of a democratic home.

10
THE IMPORTANCE OF ROUTINE

Children enjoy a sense of order in their lives. They feel secure when they can predict what is going to occur. This sense of order is not always present in the world outside the family home. Out there, children have many new situations to encounter. Starting kindergarten, school or even beginning a school year can be unsettling for many children. They are more likely to cope with change if they have a defined sense of order at home and they know what is expected of them.

Children like consistency at home. It is desirable that both parents be consistent in their approach to children but this is not always possible. It is more important that each parent be consistent in his or her own approach to raising children. Children have no great difficulty adapting to different parents' expectations or discipline methods. They may see that their father will tolerate many behaviours that will drive their mother around the twist. This sort of difference between parents is unavoidable and should not be seen as an impediment to successful child rearing. It is important, however, that parents try to be as consistent as possible with their own expectations of children and the ways that misbehaviour is handled.

An important component of an ordered environment is routine. Children love routine. It never ceased to amaze me as a teacher how children enjoyed routine at school. They would voice their disapproval loudly if I changed the set procedures within the classroom. I am not suggesting that parents abandon spontaneity and become slaves to routine. Life would then be a grind. However, a flexible order of events provides a suitable framework in which children can develop the skills needed for independence.

Morning routine

Children can often irritate parents in the morning with constant requests. They can easily put parents in their service if clear expectations aren't established. As a parent you have many tasks to do in the morning. But those jobs should not include constantly reminding children that they must dress, wash, eat breakfast, get the school bag, and so on. Children should be aware of what is required of them without constant reminders. They will become independent only if they are given the chance to think and do things for themselves. The establishment of a clear routine with each family member aware of his and her tasks places the responsibility of preparing for the day where it belongs. Young children may need extra assistance in the morning but, if possible, this can become part of the morning responsibilities of an older sibling.

Nighttime routine

Recently I met a family who had an established routine of evening activities. Each person had set tasks to fulfil and they all knew when they were to be done. The parents occasionally had to remind children to do jobs but usually they were performed without nagging. It was the mother's job to prepare the meal, which was served at seven o'clock after the evening news. The children, in the meantime, had the opportunity to play games, complete some chores, shower and clear away toys in time for dinner. Children were not invited to the dinner table until their activities were completed. Similarly, after dinner the children knew what was expected of them. Homework was to be completed before they were allowed to watch television. At the established bedtime their mother expected the children to be in their rooms. She said goodnight in her own special way and was unimpressed with distractions such as 'I need a drink'. She did not remind children to have a drink or go to the toilet. That was their responsibility.

Although you may have formed a picture of this mother as being similar to an army sergeant in jackboots, nothing could be further from the truth. She was a loving mother who had faith in her children's ability to accept responsibility for their own wellbeing. She used the advantages of establishing a routine to allow her children a great deal of freedom to regulate their behaviour within the set guidelines.

Cleaning routine

Children love to play but are not as keen to clean up after themselves. There needs to be an established procedure for cleaning. Routines vary as each family's needs vary. However, some reasonable procedures that can easily be adapted are:

- Clean up one mess before making a new one.
- Toys are to be cleaned away before mealtime.
- Bedrooms are to be tidied before breakfast.
- Each weekend bedrooms are to be cleaned well.

Daily routines provide the framework for the development of independence in children. The establishment of some simple routines should alleviate the necessity for parents to be constantly reminding their children about their responsibilities. It's all in the routine!

A–Z
STRATEGIES FOR PROMOTING INDEPENDENCE AND DEALING WITH PROBLEM BEHAVIOUR

Argumentative Children

Penny, a single mother, burst into tears as she described a torrid day to the group during a parenting course. She told us of her hard day at work and the difficult time she had experienced with her children that evening. She constantly argued with her twelve-year-old son, Ben, her nine-year-old daughter, Jessica, and her six-year-old daughter, Kate.

She had arrived home quite flustered by the events that had occurred at work. Life did not become any easier for her when she encountered her family. Ben announced that he did not like the babysitter that she had chosen to mind them that evening while she attended the parenting class. He claimed that he was old enough to look after the others and that Tania, a family friend, was a better sitter than the person that his mother had chosen. Penny pointed out that she didn't consider Ben to be quite old enough to assume the role of babysitter. She also reminded him that Tania was unavailable to sit that night. Ben continued to argue before he went off to his bedroom in disgust.

Taking a deep breath, Penny asked Jessica to set the table for dinner. Jessica replied that it wasn't her turn; besides she always had to set the table. Her mother told her not to bother, as she would do it herself. She reminded Kate that it was her bathtime. 'Can't I have one after dinner, Mum? You know I love watching this show on TV' replied Kate. Rather than get tangled up in an argument, as she so often did with her daughter, Penny gave in.

Penny wished that, just for once, her children would do as she wanted and not turn every situation into a battlefield. She was tired of constantly arguing with her children and yearned for a little co-operation. She blamed herself for the uncompromising attitude of her children but did not know how to alter the situation.

The problem of argumentative children is shared by many parents. I am often asked, 'How do I get my children to stop fighting with me and start co-operating?' Arguing is a symptom of a lack of co-operation between family members. Generally what we argue about is not the main issue. The central theme is winning and losing: a power game.

Penny had three power-drunk children. They all wanted to be the boss. They were all pulling their own separate ways instead of combining together as a family to meet the needs of the situations that arose. Their energies went into defeating one another and Penny was certainly feeling that she had fought three rounds that night, winning one against her son. 'At least I didn't give in to him,' she claimed. She thought in terms of winning and losing. That is fine on the sporting field, but it is not a healthy way to approach family life.

Penny confided to the group that she tried to argue with her children when they disagreed with her. However, she conceded that this only compounded the problem. When she won, the children would usually perform a chore in a half-hearted manner or would be unco-operative the next time she requested assistance. She also tried acting 'the heavy' in an effort to put her children 'in their place'. This approach did not work with Ben, who was too old to be bullied. He saw the heavy-handed approach as an opportunity to fight even harder – it was like holding a red rag to a bull. She was able to bully Jessica with some degree of success, but when she tried to force Kate to co-operate the other children would gang up on her and make her life a misery. Penny did not know what to do. The more she fought with her children, the less co-operative they became – yet when she gave into them she felt as if she was losing and not being a good parent.

Penny, like many parents, needed to stop viewing her relationship with her children as a contest. This was difficult when she was constantly embroiled in a running battle. Sometimes it is hard to see the total picture when you are battling it out in the trenches. It takes two people to fight. You choose to fight with children. You do not have to fight but nor do you have to give in to tyrannical children.

Change your own behaviour first

The parenting group offered to assist Penny and we followed her progress with interest. She admitted that she often provoked arguments with her brood by her heavy-handed approach and her lack of consultation. She recognised that she was locked in a power-play of her own making. She also recognised that she could only invite her children to co-operate with her. Co-operation could not be demanded or forced. The hardest thing for her to admit was that she really couldn't make her children do anything that they didn't want to do. This is difficult for many parents to admit when they are locked into the authoritarian mode of obedience. The sooner parents realise that children are capable of withholding their assistance, the closer they are to winning co-operation.

Penny made a commitment to change her own behaviour in an effort to influence her children. She announced to her family that she did not intend to argue with them over any issue. She was willing to discuss their points of view calmly at an appropriate time. Ben tested her mettle immediately. He claimed that she never listened to what they had to say. She recognised Ben's argument as an invitation to fight so she retreated to the kitchen. Ben, who was not one to let his mother off so lightly, followed her, saying, 'You're always too busy to talk to us.' She resisted the temptation to remind Ben that the reason she was so busy was that he didn't do anything to help. She walked outside into the garden with Ben still behind her. Eventually Ben realised that his mother was serious. She didn't intend to fight.

The essential task in winning co-operation in a democratic atmosphere is to encourage children to work together as a group. They should think 'What is best for the family?', not 'What is best for me?' The family should be seen as one group first, and as a group of individuals second. Penny began regular group discussions to focus the children's attention on the needs of the family as a whole rather than on their individual requirements. She also used the group to influence individual family members to co-operate with each other. The family discussion provided a mechanism for Penny to discuss the children's complaints in a calm, relaxed atmosphere.

An important ingredient in the recipe for promoting family unity is the opportunity for enjoying each other's company. Ben, the eldest, had different interests from the others, but they found ways to have fun together as a family at least once a week.

During the first week Penny ignored the children's protests when assistance was requested. She also refused to do jobs that the children didn't do. As a result, many chores were left undone, which inconvenienced the children. For instance, she sat down to eat a meal and found that the table had not been set as she requested earlier. She quietly got her cutlery, leaving the children to obtain their own. She was showing her children that she was unwilling to be their slave any longer. She was also teaching her children that co-operation benefited the whole family. During this first week Penny acknowledged any assistance that the children gave her. She also began actively to encourage her children in any way she could. She began to 'catch her children being good'.

Over the next few weeks she implemented some further strategies in an effort to elicit co-operation.

She changed her tone of voice and approach when making requests. Politeness in itself can be an effective way of encouraging children to co-operate. Statements such as 'I know you are busy but ... ' and 'I really need your help with ... ' tend to reduce conflict and elicit assistance. She also ceased demanding that tasks be done immediately, giving a realistic time frame. She decreased the number of requests that she made of children, as she had not really been giving them the opportunity to give unsolicited assistance.

Penny began to provide her children with choices which helped them to make decisions for themselves. When the children were making too much noise in the television room she did not tell them to be quiet. Instead she said, 'You may make that noise outside or you can stay inside and be quiet. The choice is yours.' When presented with realistic choices, children generally make the decision to co-operate. They are not being told what to do.

Often parents argue with children over issues that really do not concern them. In the desire to be good parents they take on many responsibilities that really should belong to children. Penny realised that she was meddling in many areas that concerned only her children. She removed a source of conflict by allowing her children to choose their own clothes within limits and allowed them greater responsibility for bedroom tidiness. This was particularly difficult for her, as she had always felt that it was her role to ensure that the children were properly dressed and kept their rooms clean. She still provided assistance and established some pertinent guidelines for the children to follow, but the ultimate responsibility for both now lay with the children.

It would be silly to suggest that Penny and her family do not still have arguments. However, through changing her approach to dealing with her children, she has elicited a spirit of co-operation that was not present before. She has ceased feeling that she is a failure as a parent, because she is no longer locked in a constant battle with her children to get them to do things her way.

MIND THE STEPS

The main issue for argumentative children is power. The result of an argument is victory for one party and defeat for the other.

You do not have to fight and argue with children to get your own way. It takes two to fight or carry on an argument. Withdrawal from an argument does not mean giving in to children. It merely means that you are unwilling to fight or argue.

When confronted with argumentative children it is better to alter your way of behaving rather than force children to change. By stimulating co-operation, as opposed to demanding obedience, you have a greater chance of maintaining harmony within your family.

The use of choices and a conciliatory approach are effective when you are confronted with children who love to argue and fight.

Attention-seeking

Attention-seeking is by far the most common form of misbehaviour in families, particularly in the case of young children who believe that the world revolves around them and their needs. Attention-seeking takes many forms: eating problems, clowning, cuteness, embarrassing parents, interruptions, shyness, showing-off and whining. The behaviours may vary but the goal is the same – to gain extra attention from parents or to keep parents involved.

When children are denied opportunities to contribute to the well-being of the family they will find other ways of belonging. Attention-seeking satisfies this need to belong. Today's children have fewer opportunities to assist parents around the house than their counterparts did even a generation ago. The increase in household labour-saving devices has made life easier but has robbed children of many opportunities to help around the house. While I am not advocating that you sell the washing machine and replace it with a boiler, it is necessary to provide children with the chance to feel useful. When children lack opportunities to contribute to their family they will gain a sense of belonging by keeping parents busy with them. Parents certainly know that attention-seekers are around, as their behaviour is very difficult to ignore.

Parents often unknowingly encourage children's attention-seeking behaviour by constantly responding to it. Christina was annoyed that her five-year-old daughter would not dress herself each morning before school. Christina was very busy, yet her daughter insisted that her mother select her clothes and dress her. She would cry when her mother refused, so Christina thought that it was easier to give in and do as the child wanted. Christina was reinforcing the child's behaviour that was aimed at keeping her mother busy with her. The goal of attention was being attained, and the young girl's belief that she belonged to the family when she received unwarranted attention was given further credibility.

Types of attention-seeking behaviours

Attention-seeking behaviours can be either passive or active. Passive attention seekers frequently depend on others and avoid accepting responsibilities. Sometimes their behaviours are considered acceptable by parents. The cute child who does nothing except receive the accolades of adults for her delightful ways is a passive attention seeker. Active behaviours, such as constantly interrupting, are very difficult for parents to ignore, as they require their involvement. Parents are often unaware that many behaviours are for their benefit, and that if they didn't give any direct attention to them then the behaviours would cease.

Here are some common attention-seeking behaviours.

- **Cuteness** is a great way of gaining attention from parents, grandparents and teachers. There is nothing wrong with cuteness itself, as long as this is not the only way a child feels that he belongs in the family or group.
- **Clowning** can be amusing, so it is an effective form of attention-seeking behaviour.
- **Eating problems** never fail to keep parents busy with children.
- **Shyness** can result in much attention. Parents and teachers take great pains to include shy children in activities. They are often noticed because of their shyness.
- **Laziness** can keep parents in children's service indefinitely.
- **Untidiness** keeps parents very busy picking up items or constantly reminding children of their duties.
- **Incompetence** is a real winner. The child who says 'I can't

do it. You do it for me!' has found a sure-fire way of keeping parents busy with her. Parents constantly perform tasks that children are capable of doing.

If you're always correcting, scolding, reminding or performing tasks for your child, then you have some effective attention-seeking occurring in your family.

Identifying attention-seeking behaviour

Consider a child who dresses in outrageous clothes. Is this attention-seeking behaviour? You must ask yourself:

'Would she dress that way if the behaviour was ignored?'

If the answer is yes, then it is unlikely to be a form of attention-seeking. Such behaviour requires feedback for it to continue.

You will generally feel annoyed by attention-seeking behaviour. Children who interrupt you when you are talking on the telephone, leave wet towels on the floor, tell tales about their siblings or tap their fingers loudly at the dinner table can be extremely irritating. They prompt reactions such as 'Stop that immediately. You are driving me crazy.' This is the response that attention-seekers want. Children who believe that they are significant only when they are noticed or being served are experts at annoying parents. The feeling of annoyance or irritation is an excellent guide to identifying attention-seeking activities.

Another useful check for such behaviour is to give your child the attention she wants. When a child receives attention, whether it is in the form of a rebuke or assistance, the behaviour will stop temporarily. The purpose of attention has been achieved. 'Mum has noticed my annoying finger tapping, so I'll stop. I wonder what else I can do to get her attention? I know, I'll hit my little sister. That is sure to get a reaction!' thinks our little attention seeker. Attention-seeking, like all behaviours, has a purpose. The goal is to keep people busy or in the service of the one seeking attention. Children may not consciously be aware of the purpose, but they certainly recognise the results of their misbehaviour.

Changing attention-seekers

You cannot change an attention-seeker unless you change the way you react to his misbehaviour. You need to prevent an attention-seeker from achieving his goal. This can be very difficult, as such behaviours are annoying and will often intensify if they are ignored. Eight-year-old Guido kept humming while his mother was writing a letter. She felt annoyed, but she recognised the game that he was playing. Determined not to rebuke him, she ignored his musical efforts. He felt miffed at being left out of the picture, so his humming grew louder and faster until his mother exploded. 'Guido, can't you see that I am trying to concentrate? Stop that noise at once!' In the manner of experienced attention seekers he ceased that activity, but five minutes later he was nagging her about dinnertime. 'Mum, what's for dinner?' 'Guido, you're impossible!' his mother shouted.

Attention-seeking behaviour should be ignored. Don't react in predictable ways that encourage children to misbehave. As Guido's mother found, this can be extremely difficult to do, as behaviour often intensifies if the desired reaction is not achieved. Guido's mother would have been better to go into another room to write her letter. If you cannot ignore attention-seeking behaviour; then remove yourself from the child or even remove the child, if appropriate. Although such behaviour gets worse initially, it will cease when the purpose is not achieved. It is a case of short-term pain for long-term gain.

MAKING ATTENTION-SEEKERS FEEL USEFUL

Encourage attention-seekers to explore more useful ways of being a part of their family. Discuss with them how they can help rather than hinder the family. Start with small activities such as putting out the rubbish or assisting a younger sibling with reading. There are many useful activities that a child can receive recognition for.

Look at how these parents changed their own behaviour when dealing with children's attention-seeking activities.

Nine-year-old Graham sucked his thumb, which really irrirated his parents. They would conscientiously remind Graham to take his thumb out of his mouth when they noticed the habit. He would dutifully do as he was told, but minutes later the thumb would make its way back into his mouth – Graham had discovered a great way to gain attention from his parents. They were disturbed by the frequency of the habit and their concern showed. So Graham and his parents were involved in a never-ending cycle: he would suck his thumb and they would react, which taught him that the behaviour achieved its goal. He could see no reason to stop it. What made them really annoyed was that they knew that he didn't suck his thumb at school.

Realising that their constant nagging was having no effect on the thumb sucking, his parents decided to change tack. They gave their son permission to suck his thumb. They told him that in future they would not remind him about the behaviour. He tested his parents' resolve by making his thumb a permanent fixture in his mouth when they were around. He soon lost interest when the habit failed to achieve the required results.

Four-year-old Emily, the youngest of three children, was very cute. She delighted everyone except her mother with her babyish ways. To friends and others in the family she was a charming child but to her mother she was a clinging vine who relied heavily on others to do everything for her. At times she was not even required to talk, as her older sister would run messages for her and answer for her when someone addressed her. Emily's mother could see that she was an attention-seeker in the extreme and feared for her future, as she was becoming so dependent on others.

Emily's mother realised that the entire family needed to change their way of treating her daughter. They had to stop babying her and let her stand on her own two feet. The family agreed and over a long period of time Emily began to assume the tasks which were rightfully hers, such as dressing, feeding and talking. The process was made easier by the fact that the whole family was involved. They ignored her tantrums and supported their mother when she had to deal with a difficult Emily.

Six-year-old Sylvana was a walking question mark. Her mother realised that her child was overstepping the bounds of normal curiosity. She answered her daughter's questions when she could, but she was annoyed that Sylvana would ask questions at the most awkward times, such as when her mother was talking to friends. Her mother pointed out that there are suitable times to ask questions, but this had little effect. She then discussed limits with her daughter and informed her that she was happy to answer questions at certain times – and she would not answer questions specifically designed to keep Mother busy.

Sylvana tested her mother out, but she soon stopped the behaviour when her mother indicated her unwillingness to answer questions that fell outside the established guidelines.

Many attention-seeking behaviours which children display are actually behaviours that we admire. Cuteness, humour, curiosity and verbosity are qualities to be encouraged rather than squashed. Life would be dull without people who display many of these qualities. However, even comedians are not funny all the time. They know when to be funny and when to be serious. Children need to exist not because they are funny, cute or smart. Their significance within the family transcends these qualities and behaviours. They need to belong through contribution rather than through their ability to gain attention.

MIND THE STEPS

Attention-seeking activity is the most common form of misbehaviour. Any behaviour that gains children unnecessary attention or places you in their service is attention-seeking behaviour.

When you punish, remind or nag attention seekers, you encourage the undesirable behaviour to continue.

You feel annoyed when confronted with behaviours aimed at achieving the goal of attention.

Whenever practical, ignore the behaviour that seeks your attention and encourage the child by making her feel valued and useful.

Bedtime

Bedtime and children's sleep habits can be the cause of nightmares – for parents, that is! Often at the end of a long day, all you yearn for is a little peace and time for yourself. It is your basic right to have a little time for yourself. After all, haven't you devoted the entire day to the service of children in some form or other? Whether it is working for money to put bread in their mouths or being gainfully employed in an unpaid position as housekeeper and cook, you deserve a break. Come on kids, be reasonable!

Nighttime should rightfully be seen as your time. It is a time when you obtain the use of the house again. The living room is changed back from a playroom to a place where quieter pursuits such as reading, conversing or relaxing to a favourite piece of music can be enjoyed. It is a time when you gain control of the television again. No more cartoons, horror shows or talking animals!

Bedtime presents problems to many parents. Children often dispute calls for bed and complain that they go to bed too early. 'None of the kids in my grade go to bed at 8 o'clock, Dad. It's not fair!' is the sort of line that is used in thousands of homes each night. Some children procrastinate with toilet time, last-minute drinks and detailed arrangements of teddies, so that 8 o'clock soon becomes half past before parents realise it. Some parents are plagued by shadowy creatures that lurk at the back of living rooms just after children have been put to bed. It is a common event in some houses to have World War III waged in bedrooms between combatants who are far from sleepy. Some children cause havoc at the other end of the day, when they get up early enough to put the rooster out of a job.

Sleeping is one of the few activities that can be regulated

by natural consequences. That is not to say children only go to bed when they are tired. You must take advantage of the fact that nature has its own way of regulating children's sleeping behaviour. Your main concern should be getting children into their bedrooms and keeping them there. Nature can then play its part.

TIME FOR BED

It is a biological fact that we all need different amounts of sleep. Children are not immune to this phenomenon, although they do need much more sleep than adults. There are no hard-and-fast rules about appropriate bedtimes. The only guideline is that they must suit both parents and children. Some children fail to see that sleep is a biological need. They often view bedtime as something imposed on them by parents.

The more you involve children in deciding their own behaviours, the less likely you are to fight with them. As bedtime concerns everyone in a family, it is appropriate to talk about the issue at a family meeting or discussion. It is amazing how reasonable children can be when they have the opportunity to be a part of a decision-making process.

Consider one family who discussed the issue of bedtimes. Ten-year-old David thought that his usual bedtime was too early, given that daylight saving had arrived. He claimed that it was difficult to go to sleep when the sun was still up. His six-year-old sister Michelle agreed with him. Their father listened to their arguments and asked them both what time they thought they should go to bed. Expecting unreasonable responses, he was surprised when David suggested that half an hour later than usual would be suitable. Michelle wanted to go to bed at the same time as her brother but her father was not receptive to this. He did agree, however, that it would be suitable for her to stay up fifteen minutes longer. Having reached an agreement, he pointed out that he would be ready to say goodnight at those times and would be unavailable for stories, kisses or drinks after that.

It is a fallacy that all children in a family should go to bed at the same time. It is a common ploy used by younger children to stay up longer than is necessary. Bedtimes should suit children's individual requirements and your need to have time to yourself.

GETTING TO BED

Agreeing to a set bedtime is one thing; getting there can be another matter entirely. You need to be firm with children at bedtime. Procrastination should not be tolerated. Usually a five-minute warning is helpful to remind children to prepare for bed. At the agreed time you should bid farewell in your usual manner and make yourselves unavailable unless an emergency occurs. One mother related to me how she would read a book to her daughter at bedtime. She would begin reading the story by her bedside whether her child was there or not. This was enough for her daughter to rush to bed, as she treasured her story time with her mother.

Another mother told me how she would be ready to tuck her children into bed at 8 o'clock. If they were late to their rooms they missed out. She would kiss them goodnight where they were. After that she did not exist as far as they were concerned. She resisted their protests about unfairness. They knew what was expected of them and they adjusted their behaviour accordingly.

It is important to distinguish between being in bed and being in the bedroom. The children should be able to regulate their own sleeping behaviour once they are in their rooms. Usually when they are in their rooms away from outside influences they fall asleep fairly quickly. Natural consequences should regulate children's sleeping behaviour. If children choose to read or play in bedrooms until all hours they will be tired the next day. If this behaviour continues they will be extremely tired. Eventually, they will catch up on the lack of sleep. It is important that children are woken at their routine time each morning if the natural consequences are to take effect.

Reluctant children

Many children seem to love to stay up and join in with the adult world. They can be reluctant to go to bed at an agreed time. In this case you need to remove all reason for children to stay up. When children are very young it is reasonable to physically remove them to their rooms in silence. With primary-school children it is easier if you leave. It is also a good idea to make sure the television is turned off. One parent who used this method claimed that when her children refused to go to bed she said goodnight, unplugged the television and took it into her bedroom. The children went to bed, as there was little point staying up once the television was gone. She only had to repeat this method once before the message sank in – she was unwilling to play games at bedtime.

Boomerangs

Some parents are faced with children who, like boomerangs, come back to join them. There are two strategies that can be employed to deal with boomerangs. The first method involves returning the children to their rooms in silence. Do not give them any feedback at all. There is no need to admonish them; merely lead them back to their bedrooms. Repeat this procedure each time they reappear. They will soon tire of this when they realise that you are not a willing partner in their game.

The alternative way of dealing with children who reappear

is to ignore them. This method works particularly well with attention seekers, who play such games to keep parents busy with them. It can be difficult to ignore some children, particularly when they share the couch with you. If you can keep a straight face as well as your cool this is an effective way of handling boomerangs.

'I CAN'T GET TO SLEEP'

'Daddy, I can't get to sleep,' moans seven-year-old Shona. What she doesn't add is 'I want to stay up for a while.' Her father needs to assess who owns the problem. In this situation it is Shona who can't go to sleep, so she should deal with the problem herself. She should be politely returned to her room where she can read, play games or listen to a tape until she falls asleep. Many parents allow their children to sit with them while waiting for their eyes to begin to droop. This is all right once in a while but habits are easily formed and often difficult to break. Also, children are often quick to seize any opportunity and quickly proclaim their rights to special treatment.

GETTING UP TOO EARLY

Many parents have difficulty getting children out of bed, particularly children approaching the teen years (see page 179). However, some children like to get up at the crack of dawn. This is great if they are willing to keep quiet or begin their daily chores. It can be a concern if they like to have company and try to wake up the rest of the household. The best approach with early birds is to provide them with some worthwhile activities that will benefit the family. This will have two possible results. Either you shall have some chores completed before you even start the day, or the children will remain quietly in their rooms to avoid doing any pre-dawn jobs.

There is little need to be concerned with early risers, as

long as they do not disturb the rest of the family.

Bedtime routine

An established bedtime routine signals the end of the day. From my experience, families that have a clear set of procedures such as drink, toilet and bedtime story experience the least conflict at night. Children know what is expected of them and are able to plan their activities accordingly. A firm, consistent approach on your part encourages children to be responsible at bedtime.

Mind the steps

You have a right to time on your own without children around.

It is a good idea to distinguish between being in bed and being in the bedroom. An agreed bedroom time needs to be discussed with children. When children retire to their rooms for the night they can decide when they go to sleep.

An established bedtime routine helps to signal the end of the day.

Ignore all efforts to keep you involved when children are in their bedrooms.

Return boomerangs and night visitors to their rooms with a minimum of fuss.

Bed-wetting

There are many myths about children who wet their beds. Theories that bed-wetters have psychological disorders or that they are deep sleepers abound. Many methods have been used over the years to counter bed wetting. Some are degrading, some are ineffective and some have been of limited use in solving the problem. Fortunately, there has been a great deal of research into bed wetting in recent years that has provided a basis for the development of successful treatment.

Some facts

When dealing with bed-wetting it is useful to consider a number of facts.

- 70 per cent of four-year-old children stay dry most of the night.
- 85 per cent of five-year-old children stay dry most of the night.
- 93 per cent of ten-year-old children stay dry most of the night.
- A child's bladder size and bladder control affect bed wetting. The bladder is controlled by the brain. When a child's bladder is full during the night, a message either to hold on or that the bladder needs to be emptied is sent to the brain. Sometimes the brain doesn't react to the message that is sent to it, so the bladder empties itself.
- By the age of five a child's bladder is usually large enough to hold a volume of urine throughout the night. If the bladder can hold 150 millilitres of urine it is generally able to cope with a night's supply.
- Many children have to learn how to remain dry during the night.
- A child can stay dry during the night either by waking and

emptying the bladder in the toilet or by holding on to a full bladder during the night. This latter child usually leads the charge to the toilet in the morning.

- There are three types of bed-wetters:
  1. primary bed-wetters – children who have rarely had a dry night;
  2. intermittent bed-wetters – children who vacillate between dryness and wetness;
  3. secondary bed-wetters – those children who have been dry at night for a period but revert back to wetness.

WHOSE PROBLEM?

Bed wetting is a child's concern that is frequently shared by parents. The smell of urine-soaked sheets and the task of continually changing and washing wet bedding can be a grind for parents. It is little wonder that parents search for ways of ending the wetting – changing – washing cycle that can place extra pressure on already busy schedules. Children sense parental concern, which only compounds the problem. There are very few children over the age of five who enjoy the idea of wetting their beds. Self-esteem suffers, particularly as children become older.

The onus is on children to overcome the problem of bed-wetting. They need to learn to control their bladders at night, just as they have learned this task during the day. The most appropriate solutions for bed-wetting are those which are child-centred. Many techniques fail because they do not take into account the physical factors and de-emphasise the role of the child in solving the problem.

INAPPROPRIATE METHODS

Waking your child before you go to sleep may avoid a wet bed but it doesn't help the child overcome the problem.

When the child is not woken and taken to the toilet he is still likely to wet the bed. When he goes on school camps or sleeps over at friends' houses the problem of nighttime wetness is still a concern.

Limiting drinks before bed is ineffective, as often a child's bladder needs to be stretched to hold more urine. Many therapists encourage children to increase their consumption of fluids before bed so that the bladder size may be increased.

The use of medically prescribed drugs is a useful temporary measure but they are ineffective in the long term when children are removed from medication. The use of medication denies children the opportunity to overcome the problem of bed wetting themselves.

The use of star charts, stickers and other reward systems are effective with younger children and those who are already well on the road to nighttime dryness. They are largely ineffective for entrenched bed-wetters because they offer no real assistance.

Some children are punished, embarrassed or labelled as bed wetters by parents desperate to see the last of saturated sheets. These degrading practices only serve to ensure that bed-wetting continues as children become fearful of their parents' reactions. Anxious children are more likely to wet at night.

What to do with a bed wetter?

The age of the child needs to be considered when determining your approach to bed-wetting. Children who wet their beds consistently by the age of seven or eight usually require some type of assistance. Some therapists suggest that parents should act if children still constantly wet the bed at the age of five. It is best to be led by the child's wishes. When a child indicates that she is concerned with bed-wetting then it is appropriate to begin some type of program. The child must want to be dry before any types of procedures will be successful. Often older children put up a false facade to protect their self-esteem. 'I don't care if I wet the bed. It doesn't worry me!' claimed one nine-year-old lad. His bravado didn't fool his parents, who noticed that he didn't go on school camp and refused invitations to sleep at his friend's house at weekends.

You may need to initiate action with older bed-wetters. Be positive and encouraging in your approach – children who have wet their beds for many years think that it is impossible to be dry at night.

Although relatively few bed-wetters have physical problems, it is advisable to have them examined medically, at least to rule out this possibility.

Provide a child who wets the bed with a thorough knowledge about the bladder and brain and know their functions. A trip to the library may provide the necessary information for you and your child. When a child understands the physical processes involved, she is more likely to gain control of her bladder at night.

A child needs to be encouraged to overcome the problem. Adults can offer assistance, advice, encouragement and general support but the thrust of a successful program lies with the child taking control. There are two basic ways to assist children to take control of their wetness. One is interventionist and generally requires the use of equipment and assistance from an outside agent. The other method places the emphasis firmly on the child, with a minimum of interference. The approach you choose will depend on your willingness to bear with wet bedding and also your child's wishes. Some children feel that they need considerable assistance, whereas others don't want any interference at all.

Enuresis alarms

The use of enuresis (bed-wetting) alarms can assist children to learn to control their bladders at night in four to eight weeks. They work quite simply. When a child urinates at night a pad beneath the child's sheet senses the moisture and then an alarm sounds, waking the child. Once awake, the child goes to the toilet, checks the size of the wet patch and changes the bedding. Children take responsibility for the mopping-up tasks relative to their age and stage of physical development. It is reasonable for a six-year-old to change pyjamas, strip the bed, help to remake it and turn the alarm back on. An eleven-year-old can be expected to take total control of all the post-wetting tasks.

The intake of fluids is restricted initially, but generally increased after a week to train the bladder to hold a greater volume. A therapeutic component (regular phone calls or visits to a counsellor) can be added.

Child-centred method

This approach places greater responsibility on children themselves to overcome their bed-wetting difficulties. It is appropriate if a child is older, reasonably confident and you are able to put up with wetting a little longer. Children gain a great deal in terms of self-esteem when they successfully tackle bed wetting themselves.

You need to discuss the issue frankly with your child, and explain the procedures carefully. When children wet the bed they are to change their own bedclothes and bedding. If they require assistance they should ask for it. You should otherwise stay out of the issue. Minimal help should be given when requested. If a child chooses to sleep in a smelly bed that is his choice, although some type of arrangement needs to be made if the room begins to smell like a toilet block at a football match. You should take little notice of bed-wetting and show faith in your child's ability to stay dry at night. There should be no need to remind children to go to the toilet before bed or to restrict their intake of fluids. That is the responsibility of the child. By shifting the responsibility for mopping up entirely to the child, bed-wetting is being treated like any other behaviour that needs to be changed or improved. The sheer inconvenience of constantly changing bedding is often enough to bring about an improvement in wetting at night. It needs to be emphasised that improvement is usually gradual when this child-centred approach is used.

MIND THE STEPS

Rule out any physical problems with a medical check-up.

A child who wets the bed must want to stay dry at night if corrective procedures are to be effective.

Provide a child with knowledge of the physical processes of urinating and staying dry.

Successful corrective techniques are those that directly involve children in handling their own bed-wetting problems.

Bullying

Bullying is an insidious behaviour that affects many children. It transgresses a child's natural right to feel safe and secure and can affect a child's performance at school, their peer relations and his or her self-esteem.

It also takes many forms and has many guises. Bullying is the selective, uninvited, intentional, repetitive oppression of one person by another person or group. It can involve some or all of the following behaviours: physical abuse, intimidation, harassment, exclusion from activities or groups, extreme teasing.

Bullying is not the domain of either gender. Girls bully just as much as boys but they do it in less physical ways. While boys will use physical intimidation or verbal abuse to wield power over others, girls are more likely to use exclusion or subtle verbal sarcasm to assert themselves over their victims.

Bullying is more prevalent in primary schools than secondary schools, although the type of bullying varies with age. As boys get older there is a gradual decrease in the amount of physical bullying but an increase in verbal intimidation. It would appear that bullying reaches a peak around the age of eight or nine years of age, which is true for girls and boys.

While children will often tease or sometimes fight physically with each other, this bickering should not be confused with bullying. The latter involves an imbalance of power as one person is powerless to stop the teasing or physical abuse.

Most schools have a range of practices in place to reduce the incidence of bullying behaviours and to support those children that are bullied. However, there are a number of recent reports that suggest that bullying is still prevalent in

Australian schools. Children who are victimised or picked on by other children need all the help they can get. The difficulty is that many children who are bullied are reluctant to discuss bullying for fear of retribution. Some children also blame themselves and feel powerless to do anything. They develop a victim mentality and expect to be picked on or to be the subject of teasing by others.

How to help children who are being bullied

Look for warning signs. Trying to find out what is happening in the lives of some children can be a little like getting blood from a stone. They can resist all your attempts to find out what is happening or see your interest as prying or meddling. Other children can be a little like open books – they are talkative and readily part with information about all manner of things. Children are often reluctant to discuss bullying with their parents so it helps to be on the lookout for warning signs. These include:

- items being continually stolen.
- evidence of physical hurt such as bruising.
- reluctance to go to school.
- change of route to school.
- deterioration in school work.
- feigned headaches or illnesses.
- withdrawal from school activities.
- rarely asked to parties.
- out of character behaviour at home such as aggression toward siblings and sullenness, moodiness or tearfulness.

Approach your child if you suspect that all may not be well at school or in their social environment. Be proactive and ask if they are okay. Even prompt them by asking if they are being picked on, teased or ostracised by others. Many children feel ashamed and are reluctant to own up to being bullied as they may be seen as a wimp or a wuss. Children are also reluctant to tell adults about bullying, as they fear that they will take the matter out of their hands, so your approach needs to be gentle and non-judgemental.

Listen to their story. If you suspect your child is being bullied or they tell you that they are being bullied take him or her seriously and avoid dismissing their complaints as tale telling. Children who are bullied need someone to believe their story. Sometimes all they may want is to know that they have their parents' full support.

Differentiating between tale-telling and real bullying can take some wisdom. If your instincts tell you that your child is being intimidated or he or she is in a situation that they can do little to change then it should not be dismissed. Children who are bullied feel powerless and need your support, understanding and ideas to help them get through their difficulties.

Avoid over-reacting. As parents are protective by nature our first reaction is often to confront the bullies or their parents and right all the wrongs that have been done. That is a natural reaction but such behaviour usually causes an escalation in bullying and invites subsequent retaliation. It is important to remain calm and avoid over-reacting.

Dealing with the feelings

A child who has been bullied probably feels scared, angry and sad. Boys according to Australian research are more likely to display anger following bullying, while girls claim that they feel sad as a result of bullying. The degree of emotional intensity of children's reactions will also usually give an indication to the amount of bullying they have received. The more angry they feel then the greater the likelihood that children are being bullied constantly rather than on a few occasions or once every few weeks.

Some children who are subjected to intense verbal abuse will repeat the same behaviours at home with younger siblings. The emotional intensity of the criticism or abuse toward a sibling can be quite a shock to parents. Esther was really shocked to hear her eleven-year-old son Tai verbally abusing his younger brother. He just wouldn't stop and the emotional intensity of the tirade was almost frightening. The younger brother was completely intimidated by his older brother whose anger was almost palpable. Tai was not only acting out what was happening to him at school but he was so angry that he was almost out of control when he abused his brother. Esther knew her son well enough to recognise that this behaviour was not part of Tai's normal repertoire. She took him aside after he had calmed down and asked him if anything was happening at school. He poured his heart out to his mother about the treatment he was receiving at the hands of two boys at school. He was constantly harassed and criticised to the point that his school-life had become a misery. He was angered by the injustice and saddened by the loss of freedom to join in activities that he used to enjoy. His self-esteem had taken a dive as well.

Before any progress or assistance is made children need their feelings recognised and validated. Let them talk about how they feel and talk through their emotions. Let them know that it is perfectly normal to feel sad, angry, scared or just plain confused when they experience such behaviour. Establishing a dialogue with your child about his or her feelings will help them work through their emotions and put you in a better position to help them and give them constructive feedback. It will also strengthen your relationship with your child, which is built largely on trust and understanding.

Get the facts

Gain a clear picture of what happens, including who is involved, the frequency of the bullying and what your child is doing before being bullied.

Get your child to be specific about the bullying behaviours they experience, even showing you what happens to them. It helps to find out what they typically do before they are bullied so you can determine if they are contributing to being bullied or if there are ways that they can avoid being subjected to intimidation.

Bullying behaviour usually follows patterns. Often the same behaviours are used, involving the same people and also happen in the same places and at similar times. An accurate picture will help you determine your next course of action, for example, whether you need to give your child some avoidance or coping strategies or gain assistance from your child's school. Bullying is such an emotive issue that pulls at the hearts of most parents. Gaining an accurate picture will help you respond rationally rather than letting your emotions take over.

It also helps to give your child constructive feedback about what they do and to challenge their perception of the situation if appropriate. Some children can catastrophise such events and benefit from a realistic or objective appraisal by an adult who can let them know that the situation won't always continue and that there are a number of options for them to take.

Give them skills to cope

Helping children who have been subjected to repeated harassment or verbal or physical intimidation is not an easy task. They often feel powerless and that there is little they can do to stand up to others. Also children's self-esteem can take a battering as a result of a constant barrage of disparaging comments. It takes courage and confidence to stand up to bullies and assert yourself. That's what children need to do – but they can't do it on their own.

Often children are picked on or bullied because they make easy targets. There is no profile of a typical child who is bullied, however, the children with the following characteristics tend to be bullied more than others:

- Children who look different – small children, overweight kids or early maturing girls are often targeted by bullies.
- Children with poor body language such as slumped shoulders or those who avoid eye contact.
- Children who have different interests, or who excel in an area that has low social status.
- Those with poor social skills or few friends.
- Passive, non-assertive children.
- A mixture of the above characteristics.

There is little that can be done to alter the physical characteristics of a child but children can learn to act in ways that don't make them easy targets. The development of a strong confident posture is a good place to start. Some kids have victim written all over them just by the way they walk. A strong, confident stance with a straight back and hands out of pockets sends a message of confidence both to the child herself and to others. Encourage children to practise confident body language in front of the mirror so they can see how they look.

Talk through avoidance strategies such as keeping away from certain areas of the school and always staying with a friend. Children who isolate themselves are often easy targets so having a buddy around for support is a good avoidance strategy.

Some children benefit from having a few non-agressive

comeback lines to use that defuse rather than inflame a situation. A suitable line for a child who is overweight maybe – 'Yes, I love to eat.' Or 'I'm not fat. I am huge.' The idea is to remove the wind from the sails of the bully and not give them any ammunition. Children who bully love to see their victims squirm, so whining or engaging in silly squabbles is exactly what a bully wants. It helps if a child moves away following such a comeback line to maximise its impact and reduce the likelihood of continued bullying. Children can also imagine themselves looking the potential bully in the eye, standing strong and tall and saying firmly: 'I don't like it when you do that. Stop it now!' The key is to practise assertive delivery of such comeback lines at home, away from stressful situation.

An assertive response to physical threats is no guarantee against being hurt but it can certainly reduce the likelihood of harm.

GET THE SCHOOL INVOLVED

After listening to your child you may choose to help him work through the problem himself. But if your child is having little success then it is important that you contact your child's school and look for joint solutions. However, before you enlist the support of the school staff, check with your child that it is okay to go ahead. One reason that children decline to inform their parents of bullying is that they fear that matters will be taken out of their hands. So involve your child in all steps of the process.

Your aim of working with the school is to find a solution rather than apportion blame or gain retribution. Many parents tell me that their child's teacher won't take them seriously or brush allegations of bullying aside. Most Australian schools take bullying very seriously and go to great lengths to support and empower victims. If you don't get the satisfaction that you want, either reconsider your approach to your child's teacher or find the appropriate person in the school to handle the issue, perhaps the school counsellor or even the head teacher. Any joint plan to handle bullying will be long-term. As bullying is generally a secretive activity it is often difficult to make it cease immediately. Sometimes conciliation between children and parents is sufficient but often schools need to put long-term strategies in place that reduce the likelihood of bullying and also support children through counselling if the bullying continues to occur.

Building their self-esteem

Children who have been subjected to bullying need their self-esteem built up if they are to have the energy and confidence to learn new skills and overcome it. Bullying by its very nature harms the self-esteem of children. When they are subjected to harassment, intimidation or verbal criticism it is very difficult for them not to take the taunts or physical mistreatment seriously and they develop doubts about their worth.

Provide children with systematic encouragement. Let them know through your words and treatment of them that they are capable and that they will get through this period. Often children who have been bullied come out stronger and more resourceful because they have experienced difficulties and know that they can defeat them. For many children there is no greater difficulty or enemy to overcome than a bully.

Building their support networks

Children need to have a group of friends to support them when they are bullied. Kids are less likely to be bullied when they have friends – loners make ideal targets for bullies. Look for active ways to help your child make friends such as inviting a friend over to play or joining a group or club that enables him or her to make a new set of friends.

MY CHILD IS A BULLY

It can come as a shock to a parent to learn that your child is not being bullied but is a bully him or herself. The profile for bullies is diverse. Many children witness bullying behaviours at home, while some have been victims of bullying themselves and others have come from homes where bullying has never been practised. As a teacher I have seen two diverse sets of reactions from parents when it has been suggested that their child either individually or as part of a group has been involved in bullying behaviour. The first reaction is for the parent to make sure their child doesn't bully anymore often using strong-arm tactics themselves. This 'sorting out' process often models bullying itself. It reinforces the notion that he or she who has power can get what they want by whatever means. Bullying begets bullying. The other reaction is one of self-denial – 'Not my child! He couldn't ever hurt anyone.' This reaction is natural in a way as our children's behaviour often reflects on us as parents, so we can find it difficult to think that our children can be anything but well-behaved.

If you find your child has been involved in some type of bullying:

Talk with them. Discuss the behaviours with them letting them know how you feel and why the behaviours are inappropriate. Find out if others have bullied your child, which will give you a guide to how you may approach the discussion.

Model appropriate conflict resolution. Make sure that bullying does not occur at home. Sometimes bullying can be such an ingrained part of family life that we aren't aware it is happening. I know one family situation where the father used bullying tactics to get his own way but he used humour and jokes to cover it up. The children and his wife had grown so used to giving in that they didn't consider this man a bully. But he would interrupt anyone who was speaking to get his point across. He would continually ridicule his wife in front of the children and would threaten to leave home whenever he didn't get his own way. This father created such an atmosphere of intimidation that his family thought it was the norm. His nine-year-old son used similar techniques at school and with his younger siblings whenever he wanted to get his own way.

Bullying is about the misuse or abuse of power. The democratic principles outlined in this book where parents use discussion and guidance rather coercion and control are anti-bullying strategies. Bullying will not occur when members of a group act in respectful ways toward each other and work toward cooperative ways to resolve issues and disagreements.

Develop empathetic skills. Bullies are usually adept at deflecting the significance of the impact of their behaviour on victims. They often have the attitude that a little bit of teasing or a biff behind the ear won't do anyone any harm. 'Get over it' is their anthem. When children develop empathy with others they are less likely to bully. Ask your child how she would feel if she were in the shoes of the child being bullied. Many know what it is like because they have experienced the same behaviour but still they won't empathise with the victims. 'How would you feel ...?' is a powerful question to ask bullies. But sometimes you have to keep asking and asking.

MIND THE STEPS

Bullying is the selective, uninvited, intentional, often repetitive oppression of one person by another person or group.

Children often don't want to admit to being bullied so handle discussions with tact and care.

If your child is being bullied:

- Listen to their story
- Avoid over-reacting
- Deal with children's feelings
- Get the facts
- Give them coping skills
- Get the school involved
- Build self-esteem
- Help your child establish support networks

If your child bullies others:

- Talk about the behaviours with your child
- Model appropriate conflict resolution behaviours
- Develop empathetic skills in your child
- Give them coping skills
- Get the school involved
- Build self-esteem
- Help your child establish support networks
- Allow them to experience the consequences of their behaviours either imposed by the school or the natural consequences that may occur

Allow your child to experience the consequences, imposed or natural. Allow children who bully others to experience any logical consequences imposed or even natural consequences that arise from their bullying. Some schools will insist that bullies miss certain social or sporting activities as a result of bullying. I know one school that isolated a boy who harassed and physically hurt many younger kids by providing separate recess and lunchtimes for him. They gradually reintroduced him to shared lunchtimes when he showed that he could mix with others without hurting them. Some children who bully are eventually ostracised by their peers but this is not a common occurrence – children who bully are generally fairly sure of their place in the pecking order. But anecdotal evidence suggest most children who bully find that they eventually will be ostracised at some point and it is then that they begin to act in different ways.

Caring for Property

Parents often complain that children don't look after their own or other people's property with a great degree of care. Children today have cupboards full of toys and are constantly bombarded through the media with a whole range of new and better items to buy. They see their parents replace the car, the video and the television set with increasing regularity. Obsolescence is a fact of life with children as well as adults.

At a parenting seminar a mother told the group how rough her two boys were with their own toys and those of other children. They would throw and bash them around with scant respect. They found ways of using toys that the designers had not thought of. Consequently, toys had a short life-span in her household. The mother complained about her children's behaviour; but she would usually replace broken toys with bigger or better items. The children learned that it didn't matter if they behaved irresponsibly because their mother would replace any broken or neglected toys.

If children misuse or fail to take proper care of their own possessions, that is their choice. You should not replace carelessly handled objects and expect children to take better care of them. Children need to feel the consequences of neglecting or mishandling their possessions if they are to learn to value them. They can either go without the broken toy or buy a replacement themselves. If the item is extremely expensive they can contribute part of the costs of replacement.

Stefan, eleven, was upset when his new bike was stolen from the nature strip in front of his house. He had left it outside overnight and someone decided that it would make a terrific souvenir. His father was reluctant to replace it as it was an expensive item and his son had been careless with it in the first place. He gave Stefan two choices. Either he could receive a new bike on his next birthday, which was seven months away, or, if he couldn't wait that long, he could contribute a significant amount towards the cost of a replacement. Either choice meant an inconvenience. Stefan decided to spend part of his savings on a new bike. He learned a costly but valuable lesson about the importance of caring for his possessions – and he took much greater care with the second bike than he did with the original model.

Mistreatment of other people's possessions

When children use items that belong to others they have a responsibility to care for them. If they mistreat them, then it is reasonable that the privilege of use be withdrawn. There is little need to harangue or punish a child for misusing a toy belonging to a friend or sibling. It is more effective to deny him the use of the toy until he can show that he can be more responsible. This consequence is logical, as it is directly related to the behaviour of the child. Similarly, when a child breaks a toy belonging to a friend or sibling, she should contribute in some way to its replacement. Children will learn to be responsible only if they are made accountable for their actions.

Children have the responsibility to look after, to share and to help maintain family possessions. If a child has the right to use a toy or a piece of equipment she also has the responsibility of caring for it. Rights and responsibility are linked. You cannot have one without the other if you expect children to respect others and their possessions.

A young girl was careless with her family's trampoline. She refused to share it with her younger brothers and always forgot to put the protective cover on at night. Her parents discussed proper care of the trampoline with her but there was no improvement evident. As a consequence, she was denied access to the trampoline until she indicated that she could use and care for it in an appropriate manner.

Tanya was tired of her family abusing their toys and mistreating their home. Her two sons were extremely rough with their possessions and delighted in playing with and inevitably breaking the toys of their younger sister. The children were particularly careless with the furniture. What really annoyed Tanya was the way they treated her prized lounge suite. They would climb on it, stand on it, jump on it and fight on it. The only thing that they didn't do was sit on it. She decided to take some firm action with her children. She discussed with them her concerns and outlined some guidelines about the treatment of their own and other people's possessions. They agreed on the following consequences for the mistreatment of possessions and property:

- If the children broke or damaged their own possessions these would not be replaced unless they wished to do so themselves.
- If the children damaged other children's toys they would either repair them or replace them. If they were unwilling to do this a deduction in allowance would be made to cover the costs of replacement.
- If the children abused items of furniture they would be denied access to the rooms that contained the furniture that was misused.

The children immediately began to treat their own toys with greater respect, knowing that they weren't going to be replaced. When they did damage their toys Tanya was unconcerned. She simply reminded them that damaged toys were their problem, not hers. The two boys continued to play on her good furniture, so she placed a ban on the use of that room for three days. This brought about a remarkable change in their behaviour – the room also contained the television! This also showed them that Tanya was willing to act rather than to nag as she had done in the past.

The boys were still careless with their sister's toys. Over a period of time they broke a number of items, including a favourite doll. They clearly could not pay for the replacement of all the damaged items – they would be years repaying Tanya from their allowances. Tanya decided that it was appropriate to place a ban on the use of all toys including their own if they continued to mistreat their sister's possessions. She explained to them that it was unfair to treat some items respectfully and others with disrespect. In future the mistreatment of any items would be treated the same way – a ban on the use of toys for a certain period. This had a magical effect on the boys' behaviour. They knew that she was willing to take action, so they decided not to play with their sister's toys at all.

Tanya was firm yet fair with her children. She brought about a desired change in her children's treatment of property by clearly stating appropriate behaviour and discussing suitable consequences before they were applied. She showed that she was willing to act rather than talk, allowing the consequences of their behaviour to teach her sons the need for a more responsible course of action.

MIND THE STEPS

If children have a right to use property they have a responsibility to care for it appropriately.

Children who wilfully damage their own toys, clothes and equipment should assist in replacing them. Alternatively, damaged possessions should not be replaced at all.

Children who mishandle or mistreat the property of others should have the right of use withdrawn until they demonstrate that they can act responsibly.

Children who care for toys, clothing and equipment appropriately should be encouraged.

Changing Children's Behaviour

A mother frustrated by the aggression of her four-year-old son complained, 'I wish I could stop Peter hitting other children. I can yell at him until I'm blue in the face and he still hits others. I've tried smacking him but it has no effect. I don't know what to do!' Another parent told of his lazy ten-year-old daughter, Rita. 'She expects everything to be handed to her on a silver platter. When I insist that she do more to look after herself she kicks up such a fuss that it is not worth the hassle to even mention the subject of helping. I'm afraid that she will never change.'

These complaints are common from parents who are at their wit's end with their children. Many children are able to engineer events at home to suit them and don't see any point in changing their way of behaving. All misbehaviour of children at home is generally for the purpose of involving parents in some way. Whether the purpose is to attract attention or defeat parents, it still has the same effect – to keep parents busy, concerned or in children's service. When the misbehaviour is to the children's advantage it is little wonder that they resist parental attempts to alter established ways of behaving. It is often difficult to achieve a change in older children, as misbehaviour can be well and truly entrenched. Laziness worked for so long for Rita that she was unlikely to change in a hurry.

There are a number of strategies that you can employ to stimulate a shift in behaviour in children. It is difficult to demand that misbehaviour cease, as children will usually fight against force. In a show of strength children usually win – in the long run. It is more effective to stimulate co-operation in children instead of demanding a behavioural change which inevitably leads to conflict.

TWELVE WAYS TO STIMULATE CHANGE IN BEHAVIOUR

1 **Make children aware that their behaviour is inappropriate or of concern to you.** By using some of the communication strategies outlined in Chapter 6, you can respectfully indicate to children that their behaviour is annoying. The use of verbal directions, behaviour statements and I-messages informs children of their misbehaviour and invites them to co-operate. If the misbehaviour continues then the use of consequences is appropriate. Effective communication about misbehaviour can effectively prevent conflict between parent and child.

2 **Check your expectations of children.** Are they positive? If you expect children to misbehave, they will not generally let you down. Parents transmit their expectations in the way they speak and act toward children. Youngsters pick up a parent's attitude very easily.

   Are your expectations reasonable? Are you expecting too much from your child? A parent who wants a four-year-old to sit quietly while adults talk is probably asking too much. Similarly, a father who complained to me that his three-year-old twin daughters were terrors on a recent all-day shopping trip was expecting a great deal from such young children.

3 **Remember the big picture.** Sometimes as a parent you get so frustrated by children when they misbehave that you lose all perspective. Suddenly, children become the enemy that you are battling. At times it is necessary to stand back from a situation and view it objectively; to realise that the sun will still rise tomorrow even if your child is being 'a horror'. A certain amount of misbehaviour is normal; children will never be perfect. There is no such creature as the perfect child, just as there are no perfect parents.

4 **Change your own behaviour first.** When children

misbehave you need to change your way of reacting. It is important to avoid an impulsive reaction, as that is generally what children come to expect. Look for the purpose of the misbehaviour and find your part in maintaining the inappropriate activity. Examine your feelings as a guide to establishing the misbehaviour's goal and respond in ways that thwart that goal. Don't reinforce attention seekers by taking notice of the misbehaviour, don't fight with power-hungry children and avoid displaying your hurt if the goal is retaliation.

5 **Tell children what you are going to do about their misbehaviour.** Inform children of your proposed reactions to their misbehaviour. It is also appropriate to invite suggestions from children about how you might deal with misbehaviour. Tell them before you act, not after you have imposed a consequence. A father caused a furore in his household when he suddenly collected all the toys lying about and announced that his children would lose them for a week. The children protested that this was unfair. They were right – they had had no prior warning of his action. It is respectful to announce: 'Any toys left lying around will be withdrawn from use for a week.' The children then know what to expect if they choose not to pack away their toys.

6 **Use the power of the group.** The family as a whole is far more effective at inducing a behavioural change than parents alone. A child's misbehaviour should be the concern of the entire family, as everyone is affected either directly or indirectly by misbehaviour. Look at a whining child. Everyone, including the person whom it is directed at, has to hear it. Your aggravation can put you in a bad mood which is felt by all.

Through discussions enlist the help of the family to

effect changes in behaviour. Anton was concerned at the way his son, Willis, aged six, spoke to other people. He would invariably demand that he got his own way by yelling out orders and being insulting when they weren't carried out to his satisfaction. Anton presented this problem to the family. He asked his two older sons for ideas. Micah, nine, suggested that Willis should be ignored if he spoke rudely or yelled at anyone. Anton pointed out that this would be difficult as Willis' behaviour generally became more obnoxious when he was ignored. They discussed ways of dealing with this, such as leaving the room. They all agreed to stop responding to Willis unless he spoke respectfully to them and they prepared themselves for the onslaught. Anton was correct in his assessment – Willis became loud and domineering when he was ignored. It was a harrowing time for them all, but eventually Willis got the message that when he spoke reasonably to people he would get a far better response than when he yelled. Throughout this process the family remained friendly with Willis so that he received the message that it was the misbehaviour they disliked, not the person.

Anton used the power of the group to bring about quite a significant change in his son's behaviour. It is doubtful whether he could have had the same result without the help of his other sons.

7 **Recognise that misbehaviour often intensifies before it ceases.** Parents are often hesitant to make changes in children's behaviour when their initial attempts often meet with resistance, and the misbehaviour often gets worse before it improves. This is particularly the case if the behaviour is entrenched. Ten-year-old Rita, who is used to being waited upon by her father, will not give up her prized position easily. Her mother died when Rita was two

and her father, in an attempt to compensate for the loss, gave her everything she wanted. She has now come to expect special treatment as her right. Her father can expect resistance in the form of tantrums, arguments and similar displays of power if he tries to increase her self-reliance. He needs to remain firm and outline the contribution that she is expected to make to her well-being. He should also allow her to experience the consequences of her behaviour. For instance, he may require her to make her own school lunches, a reasonable expectation for a ten-year-old. If she refuses, he shouldn't give in and make the lunch for her. She will soon learn that it is in her own interests to make her lunch each day.

8 **Recognise that misbehaviour does not always need to be dealt with immediately.** It is often pointless trying to deal with a child when either of you is angry or upset. It is best to try to influence behaviour when you are calm and feeling fresh. Choose the time to deal with misbehaviour, particularly if you wish to achieve a significant change. You may not be able to control your child but you can control the time and manner in which behaviours can be dealt with.

9 **Work on one behaviour at a time.** Often parents try to achieve a number of changes at once. This can be confusing to parents as well as children. Youngsters can resent parents when they try to change too much. It is a recipe for conflict. It is advisable to think big and start small. If there are a number of misbehaviours that you would like to influence, start with the one that causes the least difficulty. That will probably be the easiest to deal with. It is best not to change another behaviour until the first one has been dealt with. Many parents have told me of the 'snowball effect' that an improvement in one

behaviour has had; the change in one particular behaviour has been accompanied by a significant increase in co-operation. This occurs as a by-product of the improvement in the relationship between parent and child when the child has 'cleaned up her act' in a particular area. She is easier to like, so the parent's attitude improves, which rubs off on the child.

10 **Be consistent – don't give second chances.** Consistency is a vital factor in achieving a turnaround in children's behaviour or habits. It is by your actions that habits will change and children must know you are willing to act regardless of the circumstances. It sounds harsh but it is unfair on children to let them off for a misbehaviour on one occasion and pick them up the next time. When children know that you are consistent but fair they are unlikely to resent efforts to develop a sense of discipline. A father was annoyed when his daughter kept using his tools without putting them away. He informed her that he was unwilling to lend her any tools that he found lying around the backyard in future. She agreed to this consequence, but her father didn't always carry it out. He would find a tool lying in the backyard, pick it up and place it back in the shed, thinking that he would give her another chance. But one day, infuriated at finding his best saw lying teeth-down in the grass, he rushed to find his daughter and immediately banned her from using any of his tools again. 'You can buy your own tools,' he said. His daughter thought his reaction totally unfair. She had a point. If he had been consistent in the first place and stuck to the consequences that he had outlined she would have quickly learned the advantages of being responsible with the tools. Instead, she was angry with her father for his perceived unfairness and had been denied the opportunity to prove

that she could use his tools responsibly.

11 **Encourage children at every opportunity.** Often it is difficult to encourage children who misbehave because it is easy to think that they do not deserve it. Encouragement is not earned, it is given. Misbehaving children need to be encouraged and shown that they are valued as members of the family. It is important to show children that while misbehaviour is unacceptable, they are OK (see Chapter 5 for ideas on encouragement).

12 **Retain your sense of humour.** It is almost a contradiction in terms: deal with misbehaviour and retain your sense of humour? 'You must be kidding,' I hear you say. The use of humour is a great distractor, particularly for young children. It can also defuse a potentially difficult situation with older children. Sometimes a joke at the right time can help you both see that a situation is not as terrible as it may have first appeared. Best all, humour helps you to cope with the stress that children's activities can cause.

MIND THE STEPS

To change a child's behaviour it is essential to change your own behaviour first. Avoid the first impulsive reaction to a child's misbehaviour.

Often misbehaviour intensifies initially when you attempt to stimulate change.

Work on one behaviour at a time.

Use action rather than words to bring about a shift in a child's behaviour. Let a child know that it is misbehaviour that is unacceptable, not the child.

Remember the big picture and keep things in perspective. Misbehaviour that appears horrendous at first can appear quite trivial after a good night's sleep.

Chores

Children have a basic need to feel that they are part of a group. All their behaviour is directed at finding a place in their family. Many children believe that they belong when they force attention from parents or when they defeat them in arguments. Some feel that they belong when they are pests. Children engage in all sorts of behaviours in an effort to find a special place within their family.

Children can feel that they really are a significant part of the family when they contribute to its well-being. They can make a positive contribution in two ways. They can assist in making decisions that affect everyone and they can share the chores necessary for effective functioning of their family. Children are less likely to misbehave and cause conflict when they contribute to the well-being of their most significant group – the family.

In this age of small families and large household appliances, children often do not have the opportunity to assist around the house. One young boy remarked to me: 'Why should I do anything at home? Mum has machines to do all the jobs.' In a way it is understandable how he reached that conclusion, although he failed to mention that his mother held down a full-time paid job as well as her unpaid household duties. Until recently, children's assistance around the house was essential – families were bigger and there were few machines to lighten the load. It was easy for children to feel that they were able to make a valuable contribution to their families. However, while we may live in a more automated age than our grandparents did, our lives are just as busy. The necessity for children to pitch in and help is just as great today.

Chores are recurring activities that benefit the whole family. They should be carried out because children are members of the family. In a democratic setting they have the right to help make decisions and the responsibility to share the workload. They should not receive payment for chores. Pocket money should not be dependent on the performance of chores and is a separate issue (see page 217). When you offer incentives for the performance of jobs around the house you are not showing much respect for your children. The message is clear: 'I don't think that you can do this job willingly so I'll pay you.' Children come to expect payment for chores as their right and they begin to think 'What's in it for me? You want me to wash the dishes? OK. That will be one dollar. I'll put them away for an extra fifty cents.' rather than 'How can I help others in my family?' The performance of chores is an opportunity for a child to make a contribution to the family, not the money box.

Many parents make the mistake of waiting until children are old enough to be given chores. The trouble is, there is no definition of 'old enough'. When toddlers want to help they are often discouraged with statements like 'You are a bit small to do that. Try it when you are older'. When they are old enough and their assistance is demanded, parents are surprised when they receive a firm rejection. Children are entitled to think 'Why begin now?' since parents have done without their help for so long. Young children are generally eager to help parents in any way they can. This enthusiasm should be tapped rather than discouraged. It is unimportant that jobs will be poorly done. The pride and satisfaction that come with contribution can be nurtured from a very young age.

Allocation of chores

A mother described to me her children's unwillingness to help around the house. 'When I ask them to empty the dishwasher I receive an almighty moan. You'd think I'd asked them to scrub the pots with a toothbrush they way they carry on.' This mother experienced difficulty because she allocated chores herself. The children were unresponsive to her demands because they had no opportunity to select their jobs. It is commonsense to allow children to choose their chores – they are more likely to perform them if they have chosen them. Naturally, some tasks will be seen as undesirable and will be avoided. These tasks can be rotated among family members to share the burden.

Chores can be allocated at a meeting of the family. Initially, the necessity of sharing jobs should be discussed with children. They need to see that their participation is important and not just another plan that you have dreamed up to keep them busy. Together with the children you can compile a list of jobs that need to be done. You should select your chores. Children often receive a surprise when they see how much parents actually do around the house. This can be enough in itself to stimulate assistance. Through discussion the family determines the allocation of chores. Decisions are influenced by children's ages, social interests, school duties, sporting commitments and other factors. You may need to provide guidance and advice when children are choosing jobs. You also may find that you have to act as arbitrators if they begin to argue or accuse others of shirking their responsibilities. Children quickly adapt to this method of sharing chores, particularly when parents model appropriate conciliatory behaviour.

You could compile a roster and place it in a prominent place, such as on the fridge door. I know a creative mother who makes a job list for her three young children using symbols instead of words. When a job has been completed they place a sticker on the matching symbol on the roster. At the end of the week the children have a sheet full of bright stickers that they can put on the wall in their bedroom. It also serves as a record of their contribution to the household.

NON-PERFORMANCE

If you constantly remind youngsters to do their chosen jobs you are assuming the responsibility for the completion of the chores. It is a child's responsibility to do a chore; there should be no reminders. If a child forgets, no one else should do the job. The child should learn what happens when a chore is not done. You can use logical consequences to teach children to take their responsibilities seriously.

Consider how one mother used logical consequences to promote responsibility. One of ten-year-old Con's daily jobs was to load and empty the dishwasher. One morning his mother noticed that the dishwasher had not even been loaded. She resisted the temptation to remind Con of his task. Instead she found some clean dishes to use for breakfast. That evening, as she prepared for dinner, she found that there were not enough clean saucepans, dishes, or knives and forks. Not wishing her family to starve, she cooked toast and placed it on the table with the few remaining plates and forks. The family protested strongly, but she pointed out that she didn't have enough clean utensils to cook a meal or clean plates for the family to use. She reminded them that she was not a slave. It was her job to cook the meal and somebody else took the responsibility for cleaning and stacking the dishes. Everybody glared at Con, who was desperately searching for an excuse.

This child learned how important his chore was to the family. His mother could have taken the easy way out and stacked the dishwasher, reminding him of his neglect at a convenient time. But she would always be reminding him of the task. Con was given a firsthand demonstration in the importance of carrying out responsibilities. At no stage was he nagged or humiliated. He was allowed to experience the consequences of his own irresponsibility.

You may think that this was all right for Con, but wonder

why should the rest of the family suffer for his forgetfulness. It is important to realise that the family functions as a whole with each person relying on the others. When Con forgot to play his part the entire family was affected. You can rest assured that he didn't forget his job in future – none of the other children would let him.

An effective way to ensure that children do their chores is to link chores to eating or sleeping. Children aren't permitted to eat until chores are done. Jodie, eight, joined the other children at the table. There was no meal for her. 'Mum, where's my dinner?' she asked. Her mother replied: 'You know we agreed that dinner wouldn't be served until chores were done. You know what to do about it.' The onus to pull her weight is placed back on Jodie.

Parent strike

In extreme circumstances a temporary 'work stoppage' is an effective way of showing children that co-operation benefits everyone. It is important that you explain the procedure to children so that it is not seen simply as a show of strength on your part.

Look at how Alexei and Lisa put this strategy into action. Both parents were concerned that their children were taking them for granted. They did very little to help yet they expected their parents to be at their every beck and call. Alexei's pleading for a little co-operation fell on deaf ears so both parents decided that the use of shock tactics was the only way that the children would be shaken out of their lethargy. They chose a weekend as the best time for 'strike action' – it caused the least disruption to them and the maximum inconvenience to children without affecting their schooling. They announced to the children on Friday evening that they would provide no assistance at all on the weekend. Neither parent was going to cook but children were welcome to prepare their own meals. No lifts would be provided and no washing of clothes would be done. Any items of clothing worn on the weekend would not be washed for them during the week. Rooms would not be tidied and beds would not be made unless the children performed those tasks themselves. The nature of the strike was clearly spelt out, along with the implications for the children. Alexei and Lisa explained their reasons for such extreme action. The children were stunned and strongly protested. The two parents retired to the living room.

By Saturday night the message had been driven home in no uncertain terms. The house was a mess, which made Lisa, who was a neatness fiend, squirm. However, she managed to ignore it. The children approached their parents and claimed that enough was enough and that they understood the point that their parents were making. They all decided to sit down next day and work out some arrangements about chores.

Such a tactic is extreme and can easily backfire if not handled calmly. But as these parents found, it is a very powerful way of teaching children that co-operation is an essential element of family life.

MIND THE STEPS

Chores are a part of family life. Children share in the decision-making processes of the family as well as the many daily responsibilities and tasks associated with its organisation. They help children to see that they belong to their family as useful, contributing members.

Chores are not merely good training for later life.

Use natural and logical consequences to ensure that chores are carried out.

Discuss with children a sensible allocation of household jobs and duties.

Allow children to change chores frequently, if practical, to avoid boredom and accusations of 'It's not fair. I get all the rotten jobs'.

Competition Between Siblings

'I can't understand why Terry and Phillip are so different. They have the same parents and they are both boys. They are only two years apart. My husband and I have treated them the same. We have given them the same experiences, yet they are as different as chalk and cheese. Terry is a great little reader whereas it is a struggle to get Phillip to open a book, let alone read one. Terry is quiet and thoughtful and Phillip is loud and boisterous. Terry is always inside playing with his model aeroplanes whereas you'll always find Phillip with some type of ball in his hand. They are so different, you'd swear that the milkman had a hand in it,' lamented a dismayed mother at the start of a parenting seminar.

This mother had two competitive children. Many children view their brothers and sisters as potential rivals. All children strive for status in their family. They develop behaviours, personal attributes, interests and skills that gain them significance in their family. When children compete with each other they develop in areas that differ from their rivals. If one child is an able student then the other will be good at sport or music. She will think: 'I can't be as good at school as my brother, but I can be better at sports or music – so I'll put my energies into those areas.'

Competition is usually most evident between the closest children numerically in a family. For instance, in a family of three children, the eldest will be more likely to compete with the second-born than the youngest, who will not be seen as a rival. The youngest will be likely to compete with the second-born. The second-born is surrounded by competitors.

Why does this competition occur? The eldest child was once an only child who could command her parents' total attention. Suddenly another is capable of stealing much of the first-born's limelight. The eldest, in an effort to prove her worth, will spend a great deal of time and effort trying to prove her superiority over the interloper. Eldest children frequently develop the notion that they belong in their family by being the best. Of course, as children grow up, even older children can't always be better than younger children at everything. So the eldest will not compete with her younger brother in areas that she can't prove her superiority.

The second child is in an inferior position and tries to catch up with the older sibling. When he can't catch up he adopts behaviours that are the exact opposite to those of the first-born child. In their search for significance within the family, first-and second-born children are frequently fierce competitors. They excel in completely different areas and develop different personalities.

The first child doesn't need to compete against a third child as there is usually at least a three-year age difference. The first-born is obviously more capable than number three, so there is no point competing. The second-born can't always be more capable than the eldest, but with the youngest it's a different story. In a family of three, the second-born and the youngest frequently end up being rivals. Competition is evident when children are different in personality and interests.

It is not the position in the family per se that causes the difference in children. It is children's perceptions and interpretations of their positions that shape their personalities and behaviours.

Competition in families can be extremely destructive to family harmony. Competition by its very nature requires that there be a winner and a loser. Excessive sibling rivalry is a sign of discouragement – a child adopts certain behaviours not to contribute to family welfare or for self-satisfaction but to show that he can be better than a sibling. One child elevates himself at the expense of another in the family.

Sibling competition places limits on children's behaviours,

studies and interests. Often children will not try to succeed in an area where a sibling is successful. 'Reading is taken up by my older brother. He is too good, so I won't try to compete in that area. Now what can I excel in?' thinks a competitive youngster.

Competition between brothers and sisters is expressed when:

- they constantly fight and bicker.
- they criticise each other.
- they point out the shortfalls or inadequacies of siblings.
- they tell tales to ensure that parents know how naughty the other has been.
- one tries to be better than a sibling or show that she is 'best'.
- one child is all that the other isn't.
- one child is responsible and the other is a 'behaviour problem'.

Parents can contribute to sibling rivalry

You can often unwittingly feed sibling rivalry by adopting traditional child-rearing methods. One of the most divisive practices is the use of sibling comparisons. When you hold up the behaviour of one child as a model to be copied, you are driving a wedge between children. 'Why can't you study hard like your sister?' 'Look at your brother. He keeps his room tidy. You should do the same.' 'Tony, you always make a mess when you eat. Lucy never does that. Why don't you be tidy like her?' These are all well-meaning comparisons that do little more than create further competition between family members.

Excessive praise of one child and criticism of others is another common parental practice. This can occur over a long period of time without parents being aware. A ten-year-old boy told me that his parents always praised his sister for doing chores at home. However, they always picked out his deficiencies when he helped around the house. Nothing he ever did was good enough in their eyes.

It is common for competitive children to fight with each other. In an effort to reduce the incidence of fighting, you might sometimes interfere in their disputes. Unfortunately, when you interfere it is difficult not to take sides. Often you try to apportion blame. 'Who started it?' 'John, go to your room. I've told you before not to hit your sister.' By taking sides you are reinforcing children's mistaken belief that one child is being favoured over the other.

Accept children's differences

You can do a great deal to reduce competition between your children. It is important to accept the differences in children. The unique qualities of each child in a family need to be accepted and valued. Children must believe that they can achieve in various fields, be they academic, artistic or sporting. It is essential to assist children to identify their strengths and provide them with the means of improving in those areas that they are interested in. Help children to understand that they can all achieve in different ways and that failure is only an invitation to try again.

Encourage children to take an interest in the hobbies and activities of their siblings. This can be fostered through discussions and participation in events. Seven-year-old Chris and five-year-old Angela were fiercely competitive. Chris was interested in football and Angela was an enthusiastic little ballet dancer. Their father gave up playing football games with them, as they inevitably ended up with Angela in tears. Chris was intent on proving his superiority, while Angela just wanted to have fun. Angela refused the invitation to join her brother in an organised sport session at a local oval each weekend. Instead she chose to go to ballet lessons. The father encouraged both children to take an interest in the other's hobby. He took Angela to watch Chris play in the weekend sports event and encouraged them to talk about what his son was doing. Chris at first declined an invitation to observe his sister's ballet lesson. However, he was keen to find out what she was doing. They discussed her progress throughout the year. He even enjoyed the demonstrations that she gave of any new steps that she had learned. Eventually he asked Angela if she would mind if he watched one of her lessons. When the annual ballet concert was held Chris was the most enthusiastic member of the family.

The two children both found pursuits that they could succeed in without fear of being upstaged by the other. They gradually began to take an interest in the other's hobby, free from the need to prove themselves in the eyes of the parents.

Be liberal with encouragement

Encouragement is a child's right and is not dependent on achievement. All children thrive on encouragement. They should be valued for who they are, rather than for their achievements. Children must feel that they are worthwhile in your eyes whether they are struggling in school or not. They need to be told this – repeatedly. Acceptance is not conditional upon success at any activity. All children in a family can be encouraged.

Put them in the same boat

To overcome intense competition, children should be treated as a group when they fight or misbehave. Singling children out when misbehaviour occurs reinforces the notion of one child being 'good' at the other's expense. The 'good' child behaves well not to be helpful but to appear better than the 'bad' child.

Treating the children as a unit diminishes rivalry, as they all experience the consequences of misbehaviour. It makes each child responsible for the behaviour of the other. For instance, if a mess is made in the family room the entire family can be banned from access to the area until it is tidied up. Resist finding the culprit. Let the children work together to fix the situation. Competition is generally for your benefit. It keeps you busy in many ways. Children are capable of working as a team if you cease singling out the 'bad' child in an effort to apportion blame.

In a fight it is difficult to find who is guilty and who is not. Generally they all contribute to the disturbance. Children co-ordinate their behaviour when they deal with us. When fights occur they all help in one way or another to keep them going. When children are treated as a unit they see their inter-dependence and work as a team to resolve the disturbance that has arisen.

MIND THE STEPS

Children who are close in age or adjacent in birth order often compete with each other for parental recognition.

Competition between siblings is shown through constant fighting, criticising, telling tales and a host of other behaviours.

Competitive siblings generally display different personalities and interests and excel in different areas.

You encourage sibling competition when you:

- praise one child and criticise another
- interfere in disputes
- **compare** one child with another.

To decrease competition between siblings you can:

- accept children's differences and value their uniqueness
- encourage them to take an interest in each other's activities
- stay out of their fights
- encourage both rather than praise
- have fun – engage in activities that foster co-operation.

Coping with Change

We all feel insecure when we experience sudden change in our circumstances. Children enjoy continuity and feel uncertain when events place them in unfamiliar situations. They often can't see past the short term and they think that life will never return to normal. They sometimes waste a great deal of energy trying to return to a situation that they previously enjoyed.

Children must learn to deal with changes in their lives rather than resist them. It is useless wallowing in self-pity or blocking inevitable change. They must adapt to the new circumstances as quickly as possible, so that they can once again feel in command of their lives.

There are many types of changes that can affect children. These include being left with a babysitter, starting school, a parent returning to work, shifting house, divorce or separation, or an addition to or a death in the family. These changes take some getting used to because they cause a disruption to children's lives. As parents you can't alter the circumstances that lead to an upheaval but you can help children to come to terms with the shift from the familiar to the comparatively unknown.

Here are some key elements in assisting children to cope with change.

1 **Prepare children for change if possible.** Discuss with youngsters what will occur and let them know what to expect when new circumstances are imminent. Give them plenty of time to become used to the idea of change.
2 **Keep as many things as constant as possible.** Try to keep as many familiar routines as possible and don't alter surroundings that don't need to be different. This gives children a sense of security; not everything has changed.

3 **Be prepared for behaviour blowouts.** Children will often react adversely to change and it is generally the people with whom they feel most secure who cop the fallout when children have to adapt to new circumstances that are beyond their control. They feel secure in the knowledge that those who love them won't reject them when they react badly to different circumstances.
4 **Remain firm in the face of emotional blackmail.** Children will sometimes use emotions such as anger to make you feel guilty for imposing changes, even when they are out of your control. They may also try to force you to change things back to the way they were. It is important to recognise the purpose of children's emotions or misbehaviour and help them accept change rather than a return to the good old days.
5 **Give empathy not sympathy.** Show children that you understand their worries and concerns and display faith in their ability to handle change. Sympathy is not effective. Children must move on so that they can deal with new events. Sympathy teaches children to be dependent on other people. Changes, even if tragic, offer an opportunity for children to grow and learn.
6 **Focus on the future, not the past.** Help children to see that they will, in time, adapt to changes and focus firmly on the future.

A NEW BABYSITTER

Children may react to being left with babysitters when you have a well-earned evening off. This is more common in the under-five age group, as most older children can cope with this relatively minor change.

Cherie and Rohan were held to ransom by their four-year-old daughter Karen whenever they left her in the care of a babysitter. She would cry when the babysitter arrived and continue the tears until they reluctantly left the house. Cherie would patiently try to pacify her daughter and even offered bribes of a treat the next day if she was good. They both felt so guilty leaving their daughter that they found it difficult to enjoy their evenings out. The babysitter used to push them out the door reassuring them that the situation was under control. Her assessment was correct. As soon as they were in the car the tears would cease. Karen turned on the waterworks for her parents' benefit. She made them feel guilty for daring to leave her in the care of a sitter. The behaviour worked. They did not go out as much as they would have liked -they felt that they were not being good parents, leaving their daughter in the care of a comparative stranger.

It is difficult sometimes to separate the parent from the person. As parents we may have certain beliefs about bringing up children but as adults we have needs to satisfy. One of those needs is access to a social life. As adults we have a right to a reasonable social life. This often means that children will be in the care of responsible adults other than family members. Children must learn to accept this as part of living. Parents should not be blackmailed by children's unreasonable demands.

To minimise the problems that may be caused by leaving children with babysitters there are a number of steps that can be taken. Prepare children for the babysitter by telling them well in advance that you will be going out. Tell them the name of the sitter. If possible, choose a person the children know. Make sure the children are dressed for bed before the babysitter arrives.

Involve children in welcoming the sitter by answering the door or even helping to prepare the supper. It is a good idea for children to choose a book or a game that they can share with the sitter. If possible, choose a person who doesn't mind spending some time with children rather than merely watching the television and ensuring that they are in bed on time. Keep to the same bedtime routine and expect them to behave. Once the sitter is settled, make a quick exit and ignore last-minute tears. They generally subside once you are out of the driveway. Leave a telephone number for the sitter to contact you in an emergency – the idea being that he or she rings you rather than you contacting the sitter every hour just to check that everything is all right. You deserve a little R & R, so enjoy yourself and let the sitter; whom you are probably paying anyway, worry about the children.

OFF TO WORK – OFF TO CRÈCHE

Roslyn decided that she wished to return to the workforce after spending six years at home raising her children. Her eldest child, Ella, had started school and three-year-old Darren was becoming more independent. She felt guilty leaving her son at a creche, but knew that the family would definitely benefit from a second income. Ella was pleased that Roslyn was working but Darren was unimpressed with the idea. He made his feelings clearly known when Roslyn took him to the creche for the first time. He refused to go in when they first arrived and Roslyn was forced to carry him in. He sobbed huge crocodile tears as his mother left.

In the evenings when the family gathered at home Darren clung to his mother like a leech. He demanded a great deal of Roslyn's time. He wanted to sit with her while she prepared dinner and he insisted that she bath him and dress him in his pyjamas. He whined when he didn't get his own way on any issue. Darren was certainly making up for lost time with his mother.

This is fairly typical of many children who are left in the care of child-minders after they are used to being around you for the majority of the day. They will often protest when you leave them and demand undue attention when they return to your care. Some children will regress, like Darren, and refuse to feed or dress themselves. These are excellent ways of keeping you busy with them. They are also very effective forms of punishment for you for being so bold as to leave them in the care of comparative strangers.

If you are returning to work after a long period of raising children, you must be prepared for the protests. It is important to recognise their need for attention, generally at a time of the day when you least feel like giving it. Consider the quality of the time spent with children rather than the quantity of time. Ignore misbehaviour and provide plenty of opportunities for enjoyment and sharing at appropriate times, such as after dinner. Children quickly become used to new routines and feel reassured when you play games or read with them as you did before they went to creche.

Make the transition as easy as possible by arranging a number of visits to the creche or the child-minder before the big day when your child is left there for the first time. This helps ease the trauma for both of you. Help your child to choose some toys to take from home so that he will have something familiar with him in his new surroundings. Reassure him that you will return to pick him up. If possible leave him at the creche for a couple of hours once or twice so that he knows that you will return. Most importantly, leave the guilts at home.

Shifting house

Shifting houses can be very unsettling for both children and adults. For children, a change of neighbourhood means a new school and making new friends. Children can easily resent changing schools and leaving old friends behind. Some children take such changes in their stride and others find it difficult to respond to different situations. They may take a long time adapting to their new surroundings, forming fresh friendships and dealing with the demands of a new school. An understanding approach on your part is essential if they are to settle quickly into their new neighbourhood.

Change is often more traumatic if children have it suddenly thrust upon them. Tell them well in advance of an imminent shift. Discuss the reasons for the change and point out the advantages that the new neighbourhood may offer. If practical, involve children in selecting their new home. Let them know that their needs are being considered and that their input is valued. Arrange a visit to their new school to meet the teachers and to familiarise children with the physical surroundings. Teachers may be able to assist you with making new contacts even before the children start at the school.

Children will have many regrets and reservations about shifting houses. These should be discussed fully prior to moving. Help children to talk about their worries and concerns and reassure them that life will return to normal in time.

Help children to form new friendships by encouraging them to join clubs, sporting and interest groups. Make new friends welcome into your home and assist your children to remain in contact with old acquaintances.

Make sure that your children know that you have faith in their ability to cope with the difficulties that they may encounter. Positive attitudes are catching and are extremely effective in helping children deal with changes in their lives.

STARTING SCHOOL

Starting school is often more traumatic for parents than children. While children usually look forward to the big event with enthusiasm, for parents, children starting school can mean the end of an era. It is one of the first in a series of steps which loosens the ties between you and your child. This is something that you as a parent must deal with. There are a number of things that you can do to prepare your child for starting school.

You can assist children to develop many physical skills that help them to cope on their own. Skills such as opening lunch boxes, peeling fruit and dressing can all be developed at home before entering school.

Many preschools have orientation programs that familiarise children with the routines and physical surroundings of school. If yours doesn't have such a program or you wish to back up the organised activities, there are a number of things that you can do. You can visit the school with your child to familiarise her with the exits, toilets, taps, playground and her classroom. If possible, she could use the toilets. You could have a picnic in the school grounds, your child eating the same type of food that she will eat at school. Don't worry if you or your child are unfamiliar with many of the routines and procedures that she will encounter – the teachers will spend much of the early days familiarising children with the way their school operates.

THE BIG DAY

Children generally take their cues from you. If you are anxious and uptight, so will your child be. Remain calm, friendly and encouraging in the first days of the new experience. Confidence is catching. If you display faith in your child's ability to cope with the demands of school, she is more likely to begin school with confidence.

Take your child into school and introduce her to her new teacher. Ignore any tears that occur as you are about to leave, but assure her that you will be back at the end of school to meet her and make a quick exit. It is important that you are there on time at the end of the day, as children can become very anxious if you aren't there to meet them when class is dismissed.

In the early days parents usually have a million questions to ask children about school. 'How was your day? What did you do today? Have you made any friends?' Children are often tired and are in no mood to be interrogated until they have relaxed or had a snack. Don't pester your child but let her tell you in her own time about the events of the day. Children have a great deal to do in the early days of school and need time to relax in their own way at home.

It is important to build realistic expectations of school. Children often think it is a magic place where they learn all types of things. Let children know that it takes time to learn all the things that older siblings or peers can do.

A NEW BABY IN THE FAMILY

Carmen was pleased with four-year-old Louis' initial reaction to the arrival of his new brother. He would spend time watching the baby and proudly showed him off to his friends at preschool. As time wore on and Louis learned that the baby demanded much of Carmen's time, his resentment grew. He would throw tantrums just when Carmen was about to feed the baby. He spent less and less time with the new arrival and more time being a pest, which greatly disturbed Carmen. He was also disappointed that he didn't have the playmate that his parents had promised. He thought he would have a brother with whom he could play. All the baby did was lay around on the floor, sleep or cry when he was wet or hungry. He wasn't much fun at all!

Many children react badly to the arrival of a new infant. It is vital that children be prepared thoroughly for the changes that a new member of the family causes. Let them know that even though a baby will demand much of your time you still love and care for the rest of the family. Explain that the demanding infant will not always take up so much of your time. Children don't understand that you will be tired and that when you are not tending the baby you require some rest. They often think that it is their time for a piece of the action just as you drop into a chair, exhausted after another night of broken sleep. Prepare children for this eventuality and ensure that the time you spend with the other children is quality time.

Involve children in caring for the baby as much as possible. You may buy a doll for older siblings so that they can have their own babies to feed, change and rock to sleep. Be prepared to do special activities with older children that you can't do with babies. 'I love drawing pictures with you. I can't do that with the baby.' Don't overreact to children's feelings of jealousy. Show your children that you care for them all equally but in different ways.

SEPARATION OR DIVORCE

The separation or divorce of a couple requires a great deal of personal adjustment. Usually parents have the opportunity to prepare children for the likelihood of such an event. Children generally become angry, guilty or frustrated by the separation of the two adults that they care most about. A thorough preparation will help them to cope with the split and deal with the intensity of their emotions.

Children often blame themselves for causing a split in the family. They have feelings of self-recrimination and believe that somehow their behaviour led to the separation. Both parents need to assure children that the split occurred due to a breakdown in the marriage relationship. While the children will feel the effects of that breakdown, they did not cause it.

Help children to understand that while you as a couple had problems, you as individuals are still the same. Children look up to adults and they need to understand that the qualities they admire and respect in their parents have not changed.

After the separation, much opportunity for discussion is needed to assist children to work through their emotions and deal with the difficulties that they may encounter. Some children have difficulty accepting the fact that the family unit as they know it has changed. They may harbour secret hopes of a reconciliation between their parents. It is essential that children face the reality of the situation as soon as possible. The quicker they come to terms with a separation the sooner they will adapt to the changes that are inevitable. Help children to focus firmly on the future rather than hoping for a return to the past.

Children generally love both parents unconditionally. They do not need to hear one parent being critical of the other once the separation has occurred. Comments such as 'Your father is so lazy' are very hurtful to children. They must be able to maintain close relationships with both parents, free from the bitterness that their parents may be experiencing.

DEATH IN THE FAMILY

When a parent dies, children often have feelings of guilt or anger. 'Why did he leave me in such a way? What have I done to deserve this?' As a spouse, you must deal with your own grief. As a parent, you must help children to adjust to the reality of the death and focus on where the family goes from here. Your understanding of children's anger or guilt will help them accept the death and assist them to get on with their lives.

The death of a parent usually places extra demands on children. There is one less adult in the family to share the load of everyday life. The sole parent must seize the opportunity to teach children independence at an early age. Their contribution to the family should not be overlooked even in the time of grief.

The sense of loss and loneliness should be dealt with together. Many parents have found that their bond with children is strengthened through the loss of a spouse.

The death of a sibling is difficult for children to deal with. As in the case of a parent's death, children must face up to the life without a sibling as soon as possible. Assist them to deal with their emotions and come to terms with the death.

You must be careful not to idolise the dead child. This can place enormous pressure on the other children. It is particularly difficult for the next youngest child, who can never hope to live up to the reputation of a dead sibling.

MIND THE STEPS

If possible prepare children for the likelihood of change so they will know what to expect from a new situation.

As far as possible, keep things constant and familiar to children when they are faced with a change in circumstances.

Be prepared for a behaviour blowout. Children will often vent their feelings on those they love.

Show an understanding of the dilemma that they may face and display faith in their ability to cope with change.

Be firm when children use emotions to make you feel guilty or force you to change the situation.

Focus firmly on the future rather than the past.

Dawdlers and Procrastinators

'John, you'll be late for school. Mrs Brown will be here in ten minutes to pick you up and you're not even dressed. Have you had any breakfast?' Eve said.

'No, not yet,' John replied. 'Honestly, anyone would think that you were deliberately going slowly. Come on!' Eve said in despair. John ambled along, getting ready in his own time. He knew that his mother wouldn't let him go to school until he was properly dressed and had eaten a decent breakfast.

His assessment, as usual, was correct. When Mrs Brown arrived John was not ready. His mother explained to her that John would be there in a minute or two. She apologised for his tardiness, blaming herself for sleeping in and not waking John in time to be ready. When John came to the car he greeted Mrs Brown with a cheery smile and kissed his mother goodbye. He didn't apologise for keeping Mrs Brown waiting. He knew that his mother would have done that already for him.

Eve is more concerned with John's lack of punctuality than he is. He usually dawdles in the morning, safe in the knowledge that his mother will ensure that he is not late. She coaxes him, nags him, packs his lunch, prepares his clothes and helps him to dress. She even apologises for him when he inconveniences others. She is a good parent who will cover for her son to protect him from discomfort. John realises that his mother will protect him from the effects of his dawdling, so he takes advantage of this. The morning procrastination places his mother at his beck and call. The more slowly he moves, the faster she works to compensate for his inactivity.

Eve needs to ignore John when he dawdles in the morning. She should provide a reasonable amount of assistance for him but she shouldn't accept all his responsibilities. After all, Mrs Brown is driving John to school, not his mother. If he is late when Mrs Brown arrives, Eve does not have to apologise for him. She needs only to say, 'John is not ready yet. You go along. He will walk to school this morning.' John will have to deal with being late when he arrives at school.

You should show children that you are unconcerned with procrastination. Look behind any dawdler and you will find a parent who is eager to shield a child from the consequences of procrastination. Dawdlers can be infuriating, particularly to parents who value punctuality. They are extremely powerful because they can easily place you into their service with their time-wasting and go-slow tactics. Parents constantly nag. and remind dawdlers. 'Do this ... do that ... hurry up or you'll be late ... your dinner is getting cold ... don't miss the bus ... '

To change dawdlers, you need to alter your way of reacting to go-slow tactics. You should be unconcerned with procrastinators and allow them to experience the consequences of their dawdling. This is excellent training in independence, as it places the responsibility where it belongs.

Consequences of dawdling

Many parents who have expressed their concern about dawdlers have found that when they allow their children to feel the consequences of their dawdling, the behaviour ceases. Children do not continue behaviours that inconvenience them.

Here are some ways in which parents have extricated themselves from power struggles over procrastination and allowed natural consequences to shape the behaviour of their children.

Helena ran the bath for her four-year-old daughter, Gretel. 'Your bath is ready, sweetheart,' she said. Gretel nodded her head in acknowledgement but continued watching the television. Helena resisted the temptation to remind her daughter. She continued preparing the dinner for the family. Gretel slowly undressed in front of the television, unconcerned with time ticking by. When she eventually took her bath she found that the water was lukewarm. 'Mum, could you put some hot water in my bath? It is too cold!' she yelled to her mother. 'I'm sorry dear. I'm busy cooking. I did let you know that your bath was ready ten minutes ago. Quickly wash yourself and get out.' 'Aw Mum, it's not fair!' protested Gretel. Helena reminded her daughter that she should be quicker next time if she wanted to have a warm bath.

Seven-year-old Michael picked at his meal. 'I don't like this, Dad.' 'If you aren't hungry, don't eat it,' his father replied. 'It's not that bad,' answered Michael, who continued to take his time with his meal. His father realised that Michael wanted him to become involved in an argument over the meal. He did not accept the invitation to coax his son to eat. After everyone had finished the meal he told Michael that he could eat his dinner, which by now was cold, or he could put it in the refrigerator and eat it at another time. Michael, who was quite hungry, grudgingly ate his cold dinner on his own.

Pia reminded her nine-year-old daughter Carla that she needed to clean her room before she could watch her favourite program on television. The family had agreed that bedrooms would be tidied before the television was turned on. Carla ignored her mother and continued playing on the computer in her father's office. She eventually began to clean her room, but very slowly. When it was time for her television show to start she rushed into the lounge room and turned on the television. Her mother immediately turned the volume down and reminded Carla of their agreement. Her daughter cleaned her bedroom in a flash.

'We will be leaving in fifteen minutes!' Gary announced to his family, who were going on a trip to the zoo. Gary's eldest children, Tara, ten, and Simone, eight, were busily dressing and collecting games to occupy them in the car. However, five-year-old Danielle ambled through the house in her pyjamas. 'Come on, Danielle, we'll be late if you don't get a move on,' prompted Tara. Danielle giggled and began to annoy her sister. When it was time to leave, she was still not dressed, so her mother collected the clothes which she had previously placed on her youngest daughter's bed and took them to the car. 'You can get dressed once we arrive,' her mother said, unperturbed by her daughter's dawdling. Danielle screamed in protest but no one took any notice. Her father then gave her a clear choice: 'Either you walk to the car or I will carry you.' She quietly walked to the car and had to dress herself in the car when they arrived.

As these parents learned, the only person who should be concerned with dawdling is the person who procrastinates. You need to respect children's right to choose how they will behave, as long as you allow them to experience the consequences that dawdling incurs. Children will generally alter their behaviour when the consequences inconvenience them rather than you.

MIND THE STEPS

Dawdling is an excellent way of keeping parents busy with children.

The only person who should be concerned with procrastination is the dawdler.

Allow procrastinators to experience the consequences of their dawdling.

Dressing

'Never do for a child what a child can do for himself,' Rudolf Dreikurs wrote. Dressing provides a wonderful opportunity for teaching young children to do things for themselves. Time and again I hear of doting parents who dress their children dutifully each day. A mother disagreeing with my calls for increased independence once said, 'But I love dressing Pamela. It is a special part of the day when I can snuggle her and kiss her.' I am not denying the mother a close moment with her daughter. This is wonderful and an important part of building a relationship. However, her emphasis should be on teaching the child to dress herself, rather than doing it for her. She can still spend time cuddling while she is showing her how to put on socks, knickers, pants and so on. The task of dressing can be broken into simple skills that young children enjoy becoming competent in.

I am often asked at what age should children be expected to dress themselves. The simple answer is: when they are able to. Children vary in rates of physical maturation but certainly most children have the motor skills to dress themselves by the time they start preschool. They should be able to dress themselves before they attend school. Parents also need to be aware of children's attempts to tie shoelaces. Teaching children the complex job of tying shoelaces is a marvellous investment of a parent's time. It is a great motor co-ordination activity that helps prepare little fingers for the writing task at school.

Reluctant dressers

Some children are experts at keeping parents in their service. They will use incapability as a sure-fire way of keeping you busy with them. 'But Mum, I can't do it. I'm too small' is an often-used plea. What children are really saying is 'I can't do it. I won't try and I want you to do it for me.' You should resist such attempts to place yourself in children's service if self-reliance is to be developed.

When children are unwilling to participate in dressing tasks you should withdraw your assistance. Be prepared for a child to spend the day in pyjamas. He will soon dress himself if you announce that you are going shopping and you are happy to take him in his pyjamas. Similarly, be prepared to take children to school or kindergarten in various states of undress. Before attempting such a ploy it is helpful to give teachers some warning. They are generally responsive to any activity that reduces children's dependence on adults.

Choice of clothes

The types of clothes children wear often concern parents. Some children are fashion conscious at a very young age and 'wouldn't be seen dead' in certain clothes. Others don't care what they wear as long as they are allowed to play without restrictions. There is also that strange breed of children without any weather sense at all; they will happily venture outside on a bleak winter's day in only T-shirts and shorts. Choice of clothing can be a source of conflict between children and parents. Weather, fashion and purpose dictate the clothes that we wear. Unfortunately, children do not always have such a balanced outlook when they go to the wardrobe each morning.

There are three approaches available when you are considering who should choose the clothes that children wear each day. Each is appropriate in different circumstances.

Parent's choice

This approach is good for very young children as they need to be taught how to choose clothes. Many children will choose the same clothes whatever the occasion because they like the colour, they find them comfortable or they are easy to put on. You need to provide toddlers and preschool children with a great deal of guidance. If a child has his heart set on wearing an item and there is no practical reason for him not to, then it is pointless fighting over it.

As children grow older they often resent parental interference in delicate matters such as clothing. For these children you need to take a less interventionist approach.

Provide choices

As children progress through primary school they generally like to assume greater responsibility for choosing what they place their bodies in. They still need some guidance and you may feel that your investment in clothing gives you a right to influence your children's choice of clothing. You can influence children if you provide them with realistic choices.

'Carlo, we are visiting your grandmother today. You may wish to choose your new jeans or your blue cords.'

'Simone, it is hot today. It would be a good idea to wear a summer dress or shorts and a T-shirt.'

By limiting the range of clothes which children may choose from, you are teaching them to dress appropriately as well as involving them in decision making.

Free choice

Some children, particularly those approaching the teen years, resent any parental interference in the matter of clothing. They will often choose to wear 'those jeans with the holes' because they realise they are what you have been trying to steer them away from. It is a good idea to give older children freedom to choose their clothing within a few broad limits. For example, certain clothes are suitable for school and certain items are best suited for leisure.

Natural and logical consequences can influence children to choose clothes wisely. For instance, a child who chooses not to take a jumper to school will be cold. If this bothers her, she should remember to take one next time. If it is not a concern for the child then it should not be a cause of worry for parents. It is unlikely that she will die from cold in this country. If a child wears formal clothes to an informal gathering and everyone else is dressed casually, then he may be embarrassed and dress more suitably next time. If it doesn't worry your child then it shouldn't bother you.

Parents who give children freedom to choose their clothes may find that they need to discuss the suitability of clothes for different occasions. For instance, certain clothes are more appropriate to be worn when playing with a friend than on a visit to grandparents. Children need to learn these loose social conventions, as they are a part of everyday life.

But it is embarrassing

Some parents can be acutely embarrassed by their children's choice of clothes. One mother admitted that she almost regretted her decision to allow her three young children to choose their clothes before a shopping trip. She pushed the trolley around the supermarket, accompanied by her eldest son dressed as Batman, her six-year-old daughter wearing a fairy costume and her youngest son wearing one of his sister's old dresses. She felt embarrassed but she was happy that she had avoided unnecessary conflict at home by allowing her children to dress as they saw fit. She realised that choosing clothes is a terrific opportunity for children to accept responsibility for their actions.

Fussy dressers

Sometimes the purchase of clothes can be a contentious issue with older children. They often won't be caught dead in the clothes that you buy for them. To avoid this potential conflict it is appropriate to provide a clothing allowance for older children who have very particular tastes in clothes. They can purchase their fashion accessories free from parental interference. Children are generally more discerning when they are responsible for buying their own clothes.

MIND THE STEPS

Teach children to dress themselves and allow them to take responsibility for dressing at an early age.

The choice of clothes should not be a source of conflict between you and your children. Work out together the correct clothing for various occasions and weather conditions and allow children to experience the consequences of their decisions.

Eating and Mealtimes

Mealtimes provide the opportunity for communication and pleasant conversation. In our Western culture the evening meal tends to be the main meal of the day: breakfast is often gulped down; lunch is generally a refuelling exercise eaten on the run. The evening meal provides the only real opportunity for a family to come together and enjoy each other's company while food is eaten.

Of course, it is often difficult for families even to share a meal in the evening. Parents may work late and children may have outside interests which cause them to miss a family meal. However, whenever possible, families should come together and share a meal in the evenings. The television set should be turned off – a meal eaten in front of the television may satisfy children's appetites but it serves no social function. There is little opportunity to talk about the events of the day when children's attention is directed to the television rather than conversation.

MEALTIMES

Mealtimes should be an enjoyable experience for everyone who takes part. Parents and children have a right to eat in peace free from noisy or boisterous behaviour. To maintain a orderly atmosphere it may be necessary to establish guidelines for children. Rules such as 'We sit down while we eat' provide guidelines for children and teach them appropriate behaviours. They do not have to be listed and placed on a sign above the kitchen table. They can be informal procedures that are discussed with children as the need arises.

Children can assist you with the many tasks associated with mealtime. They can help prepare meals, set the dinner table and clear and wash dishes. Many parents of eager toddlers will grimace at the idea of young children helping to prepare a meal. The mess they make and the time taken may be counter-productive. This is a judgement that you must make as a parent. It is unrealistic for a child to 'help' you all the time, particularly when you are in a hurry. However, a compromise can often be reached. They can help some of the time and in many different ways. A male acquaintance encourages his four-year-old daughter to assist him in the kitchen. He claims he has enough difficulty organising himself in the kitchen, let alone a four-year-old. He discovered an excellent task for his daughter to do which was also a help to him. He peels and cuts the vegetables and the youngster places the various pieces in saucepans ready to be placed on the stove. With a little thought children can be encouraged to assist in ways that cause little inconvenience to you.

Shared meals provide an excellent opportunity to teach children table manners. Children are often not the neatest of eaters. To encourage neatness and promote the use of reasonable manners, some families make one meal each week a very formal affair. Children enjoy seeing the dinner table set with a tablecloth, flowers and serviettes. An occasional visit to a restaurant enables their skills and manners to be put into practice in a different setting.

TO EAT OR NOT TO EAT

How much food a child eats is the cause of much conflict in many households. Parents are often concerned about the types and quantities of food that their children consume. This concern becomes an excellent weapon for attention or power seekers. Picking at food, refusing to eat and leaving the vegetables are excellent ways of keeping worried parents in the service of children. 'Come on, finish your vegetables, then you can have sweets' is the universal catchcry of this generation of parents. Children soon learn that their parents are more concerned about eating than they are.

Eating is a child's business. There is little need to force-feed children or demand that the plate be emptied. Neither should they be praised for eating. It is absurd to think that a child should receive recognition for fulfilling a necessary bodily function. 'You have satisfied your hunger. What a guy!' When children are praised for eating all their meal they are receiving a clear message: 'My parents are very concerned about the amount of food I eat. When I eat all the meal I make them happy and I can annoy them by eating a small amount or refusing to eat.' Parents create problems for themselves when they insist that food be eaten. It is a child's decision to eat. Given the choice to eat or starve, children will choose the former every time!

When children refuse to eat, miss a meal or merely pick at their plate, they should be allowed to experience the consequences of their decision. Children who don't eat or eat very little become hungry. This is a natural consequence. There is little need to interfere in this process. However, a child who takes two bites from a meal and leaves it should not be permitted to have a snack an hour later. He should be allowed to experience the consequences of his decision. He may eat his meal cold or heat it himself. Alternatively, he can wait until the next meal, by which time he is likely to be very hungry and eat the lot. The message is simple – don't force a child to eat; allow natural consequences to regulate children's eating patterns.

A couple approached me and outlined their concern about their son's rather peculiar eating habits. The lad, ten, basically lived on a diet of Vegemite sandwiches. They were happy for him to eat the sandwiches for lunch but they objected to serving them in the evening, as they thought he wasn't getting a balanced diet. He refused to eat the standard meat-with-three-vegetables meal served up at night. His parents tried to coax him to eat a decent meal. Instead he would leave the prepared meal untouched and secretly make himself Vegemite sandwiches later on. He even made them in the middle of the night. His parents said that he was a healthy specimen who enjoyed an active life.

These parents were involved in a power struggle with their son. He used their concern about his eating habits to defeat them. He was letting his parents know that they couldn't make him do anything that he didn't want to do. I advised them to remove themselves from the power struggle by giving him permission to eat Vegemite sandwiches three times a day. He couldn't fight with his parents if suddenly he was allowed to eat as he wished. The child soon grew tired of his limited diet. Within a week of his parents granting him permission to choose what he wanted to eat, he had changed his eating habits. His parents had remained unconcerned about the food he chose to eat, so he had received no reward for his rather peculiar taste.

Fussy eaters

Children can be extremely fussy about the types of food they eat. They tend to have very conservative tastes and are often unwilling to try new or unusual food. Some children are very choosy about the vegetables that they eat. There is little need to be overly concerned with fussiness. Given time and freedom of choice, children will generally develop varied tastes.

An effective strategy for choosy eaters is to serve a meal from the dinner table. The various components of a meal are brought to the table in dishes or even saucepans. The children then choose the food they want to eat. They should be expected to eat what they choose, except if they are trying something for the first time. In this way children will vary their choices over a period of time. Be unconcerned if a child chooses only one item at first. She will soon grow tired of the same type of food. In extreme cases, for instance if a child chooses to eat only meat, the body will crave a variety to satisfy its needs.

Dessert should not be a reward for eating all their veggies. It should be treated as a part of the meal. It should be a small portion and if a child eats only dessert she will soon be hungry.

Dawdlers and late-comers

Children have the capacity to make mealtime stretch for an eternity. For some children, eating is a very social experience that is to be enjoyed. Other children will dawdle for ages, merely picking at their meals. Dawdlers are experts at wasting parents' time. Children should be expected to finish their meals in a reasonable amount of time. Meals can be removed at the end of the allocated time or, alternatively, a dawdler can be left at the table to eat his meal on his own.

All members of the family can be made aware of mealtimes. There is little need to be reminded time and again that it is mealtime. This develops parent-deafness and teaches children to be over-reliant on their parents. While it may be your responsibility to cook meals, it is not your responsibility to ensure that children eat. Cold food is the consequence of being late for a meal. Children will soon learn that you are not in the business of running a restaurant if you show your unwillingness to serve meals whenever it suits them.

Misbehaviour at mealtimes

'I've been hard at work all day. I just want to sit down and enjoy my meal in peace. Instead the children make eating a chore. They are up and down from their chairs like yo-yos and they continually argue with each other. I sometimes dread eating with my family,' complained a parent in despair.

You should be able to enjoy a family meal free from

misbehaviour. Eating should be an experience to be enjoyed rather than endured. This parent needs to discuss the possible consequences of misbehaviour with his children. He needs to be firm, consistent and willing to ignore any protests about consequences imposed. As the purpose of mealtime is eating, it is reasonable to assume that children who play or misbehave at the dinner table are not hungry. At least this is the approach that our concerned parent should take. When a child constantly disturbs others with his misbehaviour, his meal should be removed: 'I see from your behaviour that you are not hungry.' It is important to remain calm and unperturbed by the misbehaviour. Allow the child, not you, to feel the consequences of playing up at the dinner table.

Routine

An orderly routine should be maintained so that children can arrange their activities around mealtimes. Otherwise you will find yourself in the difficult position of arranging meals around children's schedules. Then you might as well open a restaurant!

Mind the steps

Mealtimes should be enjoyable times that provide excellent opportunities for communication between all members of the family.

Table manners can be taught at mealtimes in an informal way.

Children should be able to determine the quantity of food they are to eat. If they leave or refuse food then they should not be permitted to snack between meals.

Misbehaviour need not be tolerated at the meal table. Either ask misbehaving children to leave or withdraw yourself to a quieter area.

Fears

Many children have fears that surface at various times or stages in their lives. Fear is an emotion that influences behaviour. It serves two purposes: it generally leads to an avoidance of a situation and, although unintentional, it is an excellent way of gaining attention. Look how one young child used fear of the dark to achieve these two purposes. Five-year-old Kim was scared of the dark. She would cry out when left alone in her room at night if the light was off. Her mother, wishing to help her child overcome her fear, would stay with her, rubbing her head until she went to sleep. The child would not settle while the room was dark, so her mother left the light on. The youngster's behaviour, driven by fear, put her mother in her service and avoided the necessity of sleeping in the dark. Her mother's reaction did nothing to alleviate her concerns – in fact, it reinforced Kim's belief that the dark was something to be afraid of.

Children are not born with fears. They learn to be afraid of various aspects of their world. Sometimes fears are triggered by an event or unfortunate experience. Five-year-old Emilio was bitten by a dog when very young. He has been afraid of dogs ever since that unfortunate incident occurred. Whenever a dog approaches him in the street he screams and shakes uncontrollably.

Some fears that are linked to earlier events are quite irrational but nevertheless very real. Five-year-old Tom is quite convinced that any green food will make him sick. This belief is based on the fact that he vomited in public after drinking lime lemonade. Tom made the link between the colour green and being sick, and an irrational fear emerged.

Children's fears are often intensified by the reactions of adults. In some cases adults actually create the fears that children may have. Six-year-old Kylie was going to the dentist for the first time for a check-up. She knew little about the dentist except for a few shady ideas that she had picked up from watching television. She took her cue from her mother, who made a fuss about the ordeal. 'There is nothing to be afraid of Kylie. The dentist won't hurt you. When you have finished I'll buy you a little surprise,' said an anxious mother. Kylie learned from her mother's reaction that a trip to the dentist was not going to be a pleasant experience. She grew to fear the dentist before she had even put one foot inside the surgery.

Children often fear the unfamiliar and the unknown. A child who has never been to hospital to visit a relative or friend is more likely to be afraid of spending time in one than a child who has been a regular visitor. Similarly, a child who has a dog at home is less likely to be afraid of a noisy dog than a child who has had little experience of them.

It is important to distinguish between fear and caution. Caution is the sensible recognition of possible dangers and the consideration of ways of dealing with them safely. For instance, a child should use caution when crossing streets and around swimming pools. A child should not fear these, but he should recognise that there are potential hazards and consider the best way to deal with them. Fear is a debilitating emotion which diminishes the ability to cope with situations. A child who fears water will not go near a pool, let alone work out the most appropriate safety measures to be taken.

Dealing with fears

You can help children overcome their fears, but there is no quick fix or miracle cure. First investigate the source of children's fears. If there is a valid reason for children to be afraid, don't display overconcern. This only heightens the fear. 'Dad is concerned so it must be serious' is the interpretation of many children. Discuss with children the source of the anxiety and help them to realise that there is no real need for fear. Five-year-old Emilio who was bitten by a dog needs to under-stand that not all dogs will bite just because he experienced one that did. He may need to play with some friendly dogs so that he learns that they are a source of enjoyment rather than fear.

Discuss with children strategies for coping with their fears. Children who have nightmares can turn the light on and read until the fear has subsided. Don't show the anxiety you feel about your children's fears. This only makes children anxious as well. Don't ignore their fears. Show children that you recognise their concerns and you have faith in their ability to deal with them.

Sometimes children have no real reason for fear and they use it as a means of gaining attention. Fear is a very persuasive way of keeping parents in the service of children. It tugs at the heartstrings and appeals to the basic need to protect our loved ones from discomfort and harm. Children must face their fears if they are to overcome them rather than use them as an excuse to avoid situations.

Fear of the dark

Many children are afraid of the dark. A healthy imagination combined with a fear of the unknown causes many children to see all sorts of creepy-crawlies that don't exist. The use of nightlights is common, although they do nothing to alleviate the fear. They merely help children to go to sleep. Help children to understand that there is nothing to fear. It is important that you don't overreact and you treat the fear as a normal part of growing up. Let children sleep with the nightlight on if they wish. Often children decide to leave their nightlight off and are comforted by the knowledge that it is there if they need it.

Some children want their parents to be near them at night. Have faith in children's ability to cope and assure them that the fear (and the monsters) will go away when they fall asleep.

Nightmares

We all have nightmares from time to time. There are theories to explain their occurrence too numerous to mention. Help your child to deal with nightmares by explaining that they are normal and that they will occasionally occur. Provide children with comfort until they are settled and return them to bed. Don't show anxiety or they will soon learn that nightmares are to be feared.

Fear of the dentist

A friend of mine realised that the unknown is a source of fear so she undertook an extensive familiarisation process with her dentist. She took her young children into the surgery whenever she needed dental work done. She went to great pains to hide her own anxiety, although she admitted that there was pain involved. The dentist played his part by showing her children some of the instruments that he used. They even held them, although they weren't too keen to get their hands on the syringe. When it was their turn to visit the surgery for some repairs, the children were not intimidated by the noise or the instruments that were thrust into their mouths. They were aware that it may hurt a bit but they were prepared for rather than scared of the experience.

When we expect children to be scared of such situations, they will usually meet our expectations.

Mind the steps

Fear, like all emotions, serves a purpose. It gains attention for children as well as providing a reason for avoiding potentially unpleasant situations.

Investigate the source of the fear. If the fear is valid, don't display over-concern. Discuss with your child ways which enable them to cope with the source of the fear.

If the fear is largely unfounded, provide minimum attention and don't be blackmailed by your child's reactions.

Distinguish between fear and caution. Caution is a recognition of possible dangers and fear diminishes the ability to cope with situations.

Fighting Among Siblings

Cindy, nine, and Damon, seven, were watching television while their mother was sewing nearby. Suddenly Damon let out an ear-piercing yell. Their mother looked up but there was silence. Then Damon said to Cindy: 'You shouldn't hit me. I'm watching my favourite show.' 'Well, you don't need to sit so close to the television – you are blocking my view,' Cindy retorted. A few minutes later Cindy whacked Damon on the arm, saying, 'Stop wriggling about, I can't stand it.' Damon kicked his sister in the shin and she ran screaming to her mother, who listened to Cindy's complaints and went swiftly to deal with Damon. 'You should not kick your sister. How many times have I told you that only horses kick? Now go to your room and don't come out until I tell you!' Damon shuffled off to his room, determined to get even with his sister at a later date.

This scene is re-enacted in thousands of homes in many different ways. Fighting and arguing between siblings is so common that it is considered normal by many parents. Recently I conducted research into problem behaviours that worry parents. Seventy-three per cent of parents claimed that fighting between siblings was a common occurrence in their household. Forty-five per cent claimed that fighting was the behaviour that caused them the greatest concern. These are staggering statistics; sibling fighting is common in three out of every four families and is the greatest behavioural problem in just under half of the families surveyed. It may be common for siblings to fight but it is not necessarily normal behaviour. Children do not have to fight. There is no inbuilt mechanism that makes them fight with their brothers and sisters. There is no Eleventh Commandment 'Thou shalt fight and argue with thy brother or sister'.

The purpose of fighting

Children fight in order to involve their parents. Look what happens in fights. Parents almost always enter into the dispute in some way. They may assume the role of umpire who makes a ruling to end the dispute. 'That is John's toy and you have no right to snatch it from him, James. Now give it back.' 'Kim, you watched your favourite show last night. It is Kelly's turn to choose tonight.' The role of policeman is often assumed when order is to be maintained. 'Gabriela, you apologise to your sister for hitting her or you will be sent to your room.' 'Some alternative!' thinks Gabriela. Generally, when you enter into children's fighting you take sides. It is very difficult to avoid taking sides and this is what they want. Think of any fight between children and you will realise that it almost always results in a parent being involved.

Parents step into disputes for many different reasons. You may wish to avoid a child being hurt or you may want to teach children that fighting is not an appropriate way to behave. You may intervene purely to obtain some peace and quiet in the house or to ensure that justice is carried out. When you intervene you rob children of the opportunity to resolve their own disputes. You also ensure that your children will continue squabbling, as your interference is what keeps them fighting.

I recently met a couple who had different reactions to their children's fighting. Their situation demonstrated that children fight for the purpose of keeping parents busy with them. The father worked a day shift and the mother worked as a nurse at night. They had three school-aged children. Their mother complained that the children squabbled so much when they came home from school that they made her life unbearable. She had tried lecturing them, punishing them and sending them to their rooms. None of this worked – although the fighting subsided temporarily, it would continue at the next available opportunity.

The father didn't see that fighting was a problem. He couldn't understand his wife's concern, as he saw little evidence of their squabbling. In the evenings when he was home and his wife was working, the children hardly fought at all. When they did fight he was completely unconcerned. He simply moved upstairs, away from the vicinity of the dispute and resisted any attempts that the children made to involve him. The children rarely fought when he was around, as they saw little point in engaging in a behaviour that gave them no pay-off.

Children fight over a range of issues. It may be an argument over the choice of television programs, or about who has the biggest serving of ice-cream. The issues are endless but they all indicate sibling rivalry which parents reinforce when they take sides. 'Mum (or Dad) always takes the other side' is a common complaint of children.

WHO PROVOKES FIGHTS?

Youngest children often provoke fights in families because they know that parents will generally be protective of them. Five-year-old Reuben ran to his mother, claiming that his older sister was picking on him. His mother immediately rebuked Reuben's sister, reminding her that he was only little. This only encouraged Reuben to annoy his sister again, as he knew that his mother would protect him should she be foolish enough to retaliate.

Eldest children often fight with younger siblings when they feel unfairly treated. Fighting is a good way of getting even with younger brothers and sisters as well as with parents.

It is often more common for children to fight when they are playing in a group of three than when two are playing together. One child can feel alienated from a game or activity.

When this occurs, sabotage is a good way of retaliating and ensuring that she is included.

You should be unconcerned about who provokes fights and arguments. It is often impossible to work out who started a fight because children will always blame each other. It takes the detective skills of Miss Marple to find the real culprit. The concern should be about resolving the dispute rather than apportioning blame.

How to reduce the incidence of fighting

To reduce fighting in families you need to prevent children from achieving their goal – to keep you busy and involved with them. It is important to recognise the purpose of their behaviour. It is helpful to accept that children have the right to fight but they must not disturb parents. There are a number of strategies that you can employ to reduce conflict. They all have in common the fact that they encourage children to resolve their own disputes.

Permission to fight

Bill and Georgina were troubled by their children's treatment of each other. Georgina claimed that Tim, six, and Penny, eight, always yelled at each other and enjoyed seeing the other being punished by Bill or herself. Both parents agreed that there was little that they could do to stop them fighting with each other, so they gave them permission to fight. They told the two children that in future they were welcome to fight if they wished but they were not to disturb their parents. Fighting could occur in bedrooms or in the backyard. If they fought in another part of the house they would be invited to continue the fight in one of those two locations. Once the children were given permission to fight, the reason for fighting had been taken away. The incidence of fighting dropped dramatically. When they fought they were usually invited to go to their bedroom, which they shared. They usually resolved the dispute quickly, as they were not allowed to come out until they had reached a solution or an agreement.

Establish rules for fighting

It is helpful to establish rules with children for fighting. The rules may outline the types of behaviours that are acceptable and the places where fighting may occur. The establishment of such procedures teaches children that disputes of any kind should be dealt with in an orderly way. Sometimes children are unaware of appropriate ways of handling disputes and they need some guidelines to follow.

A parent told me that his children fought very little since they had formulated some acceptable rules for fighting. They never fought at night because the place for fighting in his household was in the backyard and they were never too keen to argue outside in the dark.

Help children resolve problems

When children come to you with complaints about unfair treatment by a sibling, let them know that you are willing to help them solve a problem but you are not willing to take sides in a fight. Children often need assistance to resolve conflicts and parents can play an active part in finding solutions agreeable to all. This is different from entering into children's fights.

Consider Mira, who was besieged by her six-year-old twin daughters. They couldn't agree about what game they were to play. A slanging match quickly evolved with each child blaming the other for never wanting to play her games. Mira said, 'I'm not going to help you fight but I will help you find a solution. If you wish to fight then I will continue with what I am doing.' The girls agreed to Mira's conditions. She listened to both her daughters and helped them to clarify the dispute. She made three suggestions for the girls to choose from. They could either play separately, play one or either of the girl's games or play one for a while then change to the other. The girls chose the third solution and played quite happily. Mira avoided making a choice for the children, leaving the decision making up to them. She merely outlined the choices, thus helping them to resolve the dispute rather than entering into a fight as the children originally wanted. If you can't resolve the problem and a fight eventuates, don't give up. There are still some strategies – you can bear it, you can beat it or you can boot them out!

Bear it

Parents who are able to ignore children's noisy fights find that sooner or later they will stop. This can be quite difficult for many people who simply dislike their tranquillity being disturbed. Diane related how her two children were so noisy when arguing one day that her neighbour came in to check that everything was all right. She assured her friend that her children were having a disagreement and that they were simply working it out. Her children rarely fought but when they did it sounded like World War III was about to erupt. However, Diane refused to enter into the fray. The fact that fights rarely occurred suggests the effectiveness of ignoring children's fights.

Beat it

It is important not to provide an audience for children's fighting. Diane chose to remain in the vicinity when her children fought but she gave them no response. Through her lack of involvement she refused to provide an audience for her children. You may find it easier to leave the scene of the dispute – besides it is quieter that way. When the fighting has stopped you should come back in silence, without mentioning the fight. Your swift withdrawal is an effective consequence for fighting. It lets children know that you are unwilling to be a party to their disputes.

Boot them out

Many people find it easier to allow children to fight in a particular part of the house or even outside. When they fight they should be made aware of the choices available to them. When they fight, say, 'If you wish to remain inside you cannot fight or argue. However, if you wish to fight then you must go outside.' If they refuse to go outside and they continue fighting then they should be put outside in silence. Your apparent lack of concern about the squabbles themselves will have a powerful effect on the incidence of sibling fighting.

Discuss alternatives to fighting

Sometimes children are unaware that there are alternatives to fighting. They do not have to be victims of older siblings and they do not always have to win an argument. A four-year-old once told me that his seven-year-old brother used to pinch and punch him while they watched television. They always sat next to each other on the couch when watching television. When I suggested that he sit elsewhere, he said that the couch was the best place to sit in the room. I asked him if there were other comfortable places to sit while watching television. He told me that there were but he added that he wouldn't sit in the other chairs because his brother wouldn't sit in them. This was a dispute based more on an unwillingness to concede ground. If the child wanted to avoid the conflict he could have sat elsewhere and enjoyed the television in comfort. Instead, he chose to stay and fight. Children do not have to be victims; they can usually avoid conflict if they wish. It takes two to start a fight but usually one person finishes it. This is often the point where parents step in.

You may find it helpful to discuss alternatives to fighting. For instance, children may go to a bedroom to avoid conflict or play another game. Children are able to come up with many suggestions which are useful for avoiding the inevitable fights.

When you cease to be impressed by fighting and refuse to be drawn into conflicts, the incidence of fighting reduces dramatically. Fighting is nearly always for the benefit of parents, who generally can't resist becoming involved in children's disputes.

MIND THE STEPS

Children in a family generally fight with each other to involve parents. Constant fighting is a symptom of competition between siblings.

Resist the temptation to interfere in children's disputes. It is pointless taking sides or trying to lay blame for a dispute.

When siblings argue and fight with each other you may:

- grant children permission to fight
- establish rules for fighting
- assist children to resolve their fights without you becoming involved
- ignore the fight
- leave the scene
- boot them outside
- discuss alternatives to fighting.

Forgetfulness

'I don't know why he is so forgetful,' said an exasperated mother about her eleven-year-old son, Ari. 'He forgets everything. He's forever leaving his lunch at home. I have to take it to school or else he would starve. He leaves projects at home. He forgets to take library books back and I'm left to pay the fines. He doesn't even remember to empty his schoolbag at night. I've got to remind him to do everything!' she exclaimed. 'He takes after his dad. He's just the same.'

Ari, like his father, doesn't need to remember to do various tasks when there is someone around to do them for him. Ari knows that his mother will always be around to pick things up after him, to remind him to pack his lunch and to pay his library fines. This may help his mother to feel useful but it only increases her son's dependence on her. His mother is a 'good' parent rather than a responsible parent. Generally, a child's constant forgetfulness is an indication that a parent is assuming the responsibility for his actions.

This mother was trying to work out why her son had a bad memory. She assumed that it was somehow inherited from his father. It would be more useful to ask: 'What is the purpose of his apparent lack of memory?' The purpose can be found in her own behaviour. Ari was able to put his mother in his service by forgetting things. This was not a conscious decision that he made. He learned that if he forgot his lunch his mother would bring it to school. His forgetfulness was an effective way of keeping his mother busy with him – and it worked. She responded in the way that Ari wanted and expected. To change Ari, his mother would have to change her way of reacting to his memory lapses. He should have to experience the consequences of leaving projects at home and leaving damp towels on his bed. Instead, his mother has been experiencing the consequences of his forgetfulness.

THE CONSEQUENCES OF FORGETFULNESS

Forgetful children can be extremely irritating to their parents. They leave things lying around, they have memory lapses at chore-time and they leave wet football boots in schoolbags. The list of forgotten activities is endless. Both parents and children need to be aware of the activities each is responsible for. In allocating responsibilities, be guided by the age and ability of different children. For instance, it is reasonable to remind a five-year-old child to pack her lunch until it becomes a habit, whereas it should be unnecessary to remind an eleven-year-old to do the same thing. Once children are aware of the activities they must remember, there should be little need to remind them again, as long as they are permitted to experience the consequences of their actions. For instance, a child who forgets his lunch will be hungry, a forgotten homework sheet is the child's problem at school and forgetting to put sporting apparel in the wash basket means dirty clothes next sports day. Children will learn from the consequences of their forgetfulness if they are not shielded from them by well-meaning parents.

BEING ORGANISED

Many children are naturally disorganised. They do not see the necessity or the benefits of being organised. While it is not necessary to engage an organisational consultant, a sensible arrangement of activities can help make it easier for children to remember them. It is useful for children to have established routines that rely on habit rather than on the vagaries of memory. For instance, when children come home from school they unpack their lunchboxes, put their bags in their rooms and give you any school notices. This is a small routine that makes life easier for you as well as the children. They should not be permitted to play until this regimen is followed. Children like having activities linked in this fashion. They can then concentrate on the more important things in life such as playing with friends.

Activities can be linked when the performance of one task is dependent on the first activity being completed. For example, it is an agreed rule in a colleague's family that breakfast is not eaten unless beds are made. No one needs to be reminded about the task – they will not be served breakfast!

You can discuss strategies to help children to remember, but you should not accept their responsibilities. It is a basic task of parenting to promote independence at every opportunity. If you readily experience the consequences of children's forgetfulness or constantly remind children of their obligations, you are robbing them of opportunities to learn as well as increasing their dependence on others, especially you.

MIND THE STEPS

Behind every forgetful child is a parent who is willing to remind, nag or act as the youngster's memory.

Children who experience the unpleasant results of forgetfulness are more likely to remember responsibilities in the future.

Help children to become better organised by establishing routines where practical.

Friends

Children have three life tasks that they must deal with. They need to find a place in their family, cope with school and the many situations presented there, and establish friendships. Happy, confident children are able to cope successfully with all three tasks. They are able to cope with the challenges of kindergarten or school, feel secure and valued at home and enjoy a number of significant friendships.

The nature of children's friendships changes as they grow. As toddlers, they play alongside other children with a minimum of interaction. As they grow and develop, the nature of their activity changes. They begin to play with rather than next to other children. They learn that the company of other children is pleasant and offers opportunities that don't exist in their family. As children grow, their values, attitudes and behaviour are increasingly influenced by their friends. This can be difficult for some parents to deal with because their ability to influence their children diminishes. Forming friendships is part of life and needs to be encouraged and aided as much as possible.

Making friends and keeping them

Forming and maintaining friendships requires a number of social skills. Children need the skills of sharing, communication and co-operation to make and keep friends. These skills can be formed at home but they continue to develop through interaction with children outside the family.

The nature of friendships varies with children's age and personality. Some children are naturally gregarious and have many friends, while others form close bonds with a smaller number of children. Friendships can vary like the wind, particularly with young children. They can be close mates one day and almost bitter enemies the next. This is quite natural, as they are still finding their own way in the world and are learning a great deal about themselves and other children almost every day. Their interests constantly change and influence the type of children that they associate with. Six-year-old Gino was great mates with three particular boys right through kindergarten and the first year of school. They always played with each other whenever they could. At the end of Gino's second year of school he hardly played with his former mates – their interests were different from his. They were keen on all types of sport and continually played all sorts of ball games. Gino wasn't too interested in such play. He preferred to play imaginative and adventure-type games rather than spend all his spare time bouncing and catching balls. He formed new friendships with a group of children with similar interests.

Some children have difficulty in making friends. This can occur for many reasons:

- a lack of social skills such as sharing.
- inexperience playing with others.
- a poor view of themselves.
- a strong sense of competition which is displayed through bossiness or a wish to dominate.
- an inability to compromise or a wish to get their own way all the time.
- a lack of interests or hobbies.

You can use a number of strategies to assist children to form friendships with their peers. If children are having difficulty forming friendships, you must first identify the cause. You can then deal with children individually to help rectify the situation. If bossiness is the problem, you can bring this to the child's attention and discuss suitable ways of sharing and getting on with others. Skills such as sharing can be stimulated and encouraged at home by providing situations that promote their development. With common sense and a little effort you can improve children's behaviours that may be acting as blockers to the establishment of friendships.

Many children have limited opportunities to play and form friendships with other children. This may occur for many reasons – a child might live in an area with few other children, or may have suffered a prolonged illness. In these cases you can provide opportunities to meet other children and form friendships. You can encourage children to join a club or interest group such as Girl Guides or Little Athletics. These groups, while catering for children's interests, provide ideal opportunities for them to mix with other children of their own age. Encourage children to pursue their hobbies and thus broaden their appeal to others. Children often form close alliances with children with similar interests or hobbies. Make children welcome in your house. Help make it a fun place to play. I am not suggesting that you buy an inground pool so that your child can make some new friends. There are many other ways to make a house an interesting place for children to visit.

Choice of friends

Some parents are concerned about the type of friends that children play with rather than a lack of company. When children are very young you are generally able to control the types of friendships that are formed. Children initially meet your friends' children. Parental approval is virtually assured. As they go to school and become more independent, they form associations with all types of children. At times their choice of friends is very dubious in the eyes of concerned parents. They may associate with children who are older or who have behaviour problems. Fearing the influence that these children may have, you may be tempted to prevent such friendships forming. It is very dangerous to ban certain friends, however, as, like the forbidden fruit, they may appear all the more appealing. As one twelve-year-old remarked: 'Dad has banned me from playing with Kerry, so she must be all right.' In a practical sense, it is almost impossible to forbid children from associating with someone – you cannot supervise them all day.

Rather than interfere, it is more effective to discuss your concerns with your child. Find out the reasons for the friendship and display trust in your child that he will behave appropriately, regardless of whom he associates with. Children are going to meet all types of people as they grow up – not all of them will be to your liking. However, children often surprise us with their wisdom and common sense.

Moira's twelve-year-old son had recently begun associating with an older boy who had quite a number of dealings with police over shoplifting. Moira discussed her concern with her son, pointing out his friend's poor track record. Andrew quelled his mother's worries when he replied: 'Don't worry Mum. I know that he is light-fingered. I'm not interested in that. I like Doug because he plays a mean guitar. Besides, he is one hell of a funny guy!' Andrew accepted Doug for what he was and was probably a good influence on him. Moira trusted her son's judgement and encouraged Andrew to invite Doug home. When she met him she found that her fears were unfounded and that he was a likeable boy. She could see why Andrew had grown close to him. Andrew appreciated his mother's trust in him and was determined not to let her down.

Trusting children's judgement about friends can be one of the most difficult tasks of being a parent. It is natural that we want to guide our children along the right path and protect them from danger and unsuitable influences. However, we don't always know what is right for our children. As one mother found out, our impressions of others are not always correct. Dianna discovered that her ten-year-old son Greg often played with a boy who had a reputation as a 'tough kid'. She was worried that he would be a poor influence on her son but she thought that she should get to know him before she made any hasty judgements. She urged Greg to bring his friend home so that she could meet him. Dianna found that the boy was a little rough about the edges for her liking, but he was a rather pleasant lad in his own way. She could see no harm in the friendship. A little time later she overheard a conversation between two of her eleven-year-old daughter's friends, who had come around for a visit. 'He is a real creep!' said one girl. 'Yes, he can be really mean in the playground – he loves to trip up little kids as they run past,' replied the other. Dianna thought that they must have been talking about Greg's friend. She received a real shock when she heard one of the girls say, 'Yeah, Greg can be a real bully sometimes.' It was her son that they were talking about!

MIND THE STEPS

Stimulate children to develop the skills of sharing and communication which are essential for the formation of friendships.

Provide opportunities for pre-school children to meet children of their own age.

Display faith in children that they are able to choose and maintain suitable friendships.

Make an effort to get to know your children's friends.

Getting Up and Getting Going

It was only 7.30 a.m. and already Joanne was at her wit's end. Her husband had left for work an hour ago and she had the difficult task of getting her children up and out of the house by 8.30 so that she could be at work on time. What a job it was!

Eight-year-old Belinda was no problem. As usual, she was out of bed by 7 o'clock in time to shower, dress, eat breakfast and prepare for school. She was ready early, so she played a quiet game before she went to school. Ten-year-old Jason and four-year-old Elsa were a different story altogether.

Jason ignored his mother's initial wake-up call. He remained in bed until Joanne had reminded him for the fourth time to get up. Once out of bed he shuffled around the house like a zombie, shifting from one task to another without completing anything. He half-dressed himself and complained to his mother that he couldn't find any clean socks. 'Look properly,' was Joanne's terse reply. He dawdled over breakfast and complained when the toast was cold. Joanne quickly cooked him some fresh toast reminding him that it would not have been cold if he was at the breakfast table on time. 'Now, don't forget that we are leaving in fifteen minutes. You still must finish dressing. Don't forget to wash your face, clean your teeth and pack your lunch in your bag. OK?' Joanne said.

Elsa began to whine for help as soon as her feet hit the floor that morning. She wanted Joanne to dress her, which was a trial in itself. Elsa, as usual, refused to wear the clothes Joanne had laid out on the bed for her. 'I told you I don't like that dress,' she complained. When Joanne said that she didn't have time to waste Elsa began to cry. 'Oh come on, Elsa. Just choose some clothes, please!' she groaned.

Already they were five minutes late and Joanne felt like a

wrung-out rag. Her working day had started with a vengeance. Elsa was safely delivered to her child-minder while Jason and Belinda were dropped off at school with plenty of time to spare. Joanne, however, was ten minutes late for work. She hastily apologised to her boss, who raised his eyebrows, wondering why on earth he ever hired a mother of three in the first place.

Joanne is suffering the consequences of her children's tardiness in the morning. She is caught in a situation of her own making. Until she learns to keep out of her children's affairs, Jason and Elsa will always rely on her to get them up and moving each morning. Getting up and preparing for school should be the children's responsibility. Instead, she shoulders the burden of their irresponsibility.

Mornings are often chaotic in many households, particularly when both parents work or in homes where there is a sole breadwinner. Children often keep parents occupied in the morning by lying in bed, dawdling over breakfast or forgetting to wash or prepare for school. Parents who remind children to get up, eat breakfast, wash themselves and pack school lunches are teaching them to be dependent on more capable adults. The problem can be intensified in large families in which there always seems to be someone dragging the chain.

Attention seekers and power-drunk children find that mornings are the ideal time to strut their stuff. It is difficult to ignore a child who wants to keep her mother busy with her. It is easier to dress a child than to bear the whining that may accompany a refusal. Power brokers recognise that mornings are a great time to involve parents in a fight. A busy parent is likely to give into stubbornness or dawdling just to avoid conflict.

Children have a great deal to do to organise themselves in the morning. They have to wash, dress, eat breakfast, clean teeth and pack schoolbags. Like adults, some children are slow movers at the start of the day. Some of us are morning people and others function better as the day drags on. These people are generally night owls, who become lively after dark – but before midday, you can forget it. Children follow similar patterns to adults. They must learn to cope in the mornings – the time factor is present for all people, whether night owls or morning stars. A little reorganisation of duties can assist slow starters. Packing bags, choosing clothes and showering can be done the night before rather than in the morning. This lightens the load and allows children to shake off the cobwebs without the pressure of having a million and one tasks to perform.

Reduce children's reliance on you

If your household suffers from a bad case of morning mania, the following steps can improve the situation:

- Establish a clear routine.
- Stop interfering in tasks that should be the responsibility of children.
- Ensure that children know what is expected of them.
- Remove or ignore distracting influences such as the television.
- Ensure that children feel the consequences of lateness rather than you.

Establish a routine

A regular routine is a great aid to children's memories. Like a draught horse on a milk run which knows exactly where to go and when to stop, children can easily remember their morning duties when there is an orderly routine. Through trial and error your family can establish a morning routine that best meets the needs of all members.

Don't interfere

Keep out of children's way in the morning. Children are generally able to complete most of the required morning jobs themselves without too much adult assistance or interference. When you take on children's tasks you are making them reliant on you. The aim of the democratic approach to parenting is to raise independent children. Mornings provide a great opportunity to develop a sense of responsibility, as children are capable of fending for themselves at this busy time of the day.

Most children are able to get themselves out of bed, dress themselves, wash, prepare breakfast, pack lunches and clean their own bedrooms. Some older children even make their own school lunches each morning. Children who have just started school may need help with some of these tasks but they will soon become capable if given the chance to take care of themselves in the morning.

Make expectations clear

Ensure that children know exactly what is expected of them in the morning. Clearly spell out the tasks that children are to perform. Children should be expected to get themselves out of bed. Older children can have their own alarm clocks so that they can wake themselves up. Alternatively, you can call children once in the morning. If they stay in bed then they can bear the consequences of sleeping in. Don't keep calling late sleepers, as they will only become reliant on you to get them out of bed. The object of the exercise is to place the responsibility of getting up where it belongs – with the children.

Let children know what you are prepared to do in the morning. They can then organise their duties around your activities. It is important to be firm and consistent. Giving in to undue demands teaches them that you are willing to break routine if enough pressure is brought to bear.

IDENTIFY DISTRACTIONS

Identify sources of distraction that can hold children up in the morning. That one-eyed monster commonly known as the television has magnetic powers, particularly in the morning. Children can be held spellbound by mindless programs that offer little in terms of entertainment or educational value. If television is a distraction in the mornings, ensure that it remains off. If it is to be watched, then it can be turned on when children are ready for the day.

Children sometimes choose the mornings to fight and argue with each other over a variety of issues, both big and small. This can easily distract parents as well as children from their morning duties. Refuse to be drawn into their disagreements and allow consequences to influence their behaviour. When children miss breakfast or must finish dressing in the car because they were too busy arguing, they will soon alter their behaviour.

DON'T SHIELD CHILDREN FROM UNPLEASANT CONSEQUENCES

The consequences of wasting time in the morning are generally unpleasant. Usually it means that someone will be late for school, work or an appointment. It is the children who should experience the consequences of tardiness in the morning rather than parents. When you shield them from consequences, you teach them that any behaviour is permissible because you will cover for them. The tough part for many parents is allowing children to bear the brunt of their inappropriate behaviour.

If a child sleeps in, then he will be late for school. He may even miss breakfast or forget to pack his lunch. When children are driven to school they should be informed of the time that the car will be leaving. If breakfast is not finished then they can grab a piece of fruit to eat on the way. If they are not dressed then they can dress themselves at school. One family I know keeps a set of clothes in the boot of the car for slow children. Another mother who had great difficulty getting her four-year-old to kinder on time simply carried her daughter to the car one morning in her pyjamas. She packed some clothes in her kinder bag and gave her the choice of dressing at kinder or attending kinder in pyjamas. The child chose to dress once she had arrived, although the mother had warned her daughter's teacher to be prepared for a pupil to arrive in pyjamas. The teacher was quite happy to be a part of the mother's plans, recognising that the child was being taught a hard but valuable lesson in being responsible for her own misbehaviour.

Many parents are not willing to adopt such a tough approach. However, when children experience hardship due to staying in bed, dawdling or watching television in the morning, they will alter their behaviour to avoid unpleasant consequences.

Joanne applied these ideas to alleviate her early-morning stress.

She discussed with all her children the difficulty she was experiencing in the morning. She told them that she was constantly late to work because she had to wait for her children to be ready in the morning. She was tired of reminding them to get out of bed and prepare for the day. She was careful not to accuse individual children of being slow. However, she asked her children to help her find a solution to the morning dilemma.

She discussed with Jason the need to become better organised in the morning. She helped him to establish an orderly routine and suggested that he complete one task before moving on to another. She bought him an alarm clock and showed him how to use it. As he was a slow mover in the morning, he agreed to set it fifteen minutes earlier than the time his mother had been waking him. Joanne told him that she was not going to call him in the morning. If he chose to remain in bed that was his business, but breakfast would be ready by 8 o'clock. If he was late he could eat it cold or cook his own breakfast. She would be leaving for work at 8.30. If he was not ready he could either walk to school or get dressed when he arrived. He was surprised by the new approach but he agreed to give it a try.

Joanne gave Elsa much more responsibility than she had been given before. She allowed her to choose her clothes and wash herself and clean her teeth. She recognised that Elsa needed some assistance, so she enlisted the help of Belinda, who was always well organised in the morning. Joanne also addressed Elsa's whining. She told her that if she chose to whine in the morning that she would leave the room. Joanne also asked Belinda not to assist Elsa when she whinged. She encouraged her children to work as a team in the morning, assisting each other to prepare for the day.

Joanne was not surprised when Elsa tried to become even more reliant on her. She liked the old way of keeping mother busy with her. This had served her well for a considerable time. At first she refused to choose her clothes and tried all sorts of tricks to involve Joanne. 'I can't reach my coat. It is too high up.' 'I haven't any clean knickers.' 'Can you find my shoes for me?' Joanne stuck to her guns and steadfastly refused to be drawn into a game of her daughter's making. Eventually Elsa came around, as she was more inconvenienced by her dawdling than her mother was.

Jason surprised everyone with his morning preparations.

He didn't exactly move like a speeding bullet, but he did usually manage to be ready on time. Occasionally he walked to school, but Joanne noticed that whenever rain was imminent he was always ready in time. She thanked all her children for co-operating in the morning and remarked that she was hardly ever late to work any more.

Modelling

It is useless expecting children to be organised in the morning if you are in a muddle yourself. Set a good example by being as methodical as possible and don't sleep in yourself unless your children are so well organised that they get you breakfast in bed. And pigs might fly!

Mind the steps

An established routine helps mornings to run smoothly. Ensure that each person knows what is expected.

Reduce children's reliance on you by making them responsible for morning matters. You may even wish to make yourself scarce.

Remove distractions, such as the television, which keep children from performing their morning duties.

Allow children who are slow to arise or who dawdle to experience the consequences of their actions, such as missing breakfast.

Homework

'Dimitri, have you done your homework yet? Why are you watching TV when you have homework to do? When is that project due?' said his father, Alex. 'What is this? Twenty questions or something? I'll do it in a minute. Don't worry!' answered Dimitri, who didn't intend to budge until his favourite program was over.

Homework is the source of many arguments in families. Parents often assume the responsibility of ensuring that homework is completed. This is unfair, as homework is set for the child by the teacher. There should be no need for you as a third party to interfere. It is the responsibility of the child to do and of the teacher to ensure that it is completed. As a parent, you should support the teacher's implementation of consequences when the work is not completed, but it is pointless assuming the role of police officer to ensure that tasks are done. This is the role of the child's teacher.

Education is most effective when there are close ties between school and the home. It is a good idea to meet your child's teacher and discuss the homework require-ments for the year. The teacher can outline ways that you can assist your child with home tasks and also provide you with some informal learning activities that may supplement the program at school. The establishment of a friendly relationship with your child's teacher can be helpful if problems occur throughout the year.

THE EARLY YEARS

Reading is the main home task for children in their early years of schooling. However, you can assist children informally to develop basic mathematics, reading and writing skills. Many schools conduct parent programs in various subject areas that promote learning in the home. Programs such as 'Family Maths' and 'Readers, Writers and Parents Learning Together' inform parents of current learning strategies and provide many practical ideas for assisting children's development at home. If you wish to gain an insight into the activities your child is involved in at school, volunteer to be a parent helper. Many modern classrooms use parents to assist in a variety of ways, not merely as 'reading mums'.

The most valuable way of assisting young learners is to share books with them. It is best to set aside a regular time each day for sharing books with developing readers. The activity needs to be as enjoyable as possible or children will be turned off reading. Choose a comfortable location away from disturbances and share the books brought home from school. You may listen or you may decide to read together if the book is too difficult. Perhaps you might include a short discussion before and after the book – but don't labour the point, as pleasure is the key component in the exercise. Reading to your children exposes them to literature that they can't read themselves.

Projects and assignments

As children progress through school they are exposed to more formal homework requirements. You should offer guidance and assistance when you can, but it is best to avoid fights about the completion of set tasks. The teacher who set the homework should ensure that it is adequately completed. You can assist children by helping them plan study times, providing quiet work areas and discussing problems that may arise. You can help them to locate information and present it attractively in projects. There are many subjects, such as maths, which you may not feel confident to assist with. As a rule of thumb, help children with homework when you can, and refer problems that you can't deal with to the teacher.

These days there is a trend for less homework to be set for children. There are doubts about the educational value of setting homework for children in primary school. Often work can be set purely because it is expected that children be given home tasks. If a child is having difficulty, the most appropriate place to improve is at school, under the supervision of a trained teacher. If homework is set it should be interesting and build on the activities that occur at school.

Children today are often involved in a variety of afterschool activities. The range of sporting, creative, cultural and adventure activities available for young children these days is mind-boggling. They offer valuable learning experiences, extending children in ways that schools cannot. Involvement in afterschool activities contributes to a child's education in a broader sense.

Parent participation

Children are more likely to have a positive attitude toward school when they see their parents actively involved. There are many ways that you can contribute to your child's school. You may:

- assist with the preparation of learning materials.
- assist with small groups in the classroom.
- help with excursions and camps.
- assist in a club or activity program.
- be a resource person if you have specialised skill or knowledge.
- become a member of a committee or the school council.
- assist in the canteen or attend working bees.

MIND THE STEPS

It is the responsibility of children and teachers to ensure that formal homework assignments are completed. Assist children with homework tasks when you are able, and refer difficulties back to the school when you don't feel able to assist.

You can best help young learners by assisting them with their reading.

Research has shown that education prospers when there are close links between school and the home. Establish close ties between school and home by:

- meeting your child's teachers
- assisting the school in a variety of ways
- keeping informed through newsletters, information nights, etc.
- attending parent participation programmes.

Interruptions

Interruptions are a common form of attention-seeking behaviour. They can take many forms and occur when you are busy with a task or another person. You may be interrupted by an argument when you are talking on the telephone. You could be disturbed by whining when you meet a friend in the street or you may be distracted by demands for a drink when you are busy writing a letter or an email. Children's interrupting behaviour may vary but the intent is the same – to divert your attention from whatever you are doing and to focus the spotlight on them. This annoying form of misbehaviour is not confined to young children. Primary- and secondary-school children can also be experts at making unreasonable demands on parents.

Interrupting behaviour is indicative of a lack of co-operation between parents and children. In a family each member should behave as situations require. If you are speaking to a friend on the telephone, common courtesy demands that you be allowed to talk in relative peace and quiet. When you open the front door to a visitor, you should be able to greet that person without your child nagging you to play a game. Children's behaviour should be dictated by the needs of the situations as they occur. It is reasonable for adults to expect to converse with each other and complete their normal daily tasks with a minimum of undue interruptions and demands placed on them by children. Similarly, it is reasonable for children to expect to receive positive attention from parents during the day. Parents can initiate pleasant conversations, play games, read books, tell jokes or merely listen to accounts of the day at school. Children are entitled to this type of positive attention. If they don't receive it they will find other ways of keeping parents busy with them.

There are a number of ways that you can approach the problem that interrupting behaviour presents. Common sense and a willingness to change your own behaviour are key elements. The art of distraction (remember the technique that grandparents are so adept at using) is an excellent way of avoiding such behaviour.

A DOSE OF PREVENTION

Susie, the mother of four young children, decided to resume her career as a solicitor on a part-time basis. As she was unable to find suitable childcare for her two children, who were too young to attend school, she established her office at home. Her children were fairly co-operative, enabling her to work successfully from home. They were co-operative, that is, until she used the telephone. They took this as an opportunity to create havoc. They made so much noise that one client remarked during a telephone conversation that it was odd that a law office would be situated next to a school. She tried shutting the office door when there was a telephone call but this merely invited the children to yell louder. When they began to bang on the door she thought that it was time to abandon this ploy. She tried threatening the children with all sorts of horrid punishments but they knew that she was too busy to carry them out. Besides, punishment was not in her gentle nature. There was little that she could do to change her children so Susie decided to make some adjustments to her own behaviour. A sensible place to start! She knew that she was at least capable of controlling herself, even if she couldn't control her children.

Susie decided that prevention was the best cure. She also decided to employ some shock tactics. She gave her children permission to yell when she spoke on the phone. She tried this out first during a few bogus calls to friends. At first, seeing their mother talking on the telephone, the children saw their opportunity to have some fun at her expense. When they found that she was quite unconcerned they turned the volume level up a few turns. They were stunned when this had no effect. So Susie succeeded in achieving peace for a while. Realising that attention-seeking behaviour takes many forms she knew that they would find another way of disturbing her unless she could engage them in useful behaviours. So she sat down with them and talked about all the activities that they could do when she was speaking on the phone. The children came up with a long list of suggestions. Together they recorded all the ideas using pictures and symbols in the place of words. The children were able to read the list, which was placed on the back of the office door. Whenever the phone rang the children were to choose an activity to do from the list. They agreed to do this. This plan was put into practice with great success.

Susie diligently acknowledged the children when they participated in an activity from the list. She took an interest in what they were doing and encouraged their efforts. She became an expert at catching them being good. She persevered with this approach and gradually the children altered their behaviour.

Modelling

A friend complained to me that her children would constantly interrupt her while she was engaged in a conversation. They would even contradict her statements in front of others which was a source of great embarrassment. She had spoken to her children, aged eight and ten, about this irritating habit and explained her annoyance to them. They agreed to stop but their behaviour didn't change. My friend was sure that her children didn't believe that they were misbehaving when they interrupted her.

I had the opportunity to observe my friend's family during a recent camping holiday and it was interesting to see how they all related to each other. They would constantly interrupt each other whenever they wished to speak or make a request. My friend was the worst offender. She would interject in her children's conversations in mid-sentence to disagree, make a point or to ask for assistance with a chore. She displayed little respect for her children, their conversations or their activities. It was little wonder that the children showed her the same lack of respect.

She was correct in her assessment of her children; they did not think that interrupting and contradicting others was inappropriate, as their mother had shown through her actions that such behaviour was commonplace. The children were merely copying the model provided for them.

My friend needed to change her way of relating to her children. The family needed to observe some basic guidelines when speaking and listening to each other. The mother was in an excellent position to influence her children's behaviour by setting a good example for them to follow.

Consequences

The use of logical consequences can be an effective counter to children's irritating and unreasonable demands (see page 43). Children who make constant intrusions into parent's time and activities generally seek attention. When disturbances occur you should make a quick withdrawal from the situation. This usually is effective if you are cooking a meal or involved in an activity that benefits the children. If withdrawal is inappropriate, then you should stop what you are doing and calmly, without speaking to the offenders, remove them from your presence. This procedure should be repeated if there are subsequent interruptions. Sooner or later the interruptions will cease when no attention is given to the misbehaviour. It is important that this procedure is carried out in silence, because even a reprimand provides children with attention. Children should receive recognition only for useful activities.

Attention seekers detest being ignored. They will generally alter their behaviour if they don't receive feedback for interruptions. They should also be given plenty of encouragement for appropriate behaviour.

Sometimes the use of consequences can cause short-term inconvenience but the results make the effort worthwhile.

Trish attended a friend's house for morning coffee once a week, where she was constantly hounded by her four-year-old daughter Tanya. The child had the opportunity to play with other children. Instead she hovered around her mother like a satellite, making a nuisance of herself. Trish decided that she had to do something about her daughter's behaviour, as it was making the entire gathering feel uncomfortable.

Before she left home for one of her regular visits, she told her daughter that she could spend a few minutes with the adults to allow her to settle in and then she was to join her own young friends. If she continued annoying her, then they would both leave immediately. Her mother was not going to nag or remind her to go and play as she had previously done. Trish had the foresight to warn her host of her strategy and to be prepared for an early departure. She was not surprised when Tanya tried her usual tricks. When Tanya refused to leave the company of the adults, Trish said goodbye to everyone and departed with her daughter following close behind. This was a rather drastic measure which taught Tanya two important things. First, her mother was unwilling to put up with her interruptions in public any longer and second, she was willing to act rather than make useless threats.

Trish learned firsthand the effectiveness of taking action when Tanya asked her if she could go to the next morning coffee so that she could play with her friends. Trish may have missed one coffee morning, but the ensuing sessions were much more pleasurable for all.

INVITE CHILDREN TO JOIN IN

Sometimes it is appropriate to invite children to participate with adults rather than push them aside.

Some activities such as cooking and letter writing present ideal opportunities for children to assist or work beside parents. This is not to say that it is always appropriate for children to join in. The last thing parents need when they are frantically preparing dinner is the kind of help that a four-year-old can provide! However, there are times and activities which are ideal for shared participation between adults and children.

As with all situations that require increased co-operation between parents and children, the family meeting or discussion provides an excellent forum. Your concerns can be posed in a manner that invites suggestions from children. 'I need to be able to drive the car without being hassled by noisy passengers. What can you do to help?' This approach states the problem and invites co-operation.

Children should be encouraged when they are engaged in worthwhile activities instead of interrupting their parents. Recognise that when children are happily occupying themselves, they are making a contribution to the organisation of the household as well as to your well-being.

MIND THE STEPS

Constant interruption is a common form of attention-seeking misbehaviour. You should expect a reasonable level of co-operation from your children.

Preventative measures (which take into account children's needs) and the application of consequences are effective measures for interruptions.

Lies, Untruths and Fibs

There are many categories of untruths. They range from little white lies and fibs to full-blown whoppers, and they always serve a purpose. Children often bend the truth to suit themselves. They sometimes tell fibs to escape punishment or avoid being caught when misbehaviour occurs. They can also try to put one over their parents as a display of power. 'I can do as I please and I'll lie to cover my tracks' thinks a power seeker. Some youngsters fantasise about their exploits to make themselves appear bigger, more daring or more exciting than they really are. These children often think that they are not much good and so invent a few tales to make themselves seem more interesting. Of course, some children fantasise purely because it is fun to stretch the truth a little. It is more fun to run away from 'a ferocious man-eating tiger' than be scared of the next-door neighbour's mutt.

It is helpful to identify the purpose of a child's untruths. This indicates to parents how they should deal with the behaviour.

Escaping punishment

When children tell lies to avoid being blamed or punished for particular incidents, it is important to ensure that they face the music. It is often difficult to separate fact from fiction where children are concerned. However, if you are able to work out the truth and ascertain that a child is being less than truthful, she should feel the consequences of the misbehaviour that she wishes to avoid. There is little point lecturing or punishing her for telling lies. Then you have two misbehaviours to deal with: the misdemeanour that she is dodging and the lying. It is better for the child to learn that telling lies doesn't achieve a satisfactory outcome. Let children know that you appreciate it when they own up and tell the truth.

Eight-year-old Pamela spilt a container of milk on the

kitchen floor. She panicked, replaced the empty container in the refrigerator and went off to her bedroom to read. When her mother saw the mess, she asked Pamela if she knew what had happened. The child denied any knowledge of it. 'What milk do you mean, Mum?' said Pamela, with an innocent look on her face. Her mother, knowing immediately that her daughter was responsible, asked her to help to clean up the mess. She avoided apportioning blame, however, she made sure that her daughter didn't escape the consequence of cleaning up the mess that she had made.

FANTASISING

Some children continually exaggerate to make everything appear bigger or better than in real life. In this way they appear more exciting or interesting than they think that they are. This is a sign of discouragement. It is best to go along with these children's tales, although you should let them know that you are aware of the truth without bursting their bubble. It is fine to exaggerate, but they should never be too far away from reality.

Persistent fantasisers often need plenty of encouragement. Let them know that they are OK as they are. Fantasising and telling tall tales may be fun but they don't need to fantasise to build themselves up. Youngest children in the family often tell whoppers in an effort to make them-selves seem important in the eyes of older siblings.

One young boy enjoyed the company of an imaginary cat. This feline was able to perform fabulous uncatlike feats. His family tolerated his 'pet' without ever letting him become too carried away with the fantasy. His mother asked him one day: 'Who made the mess in the bathroom?' He told her that the cat did. She replied: 'Could you please ask him to clean up the mess?' 'OK, Mum,' the child said. The illusion was maintained but the needs of the situation were met.

Putting one over you

Eleven-year-old Britta was refused permission to visit an older friend after school, as her mother thought the friend unsuitable company for her daughter. She was also concerned that the friend lived a long way from their home, which meant that Britta had to ride her bike along a busy road at night to visit the girl. Her mother gave her permission to visit school friends who lived much closer to home.

Britta resented her mother's interference and frequently visited her older friend. When her mother asked her where she was going after school she would lie and tell her that she was visiting a friend that her mother approved of. Eventually her mother found out through an acquaintance that Britta had been lying to her about her visits. She confronted her daughter with the truth. Britta was in no position to deny the claims. Her mother dealt with the matter of the illicit visits. She was not permitted to go out after school for two weeks. This was an appropriate consequence that matched the misbehaviour. She dealt with the matter of lying separately. She pointed out to Britta that it was difficult to trust her when she told lies. This was an unfortunate but natural reaction to her bending of the truth.

Don't overreact

Be careful not to overreact when children tell lies. It is better to recognise the child's goal and act in a way that prevents the behaviour from achieving its purpose. There is little point moralising about the evils of lying. Children know that they should be good; they don't need to be reminded all the time. Children will continue behaviours that serve a purpose, regardless of whether the actions are morally good or bad. It is more useful to ensure that lying doesn't achieve its goal and to encourage children at every conceivable occasion.

Separate the deed from the doer

Let your child understand that you disapprove of his misbehaviour but not him. You don't approve of lying but you still like the child who told the lie. It is important that the deed is separated from the doer. There is no such person as a liar, only someone who tells lies. It is easy to label a child as a liar or a thief but such names have a habit of sticking. Children are always capable of changing their behaviour; they cannot always change themselves. A child can stop telling fibs but it is more difficult for a 'liar' to change.

Modelling

Take care that you don't, through your own actions, teach children that lying is sometimes acceptable. A parent who telephones the boss and reports that he is sick then goes off and plays golf is setting a poor example for children. Similarly, writing sick notes for children when they have had a day off school to visit relatives teaches them that bending the truth is acceptable as long as you are not caught. It is better to induce respect for honesty by being truthful at every opportunity. Children are quick to pick up double standards and will generally follow a lead set by their parents.

An open atmosphere

Parents who develop an atmosphere of trust and freedom of expression in their families remove the need to tell lies. When children are confident that their point of view is valued, they are less likely to bend the truth to defeat parents or avoid punishment. This open atmosphere can be fostered when there is a willingness to discuss matters with children rather than imposing sanctions upon them. Regular family meetings or discussions provide a forum for children to express their views and concerns in a conciliatory manner.

MIND THE STEPS

Look for the purpose of children's lies. This will provide a guide to your reactions.

When dealing with untruths it is important to separate the deed from the doer. You may disapprove of the lies but you must let your child know that he is OK.

Develop an atmosphere of honesty in the family that precludes the need to tell lies to parents.

Be aware that you are a model for your child.

Nagging

Parents and children who nag show little respect for other people. Nagging is an irritating behaviour that occurs in many households. Parents who constantly remind and pester children about their responsibilities not only make them less independent, they teach them that this annoying behaviour is acceptable. Children who demand service by nagging treat parents as little more than servants. The trouble is that parents and children are stuck in a continuous cycle of nagging and pestering each other to get what they want. It is usually effective in the end, but it is also extremely annoying.

Nagging parents

A mother lamented that she had to nag her children to do everything around the house. She was convinced that if she wasn't on their backs the whole time they wouldn't remember to do anything for themselves. This mother robbed her children of initiative, as she didn't give them a chance to do things for themselves. They became totally reliant on her to remind them of their own responsibilities.

When you nag children you assume responsibility for their actions. You send the message, 'I don't think that you can do it on your own so I'll remind you.' Youngsters are quick to learn the habits of their parents and will happily sit back and be reminded about all types of tasks.

Recently I asked a group of children to outline the things that parents nag them about. They readily provided me with a long list of complaints. Their parents nagged them about:

- picking up toys.
- tidying their bedrooms.
- doing their homework.
- cleaning their teeth before bed.

- getting ready for an outing.
- doing chores.

These are all activities and responsibilities that belong specifically with children. Parents who nag children about such matters are interfering in areas that are primarily the children's concern.

It is no coincidence that parents who nag often complain of 'deaf' children. There is usually nothing wrong with the children's hearing. They simply listen to what they wish to hear. They know that their parents will remind them a number of times to perform a task so they think, 'Why should I act when I'm asked to do something the first time? I'll be reminded again'. 'Parent-deaf' children train their parents to react on their terms. They set the agenda for the parents to follow.

To break from the habit of pestering, nagging and reminding children, parents should use the power of consequences to achieve their aims. Talk is best used for conversation and encouragement, not nagging. If children are to be reminded about a duty or task, they should be told only once. If there is no response, then it is appropriate to take action. Generally, there is little need to remind children about their responsibilities, as they are quite aware of what is required. They have heard it often enough! The children who presented me with their list of grievances would not need to be nagged if the following consequences were applied:

- Toys which are left lying around are confiscated for a set time or until the children have indicated that they are responsible enough to pack them away when required.
- Parents do not have to enter untidy bedrooms. Children put their own clothes away and are not tucked in at night.
- Children who don't do their homework must deal with the punishment or consequences of their school.
- Children who don't clean their teeth miss ice-cream or

sweets the next day, as these can cause decay.

- Children who are not ready for an outing go as they are or dress themselves when they arrive. They may also forget to take favourite toys or items.
- Chores that are forgotten are not done by anyone else. Although this may annoy parents it will usually inconvenience children; chores are for the benefit of everyone.

Independence, resourcefulness and self-reliance are taught by allowing children to experience the effects of their inactivity, not by constant pestering and badgering.

NAGGING CHILDREN

Children can be quite proficient in the art of nagging. Generally, they pester adults when they want something badly and you as a parent are unable or unwilling to satisfy their whim. Children need to learn that you can't always get what you want. You need to be firm when faced with nagging and demanding children and indicate that you are unwilling to respond to such behaviour. Parents who give in to nagging are showing little respect for themselves or children. A busy mother who was pestered by her young daughter for a drink responded: 'I only get drinks for people when they use manners.' This mother indicated to her daughter that she would only provide assistance when she was treated fairly and in a respectful manner. She wasn't going to be anybody's slave!

Nagging behaviour, like whingeing, should be ignored. This can be difficult, as pestering can be extremely irritating. Sometimes it is best to stop what you are doing and make a hasty retreat from a nagging child – she will soon learn that such behaviour is successful only in emptying the room.

When faced with nagging children it is advisable to examine your own behaviour. Children only engage in behaviours that achieve a purpose. They also adopt ways of acting that they see work for others in terms of achieving a desired result. If children see that nagging works for their mother or father, then they are likely to adopt that behaviour. Children learn a great deal from the models around them.

MIND THE STEPS

Nagging is a sign of disrespectful relationships.

When you nag and constantly remind children of their duties you teach them to behave in the same way.

Speak to children once, then take action rather than constantly nag.

It is best not to respond to children who nag you. Teach children that you will assist them only when you are treated respectfully.

Night Visitors

Effie was curled up in bed asleep when she felt a tap on her shoulder. 'Mum, I can't go to sleep,' whispered her five-year-old daughter, Sophia. 'Darling, go back to bed and you'll fall asleep in no time,' replied a bleary-eyed Effie. 'But Mum, I can't sleep. I keep hearing noises. Can I come into your bed?' 'Oh all right, just for a little while,' said Effie, too sleepy to get up. They both fell asleep in an instant and were woken by the sounds of the alarm clock in the morning.

It is quite common for children to wake up and visit their parents' bedroom. It is generally of little concern if it happens once in a while, but it can be very tiring when it is a frequent occurrence. Parents, like children, need a decent night's sleep. It is often difficult to function properly when you are tired, and you are busy enough with children throughout the day without having to face them unnecessarily in the middle of the night.

Night visits occur for many reasons. Some children wake up and don't try to go back to sleep in their own beds. Instead they seek the comfort of their parents' bed. It feels good to snuggle against a warm body in the middle of the night. But this is best done in the mornings. Parents often give in and let children into their beds at night. The trouble with this is that a privilege is easily interpreted as a right. 'You let me in bed last night. What's wrong with me tonight? It's not fair!' thinks a confused young child.

Some young night visitors have not broken habits established as babies or toddlers. Their parents found it more convenient to soothe them to sleep in their bed rather than return them to the cot and let them cry. As a baby grows, the same behaviour pattern continues and parents are confronted with a regular unwanted guest in their bed. Some older children see a baby in their parents' bed and think: 'If it's good enough for baby then it's good enough for me.' They see it as their right to be able to wake their parents when they can't go back to sleep.

When children are ill they often require special care at night. After they have recovered they may expect this special service to continue. They strongly resent any efforts to ignore them at night. They may enter your room or cry out from their own bed. Children who have nightmares often seek the comfort of their parents' bed. This is understandable, as bad dreams can be very frightening for children, who are less able to deal with them than adults.

A parent who adopts a responsible approach believes that children are capable of dealing with their own problems as much as possible. Waking in the night is a problem that belongs to the child. When he comes into his parents' room it quickly becomes their problem as well. Not only is this unfair but it is asking other people to handle his difficulty. Waking in the night is just one of many problems that children should learn to deal with.

Discuss with children what they may do when they wake in the middle of the night. There are many options available for children to choose from. They may simply roll over and return to sleep or they may turn on the light and read. Ensure that visiting your room is the last option, rather than the initial reaction, when they wake up at night. They should disturb you only in an emergency or when they are having a nightmare.

Set limits

Sometimes night visits occur in homes where there are few limits placed on children. To learn to respect the rights of others, children should be aware of the boundaries that exist. It is helpful to discuss with the children some simple rules regarding parents' bedrooms. A workable rule is that children remain out of parents' bedrooms until a certain time in the morning. This can allow you to shower and dress in peace without children constantly around. Children must respect your need for privacy, just as their need for privacy should be respected.

Many parents sleep with their bedroom door open. This is a legacy of having babies – parents generally need to leave the door open so that they can hear when baby wakes in the night for a feed. Somehow, as children grow older the bedroom door never closes. An open door is an invitation for night visitors.

Excessive night visiting

It is so easy to give into night visitors and let them in your bed or spend time rubbing their heads until they go to sleep in their own beds. When you are tired you are more willing to do anything it takes to allow you to get back to sleep. By giving in to children, you may be getting back to sleep in a hurry but you are not solving the problem. A child is likely to come back again the next time she wakes if she knows that you will give her the comfort she wants. When a child comes to your room in the middle of the night with that familiar refrain of 'I can't go to sleep', remove her in silence. Lead the child back to her own bed, then leave. This procedure should be repeated if the child returns. For repeated visits, make sure that your bedroom door is closed. Children will eventually cease visiting your room when you cease making their effort worthwhile.

Avoid letting night visitors sleep in to compensate for their broken night. Wake them at their normal time. If they are tired they are more likely to sleep through the night. Young children can be cranky and difficult to put up with when they are tired. But remember that the aim is to regulate their sleep and to break the habit of visiting your room at night. To achieve this it may be necessary to put up with tired children during the day.

If there are two parents, both should share the load when dealing with night visitors. A joint effort not only strengthens your resolve but ensures that there is consistency in your approaches. Children always know which parent will be more sympathetic to their plight when they can't go back to sleep. They won't wake a parent who is more likely to growl or put them straight back to bed.

A mother who was hounded by her seven-year-old son night after night broke the cycle with some effort. She explained to him that she was going to ignore him when he came into her room at night. She also discussed ways he could help himself to go back to sleep. When the child appeared in her room that night she asked him to leave. When he didn't budge she quietly took him back to his own bed. He reappeared a number of times but she repeated the procedure. Eventually she closed the door. When she awoke next morning she found her son curled up asleep under a blanket outside her door. She complimented him on finding a workable solution to his dilemma.

Over the next few nights he entered his mother's room but he always received the same response. His mother was extremely tired, of course, but she managed to break her son of this energy-sapping habit. The child stopped coming to his parent's room at night, preferring instead to sleep in a sleeping bag outside her room when he had the need to be close to someone.

When children have nightmares or are frightened they should spend only as much time with parents as is needed to allay their fears. After being comforted they should return to their rooms.

MIND THE STEPS

You have a right to privacy and an uninterrupted sleep at night.

Establish with children clear limits about visiting and using.

When children visit your room at night, provide minimum comfort and take them back to their own bedrooms.

Personal Hygiene

'Robert, it's time to have a bath. Make sure you wash behind your ears and in all those places that don't see the light of day but still get dirty.' 'Yes, Mum,' groaned eight-year-old Robert.

Many children have to be constantly reminded to perform even the most basic personal hygiene activities. When you take them to the beach in the middle of winter they are attracted to water like pins to a magnet. Yet mention the word 'bath' and they run in the opposite direction. Children often don't see the point in washing. Unless they are caked in mud from head to foot they don't believe that they need to bath or take a shower. Their standards of cleanliness are generally different from adults'. A bit of grime on the face and on the knees is neither here nor there in their eyes.

It is easy for parents to become too heavily involved in children's hygiene habits. While supervision is essential, the task of toileting and keeping clean needs to belong to the children. They should become responsible for their own personal hygiene at the earliest possible age. If children are to become independent they should learn the basic skills of cleanliness as soon as they are physically capable.

Personal hygiene includes cleaning teeth, washing hands after the toilet and before a meal, taking baths and showers, washing hair and going to the toilet in the correct place and cleaning up any misses. Your lives as parents and providers are busy enough without the added burden of keeping children clean. It is hard enough keeping the house clean without the added responsibility of washing mobile dirt collectors.

Teach the skills at an early age

Cleanliness does not necessarily come naturally to children. They need to be shown how to take care of their hygiene requirements. This means that you should show children how to wash themselves, run showers or baths, clean their teeth properly and wipe their bottoms instead of doing those jobs for them. Teaching leads to independence. It is also a worthwhile investment of your time as a parent. Five minutes a day teaching children how to keep clean will save a great deal of time later on if they are able to do it all themselves.

Many parents continue to perform basic hygiene tasks for children to avoid the mess that so often occurs when they have their L-plates on. It is easy to fall into the trap of doing things for children to avoid messes or because it is quicker. Acquiring new competencies usually results in less than perfect efforts but with perseverance children will improve and become less clumsy. It is also reasonable to expect children to clean up any excessively wet or messy cleaning areas.

Maureen had just taught her five-year-old daughter to clean her teeth and had given her the responsibility of performing this task by herself. The child delighted in sitting on the edge of the basin and watching herself in the mirror while she cleaned her teeth. This resulted in the bathroom mirror being covered in a spray of toothpaste, which was difficult to remove. Maureen asked that she kindly refrain from this habit and suggested that splatter painting be done at school. When the mirror continued to be covered in toothpaste, Maureen insisted that her daughter help to clean the mess. The splatter effect on the mirror quickly stopped happening as the child suddenly became a great deal more careful when she cleaned her teeth.

Personal hygiene skills should be taught as children become physically capable of handling various tasks. It is a good idea to ask yourself: 'Am I doing things for my children that they can do for themselves?' If the answer is yes, then it is appropriate to hand the responsibility for performing these tasks to children. With regular supervision and a little teaching, children will quickly develop the competencies needed to take care of their hygiene needs.

Hygiene is habit-forming

Cleanliness habits should be part of the daily family routine. Children can be expected to bath, shower or wash themselves before breakfast or the evening meal. Teeth cleaning can occur immediately after a meal or as children prepare for bed. By linking hygiene with regular activities, children easily develop the cleanliness habit. Children enjoy routine because it removes the pressure of having to remember to do a myriad of tasks. It also allows you to use consequences to influence children to adopt reasonable standards of cleanliness.

Barbara and Zac were fairly fastidious when it came to personal hygiene. They encouraged their two children to have similar standards. They regularly discussed with Rita, seven, and Ali, eleven, the importance of personal cleanliness. They also spent a lot of time training their children in the various tasks required to maintain a reasonable standard of hygiene. They used consequences to keep their children up to scratch instead of nagging or lecturing them. When either of the children forgot to shower before dinner, which was the agreed procedure, the meal was not served until the offender had showered. Barbara indicated to her children that she was not willing to serve a meal to anyone who was grubby or smelly. Similarly, dirty children were not allowed to use the lounge room furniture. Children who forgot to clean their teeth were not given sweets the next day. The consequences that Barbara and Zac chose were fair and reasonable. The children could see that it was in their own short-term interests to adopt acceptable standards of personal cleanliness.

SOILING

Some young children delight in the habit of soiling their pants. This can be irritating, to say the least, and keep parents very busy in their service. First, it is advisable to seek medical advice to ensure that there is no physical problem such as a lazy bowel. Usually it is a case of lazy children, particularly when they are preschoolers. Don't overreact to such behaviour – you will often only compound the problem. Keep in mind that all behaviour serves a purpose. Pants soiling is no exception. It can sometimes be for the purpose of attracting attention, perhaps when a new baby has arrived in the house. A child can reason that soiling nappies keeps parents extremely busy with baby, so it may as well work for him. The same behaviour can work for a little power-seeker. Try as you might, you can't make a child stop messing his pants. Children are generally aware that really you can't make them do anything that they don't want to do. Soiling is also an excellent way of retaliating against parents. 'You keep paying all that attention to Mary and not to me. I know a good way to punish you,' thinks a typical revenge-seeker.

Whatever the goal of soiling, the outcome is still the same – parents become involved in an area that should be the child's concern. The behaviour will generally cease if the consequence of soiling is more unpleasant for the child than it is for parents. When children soil they should clean themselves up and help to dispose of the offending article in the appropriate manner. If they are too young to clean themselves completely, then assistance can be given. There is no need to chide the child. Remain as calm as possible and show the child to the laundry door. When the child sees that you are unconcerned with soiling, the behaviour will cease – there is no point in engaging in a behaviour that doesn't achieve a desired goal.

A mother complained that her four-year-old daughter constantly wet or soiled her pants. She was particularly perturbed because the youngster was perfectly capable of controlling her bladder and bowels when it suited her. Generally she messed her clothes when she was busy playing with friends or was involved in an enjoyable activity. She would always run to her mother, claiming that she couldn't make it to the toilet. Her mother would scold her before changing her. Clearly her mother was more perturbed by the behaviour than the child.

This mother changed her tactics. She agreed that it was better to ignore the behaviour and leave her child to change herself. She also helped her daughter to recognise the physical signs of impending doom. She made light of any accidents but she refused to offer assistance unless the mess was too great for the child to clean by herself. The problem then disappeared fairly quickly, because the child was inconvenienced more than her mother by the soiling. By experiencing the consequences of being 'slow' to go to the toilet, the child learned that it was in her best interests to alter her behaviour accordingly.

MIND THE STEPS

Children should be responsible for all aspects of personal hygiene from the earliest possible age.

Teach children the skills of cleanliness and hygiene on a regular basis.

Hygiene can easily be linked to other activities in the daily routine.

Pocket Money

Dennis, aged ten, kept asking his father for some batteries for his remote-controlled car. 'Dennis, I just bought you batteries last week. You shouldn't waste them. Be careful how you use them,' he said. 'But Dad, the car uses up heaps of power. Can I please have some money for some new batteries?' continued Dennis. 'No, money doesn't grow on trees, you know,' answered his father. 'Ah Dad, it's not fair!'

Dennis does not receive regular pocket money. He is dependent on his parents to provide all his monetary needs. When he wants sweets, treats or toys he must ask his parents for the necessary money. This is an imposition on his parents and a source of frustration for Dennis himself. The simple solution is to provide the child with a regular allowance which he can use as he pleases within limits. When Dennis asks for batteries his father can reply, 'Buy them with your money.' Dennis will learn the necessity of planning for his regular purchases instead of impulsively asking his parents to provide for his every need.

Regular pocket money is an excellent way of developing independence. Children are able to regulate their own financial affairs without continually asking their parents for money. They soon learn, with a little parental guidance, how to handle money sensibly. Many children become thrifty savers as they learn that amounts quickly build up when they are not spent. They are also more likely to establish saving goals. One seven-year-old boy saved for nearly six months for a mountain bike. He combined his savings with cash birthday presents that he requested from relatives to buy his new bike. As it took a great deal of effort and sacrifice to save the money, he cares for his bike like no other possession.

In a democratic family an allowance is seen as a child's

right, rather than a privilege granted by parents. In families we share the responsibilities and the wealth. This is not to say that the family income is divided equally between all members. Rather, children are provided with a realistic sum of money, given their age, needs and ability to deal with money. There should be no connection between chores and money. Children do chores to contribute to family welfare. An allowance is the division of the family benefits. Democratic families share decisions, responsibilities and benefits.

Allowances should not be used as rewards or bribes. 'If you clean the floor I'll give you a dollar,' said one mother to her ten-year-old daughter. This approach teaches children to help only when there is something in it for them. One of life's demands is that we assist each other as needs arise. Offering children bribes for good behaviour or assistance promotes a self-centred approach to life. Similarly, allowances should not be withheld from children as a punishment for misbehaviour. Keep allowances and misbehaviour separate. An allowance should best be viewed as a right which cannot be withdrawn.

It is sensible to provide children with guidelines to help them regulate their use of pocket money. They should know what you are going to provide for them and the types of expenditure that they are responsible for. When Stewart gave his seven-year-old daughter a significant increase in pocket money, he warned her that he was not going to buy her any sweets. Also, he was going to give her sufficient money to buy two lunches per week at the school canteen. She was welcome to make her own lunches at home and save the canteen allocation if she wished. Stewart suggested that his daughter save for the annual summer holiday, because he was not willing to keep buying her ice-creams as he did the year before. He pointed out that he was budgeting for the holiday and that it would be a good idea if she did the same.

Teaching responsibility

'I just hate going to the Show,' complained Fazal. 'I can't stand the crowds and I just loathe it when the kids keep asking for showbags all the time. When I say that enough is enough, they treat me as if I was the worst father in the world. They whinge and carry on. I bought them all four bags each and still they wanted more. They are so ungrateful. Never again!'

Fazal should not despair. He should change his approach to handling the children's finances. Next year he could adopt one of two approaches: either he increases his children's pocket money slightly, so that they can save through the year for their show-bags; or he provides them with an allocation of money before they leave home. Of course, he should let them know that they can spend it how they wish and that there is no more cash where that came from. Fazal could also discuss with them the types of things that they might be able to buy. In this way he could solve the problem of his children making constant demands on his pocket while providing them with a terrific learning experience.

Budgeting

Pocket money can be used to promote real independence. With proper guidance children can quickly learn to control their own spending. They will experience a great deal of satisfaction and a feeling of control when they are not constantly dependent on you to make all the decisions for them.

Bob decided that he wanted to stimulate his children to accept a greater degree of responsibility for their own welfare. His wife had just returned to the workforce and they both had less time to spend with the children each morning. He sat down with his family and discussed the new arrangements. Donna, twelve, Steve, nine, and Paula, six, were excited when they heard that they were receiving hefty increases in their regular allowances. As Bob outlined their new responsibilities they soon realised that they were required to do some careful planning.

Donna was given a significant amount of money each week. This included her school bus fares, her lunch money and an allocation for clothing. Donna was becoming quite fashion-conscious and her parents could not afford to buy her all the clothes that she wanted. She continually complained about the clothes that her mother bought for her. 'Daggy' was the word that was always on her lips when she saw the outfits that her mother bought for her. To avoid conflict, her parents decided that she should be responsible for buying her own clothes. They would still provide her with her school clothes.

Steve's allowance was significantly less than that of his sister because his needs were not as great. He was now responsible for buying his own canteen lunches and paying for his weekly karate lessons. Paula was responsible for buying her own lunch at school. All the children were given extra money to use as they wished. This included the purchase of toys, sweets and other luxury items.

Bob discussed with his children the need for prudent planning. He showed them how to plan a budget that would meet their needs. He also discussed the benefits of saving and explained that large purchases could be made if they set some money aside for this purpose. Donna immediately decided that she would save ten per cent of her allowances. Steve couldn't see the point in saving. All he could visualise was a school canteen full of goodies that he could sample with his new-found wealth. Paula was unsure of the whole procedure. She was used to her mother making all the decisions for her, so she wasn't too keen on the idea at first. Bob was willing to help his children make adjustments to the scheme, but he was not going to interfere in the process that he had set in motion.

Steve was fairly predictable. He spent his initial allowance by the first day of the school week. He bought up big at the tuck-shop and purchased an expensive plastic gun from the toy shop on the way home from school. He asked his father for an advance on his pocket money so that he could buy some lunch at school. Bob refused, reminding him of the original deal. He did say, however, that he was welcome to make his own lunches in the morning. Steve made his lunch each morning except Friday. He slept in and didn't have time to prepare it. His mother resisted the temptation to make him a sandwich and suggested that he grab some fruit instead. She agreed to pay for his karate lesson this time but reminded him that she would not do so again. She made this concession as it was only the first week and he had already learned a valuable lesson in budgeting.

Donna, who was a well-organised girl, thrived on the new arrangement. She immediately began to save for a new pair of jeans. She made her lunches each day and walked home from school on a number of occasions, using her bus money to boost her savings. She enjoyed having control over her own affairs. Paula quickly became used to the idea of being responsible for buying her lunch and soon saw the benefits of saving.

At the end of the first week the family discussed the new financial arrangements. Steve asked for a raise as he had quickly run out of money. Bob pointed out that the money was sufficient to provide for his requirements as long as he spent the money wisely. The ensuing discussion proved fruitful as the children shared their experiences. Steve learned from his sisters how to budget effectively so that his allowance could last for the full week.

Eventually Donna supplemented her allowance by taking a part-time job as a sales assistant at a milk bar on weekends. As the children grew older and were able to accept more responsibility for their spending, their allowances were increased. Steve developed a keen interest in music. He was able to buy records occasionally from his allowance. Donna began to go out more on weekends. Her pocket money increased to take into account her changing needs. By the time Donna was in her final year of school she was even given the task of buying her own school books and stationery. Her parents built this component into her allowance.

Steve and Paula had considerable control over their own budgeting. Steve learned to appreciate the benefits of saving. He even bought himself a CD player. Paula learned to be very careful with her money. She enjoyed seeing her bank account grow and hardly ever bought sweets or other trivial items. She considered this a waste of money. All the children became far more independent and certainly learned a great deal about managing money.

Young children

Preschool children should be given allowances, even though they have little knowledge about relative values of money. Most young children are aware of the kinds of sweets and supermarket rides that certain coins will buy. One mother told me that she was tired of her four-year-old daughter always asking for a treat whenever they went to the shops. There was a horse outside the supermarket which was the source of many requests. This mother gave her daughter two dollars pocket money each week. This was sufficient to buy a bag of sweets and a ride on the mechanical horse. Her daughter was free to decide when she spent the money and how it was to be used. She stopped constantly asking her mother for money when she was able to decide for herself how she was going to spend her allowance. Her mother was relieved not to have to continually refuse her daughter's requests – she used to feel that she was giving in when she bought her daughter a treat.

Be realistic

Children are very aware of other children's possessions. Considerable pressure can be placed on parents to buy this or that to keep up with the other kids. 'Ken's mum bought him a new skateboard. Can I have one, please?' is a typical request. This sort of unrealistic demand can be difficult to refuse. It seems that parents are forever saying no to children's requests.

The provision of pocket money helps to remove some of this pressure. Allowances should relate to both the needs of children and the family income. It is pointless giving a certain amount because that is what 'the other kids get'. This is not being realistic. Don't try to keep up with the Joneses – they are probably trying to keep up with the Smiths.

Starting out

When beginning the budgeting process with children you might find that it is necessary to scrap your first arrangement and make a fresh start. Some children, like Steve, spend all their money immediately and have no money for essential purposes such as bus fares. They are given an advance or receive a loan from an older sibling and then find that their money doesn't stretch to loan repayments.

Budgeting should be seen as a learning process. Children have to develop the skills necessary for them to handle money wisely. Experience is a great teacher, but in the world of money it can be downright cruel. Be a little forgiving when children overspend, particularly if they are just starting out in the budgeting process.

MIND THE STEPS

The use of allowances can be an excellent way of developing a sense of responsibility in children.

Before granting children allowances, establish what the money can be used for and provide guidance about budgeting, spending and saving.

Preschool children can receive a small allowance to be spent within known limits.

Older children can be given greater freedom to spend their allowances. They can be taught how to budget for a week's expenditure.

Power-hungry Children

'Wash your hands Giorgio. They are filthy. They will make a mess all over my furniture.' 'They aren't dirty, Mum,' replied Giorgio. 'Yes they are! I want you to clean them now, Giorgio,' his mother responded. 'No, I don't want to!' yelled the child. 'Giorgio, I told you to wash those hands of yours and I want it done now!' screamed his mother. 'Make me!' said Giorgio, issuing a challenge. His mother, who was gathering a full head of steam, stormed over and grabbed Giorgio by the ear and led him to the bathroom. 'Now wash those hands and do a good job of it,' she demanded. Giorgio, with his ear still stinging, rubbed a damp flannel lightly over his hands and said defiantly: 'There, I've done it. They're clean enough now.' His mother was not finished yet. She took his hands and plunged them under the hot water tap and began scrubbing them until Giorgio screamed out in pain. 'Now, next time you do as I say, Giorgio,' she yelled angrily.

Giorgio was locked in a fierce power struggle with his mother. This time she won, but you can be sure that the fight will flare up again. She achieved what she wanted, but at a price. The hands are clean but the power struggle has been intensified. She has just shown her son that power and force are important. Giorgio is very unlikely to co-operate with his mother unless some type of power is used. If she asked him to do a chore right now she would be unlikely to receive a positive response!

Power struggles, although perhaps not as intense as in this example, are common in many homes. They are particularly prevalent in households that are dominated by autocratic parents. Children, in an effort to prove their independence, are intent on defeating parents at every opportunity. The quest for power usually emerges in arguments over the more trivial issues such as room tidiness, choice of food and bedtimes.

Parents and children combine to maintain power struggles. When they meet with defiance, parents often try to dominate children. This usually only provokes conflict and makes children try harder to have their own way. Simple orders and demands become invitations to enter a struggle for dominance. It is important to realise that you cannot demand co-operation from children. You can, however, influence children to behave in appropriate ways when you stop demanding compliance.

The things that parents and children fight about are not the real issues. Look at any conflict situation and you will find that it is about power, prestige and position. When children are obstinate or unco-operative they threaten your position and prestige as parents. Power is about winning and losing. When parents lose they feel insecure that their position as parents has been undermined. 'What would others think if they found out that I can't make my children do as I want?' Our traditions tell us that children should do as they are told. If we can't control our children then we are failing in our job as parents. However, the truth is we must control ourselves rather than our children. In this way we can stimulate co-operation and self-reliance.

Giorgio's mother felt extremely threatened when her son refused to wash his hands. The issue of clean hands was replaced by the desire to dominate her son. She believed that children should do as they were told and had no right to defy parents' wishes. She treated him with little respect and received none in return. With a little more tact and careful handling, the conflict would not have occurred. She could have said to her son after he initially claimed that his hands were clean, 'All right, but could you please help to keep the furniture clean and tidy?' An invitation to co-operate has more chance of being accepted than a command to comply.

Parents who are embroiled in power struggles with children have good intentions, but they are generally guided by a wish to control rather than the realities of the situation. Beth asked her six-year-old daughter to pick up the toys in the living room before dinner. When the child continued playing Beth grew angry and reminded her about her job. The child resisted, saying that she didn't want to clean the room at that time. Beth exploded at her defiance and yelled, 'Pick those toys up right now or you'll get a smack.' 'No, I'm not going to. I don't care if you smack me.' Beth gave her one more chance. 'I'll count to three and if you don't pick those toys up I'll come over and smack you on the legs.' 'No, I hate you anyway,' yelled the child as she ran off to her bedroom, leaving her mother feeling angry and frustrated.

In this example the young girl had a hollow victory. She retaliated against her mother's threats by calling her names and ran off when it appeared that she might lose. Really there were no winners, as Beth became angry, the child was upset and the room remained untidy. If Beth was so concerned about cleaning up the room she should have picked up the toys herself after the initial refusal. She could have withheld them for a period of time to teach her daughter to be responsible for her toys. Beth was more concerned about making her daughter pick up the toys than having a tidy room. This became her secondary concern.

Behaviours that demonstrate power plays vary, although their purpose is similar. Behaviours such as arguing, defiance, refusal, and temper tantrums are active ways of exhibiting power. They inform parents that children can do as they wish. Other behaviours such as dawdling, stubbornness and forgetfulness are passive ways of letting parents know that they cannot make children do anything that they don't want to do.

The purpose of power-seeking behaviours is to defeat parents, who invariably feel angry when confronted with such behaviours.

WHAT TO DO ABOUT POWER-HUNGRY CHILDREN

Parents need to recognise their own part in maintaining a power struggle. A quest for dominance cannot exist on its own. It takes two parties to fight whether it is an international skirmish or a dispute between a parent and child. Parents can refuse to be drawn into a fight with a child. As in the case of the messy living room, Beth could have refused to enter the dispute with her daughter and removed the toys herself. Refusing to fight is not giving in to a child. It is reacting sensibly to meet the demands of the situation. If a child refuses to eat then he will be hungry and he will eat at the next meal. When a child procrastinates at bedtime you can say goodnight at the regular time and have nothing further to do with him. Indicate your unwillingness to be drawn into an argument or dispute. A child cannot win if there is no fight.

It may come as a shock to many people but parents cannot make children do anything that they don't want to do. But you are not powerless because you are able to control yourselves. By changing the way you act, you can influence power seekers and achieve greater co-operation within families. The fact that co-operation is stimulated rather than demanded is taboo to many hardline authoritarians. However, it is a behavioural phenomenon as well as a law of physics that the use of force always causes an equal amount of resistance.

Power-seekers challenge your authority. When you are involved in a power struggle, ask yourself: 'What do I have at stake in this matter? Will my prestige or position as a parent be diminished if my child defeats me?' If the answer is yes, then you are in a game that the child will invariably win.

Power-seekers are generally very skilled in the art of defeating parents. You may win one issue but they are sure to fight over the next matter.

Power-seeking behaviour is generally easy to identify. Just examine how you feel when confronted with a misbehaviour or lack of co-operation. If you feel angry, frustrated or defeated then the purpose of the misbehaviour is power. Check the tone of voice that you use with children. If your response to misbehaviour is loud or yelled then you are more than likely angry. A firm approach is generally indicated by a calm, friendly voice. A further check for behaviour that has the goal of power is to correct a child's misbehaviour. A power-seeker will not stop the misbehaviour upon correction -the aim is to defeat you. A child who taps her fingers loudly will continue tapping when asked to stop, if power is her goal. She is issuing an invitation: 'Go on, try to stop me.'

When confronted with power-seeking behaviour you need to change your way of reacting. Indicate your refusal to fight and don't give any attention or feedback to the misbehaviour. Our finger-tapper will soon stop if her audience ignores her or even leaves the room. In this way the child learns that you don't intend telling her to stop what she is doing but you are not going to listen to it. Children will only use power if there is someone to contest it. Refuse to fight and you take away the purpose of the behaviour.

Often the way parents talk to children invites resistance. If you believe that children are our social equals then they should be spoken to as such. Adults don't take too kindly to people who issue demands and provide instructions in the manner of an army drill sergeant. An adult is more likely to comply with a request issued respectfully, such as 'Could you please close the door?' An order such as 'Close that door, will you!' is more likely to get the door shut in your face. Children respond more readily when they are asked to help rather than told what to do.

Children may try to exercise power over other people when they feel that they have little control of their own lives. Children who pursue the goal of power are often frustrated by parental interference in many areas. By giving children a reasonable amount of autonomy you are utilising the quest for power in a positive way. This does not mean that children do as they wish. That would lead to chaos. You should identify areas where children can take greater control, such as television viewing, types of clothing worn and morning routines, and allow them some freedom of choice within reasonable boundaries. Discuss with children their ideas about such matters and come to an agreement that accommodates everyone. Discussions should take place when everyone is calm -no one really listens in the heat of the moment. Angry conversations achieve nothing except a widening of the gap between people.

An excellent technique to use with children who like to flex their muscles and exercise power is the use of realistic choices. Provide a child with two options and ask him to choose one. A power-seeker will generally take one of the options offered when he feels that he is able to exercise some control. These realistic choices may be presented to children at various times.

- To a noisy child playing inside – 'You may play that game outside or you may choose a quiet game if you wish to remain inside.'
- To a child who refuses to wear a raincoat on a wet day – 'You may stay inside without your raincoat but if you wish to go outside the coat must be worn.'
- To a child who is dawdling in the morning – 'You may hurry up and get a lift with me or you are welcome to ride

your bike to school. The choice is yours.'

- To a child who refuses to wear the clothes you have chosen – 'You may wear your pink summer dress or the blue shorts and matching T-shirt.'

Children are less likely to fight with parents when they participate in the decisions that directly affect them. Whenever possible, allow children to exert influence in positive ways.

PUTTING THE THEORY INTO PRACTICE

Marion was involved in a long-running dispute with her nine-year-old daughter, Brenda, over the amount of television that she watched. They constantly argued about her viewing habits, with little success. Marion would generally demand that Brenda turn the set off, which would invariably lead to a heated battle. Brenda would dig her heels in and refuse to turn the television off when her mother wanted.

When she examined her feelings, Marion realised that she was involved in a power struggle with her daughter. She felt angry and defeated. She realised that the matter of the television viewing had become secondary to the issue of power and prestige. She felt that, as a parent, she should be able to make Brenda comply with her wishes. She also realised that the more she interfered, the more television Brenda watched. Brenda had discovered a great way to defeat her mother.

Marion decided that it was pointless to fight any longer about television. She was unwilling to give Brenda total control of her viewing, as this was unfair on the other children in the family and not in Brenda's best long-term interests. She discussed the issue of television viewing with Brenda and outlined her concerns. She pointed out that ten hours television viewing a week is considered to be reasonable by most experts. Brenda wanted to watch more than that. Marion reached a compromise and allowed her to watch twelve hours a week. This was a considerable improvement on the amount she used to watch. Brenda was happy to co-operate when she discovered that her mother was willing to be flexible. They discussed how the amount would be monitored and agreed to a consequence if she overstepped her limit. The amount of time would be deducted from next week's viewing. Marion agreed not to interfere in the matter any more.

By refusing to be drawn into the fight, Marion had defused the issue. She was able to reach a solution to the problem that best met the needs of them both. It may not have been the ideal solution as far as Marion was concerned. She would have been happy if her daughter watched no television. However, the solution was the most realistic, given the situation at hand.

MIND THE STEPS

Power-drunk children challenge parents' authority.

Refuse to fight with power-seekers. Avoid being drawn into conflict, as this is generally the purpose of the behaviour.

You generally feel angry when confronted by power-seekers.

Provide power-seekers with simple, realistic choices. Tell them what you are going to do rather than what they should do.

Develop children's sense of personal power by increasing their control over their own well-being.

Public Places

There is nothing more mortifying for parents than their children misbehaving in public. It is easy to believe that children's misbehaviour reflects poorly on them as parents. 'If I was doing my job properly my child would not be naughty or misbehave,' claimed a concerned mother. This attitude places unfair pressure on parents, who, realistically, can only expect to control their own actions. Children, with minds of their own, are able to choose how they behave. Unfortunately, some of these behaviours can be downright embarrassing to parents. We can be judged as parents only by our own behaviour, not the behaviour of our children.

Children realise that parents are extremely susceptible to their misbehaviour in public. The tantrum that gains little attention at home is extremely hard to ignore in a shop, on the train or at a friend's house. Misbehaviour in a public place is a type of emotional blackmail: – 'Do as I want or I'll misbehave.' Our reactions to inappropriate behaviour are usually intensified in public. Feelings of annoyance or anger are magnified in proportion to the number of people around.

At a Fathers' Night at my daughter's kindergarten once I witnessed a father's anger at his son's refusal to leave when requested. The father and child were having a great time playing together until it was time to leave. The child refused to budge. The father tried to reason with the boy, reminding him that he was due on nightshift very soon. The child screamed at his father at the top of his voice, threw himself on the floor and refused to move. The father, who was obviously aware that by this stage there were forty pairs of adult eyes trained on him, felt extremely embarrassed. He shouted angrily at his son, spanked him hard on the bottom, picked him up and carried him screaming out the door. The father was fuming, to say the least. His reaction reflected the way he felt about the total situation. He was, in effect, trapped by his son's tantrum. If he agreed to stay, he was giving into the tyrannical behaviour of his son. His dilemma as apparent: 'What do I do with a screaming child and still maintain my status as an effective parent?'

The rule of thumb in public is to do as the situation requires and maintain order with a minimum of fuss. The situation required that they both leave, so that is what had to occur. The father would have been better to simply pick his child up and carry him to the car. Alternatively, the child could have been offered a choice: 'Either you walk to the car or I shall carry you.' Even children in the midst of a full-blown tantrum usually choose a course of action that allows them to maintain their dignity. My bet is that he would have walked. The father needed to realise that there was little he could do about the tantrum, so a quick, painless exit was the best alternative.

When children misbehave in public, firm action is the best approach. Talking and reasoning is often ineffective, as children are less likely to listen to parents in public. Talk often becomes a type of pleading, which has little effect on unco-operative children. Words are best used to prepare children for an outing or to explain the nature of inappropriate behaviour at home after it has occurred.

Prepare children beforehand

It is common sense to discuss with children what they will encounter on an outing. Details such as departure times, planned activities and people they could meet may be obvious to you but are unknown to children, particularly if they have not previously experienced the visit or outing.

Let children know the type of behaviour that you expect of them before a trip, visit or outing. Discuss appropriate behaviours in positive terms rather than in language sprinkled with liberal doses of don'ts. Tell children how you expect them to behave rather than how you expect them not to behave.

If possible, involve children in planning an outing or trip. Children are less likely to misbehave when they feel that they have had some input into a visit.

When planning a public outing, the needs of children should be considered. For instance, during a visit to a friend's house, a young child may need to spend some time with you, settling into new surroundings before she wanders off to play with other children. While this may be frustrating, it may be realistic in terms of a child's needs.

Consequences of misbehaviour

Unfortunately, the most effective consequences of children's misbehaviour can be as unpleasant for adults as they are for children. When children misbehave in public they should be taken home immediately if possible. Although this is inconvenient in the short term, the results of such action will be well worth it in the long run. It is best to remind children once about their inappropriate behaviour, then act if the misbehaviour continues. The best course of action is for them to miss the outing. The message is clear: 'I see that you are not willing to co-operate so we shall return home.' Discuss with children at a later date the nature or their misbehaviour and suggest how they may act during the next outing.

Eating out

Ted and Paula took their two children to eat out at a local family restaurant one evening. Seven-year-old Jarrod and five-year-old Kimberly turned what should have been a pleasant evening into a nightmare for their parents. As soon as they arrived, both children asked for a drink. Paula reminded them that they had to wait until a waiter attended them before they ordered. Jarrod, who was used to getting what he wanted immediately, yelled out to the nearest waiter: 'Give me a drink, please.' This set the tone for the outing. Both children were noisy and boisterous, were up and down from their seats like yo-yos and ate with atrocious manners. Ted and Paula both felt powerless against the combined efforts of their children. The most effective and least intrusive action would have been to leave as soon as Jarrod issued his first order to the waiter for a drink. 'I see that you are not willing to co-operate tonight, Jarrod. We shall go home and try again another night.' This would have indicated to Jarrod that his parents were not willing to be held to ransom in public.

Children need to learn that they are to modify their behaviour according to the requirements of different situations. When they're at the football, it is acceptable to yell and scream. However, this behaviour is inappropriate at a restaurant. It is important to explain to children the type of behaviour required of them before they go on an outing.

Ted and Paula could discuss the correct ways to act in a restaurant after their disastrous trip. They could spend considerable time training them at home for a return trip. They could establish restaurant conditions in their own home, with Ted as the waiter taking orders. They could practise using correct table manners, talking quietly, waiting to be served and sitting until others have finished their meals before they leave the table. These are all requirements of those who eat out in restaurants, hotels or other people's homes. When the children have demonstrated that they are ready to eat out, then another trip to a restaurant can be organised. This training process can be fun, particularly if it is sprinkled with liberal doses of encouragement and parents get into the spirit of things by hamming it up.

VISITING FRIENDS

One question that I'm always asked during my parenting seminars is, 'What do I do with my children when they misbehave on visits to my friends' homes?' This is an extremely difficult situation for parents to deal with. They must consider their own needs for relaxation, the accepted rules of the host's household and the host's expectations of the visit. It is often unclear who should discipline children when visiting friends – the host or the visitor. My rule of thumb is that both parties should be responsible for discipline. The host should feel comfortable enough to discipline children who infringe the accepted rules of the house.

Elizabeth attended a dinner party at the house of one of her workmates. Her children, aged ten and six, accompanied her, the plan being that they would all sleep the night. This idea soon flew out the window when her two children combined with the host's two sons to create havoc. They were noisy and refused to go to bed at the agreed time. Instead they wanted to have a party of their own. Both parents were unsure of their role, neither wishing to offend by disciplining the other's children. So nothing was done. The other guests squirmed as the children popped in and out of the dining room with requests for chips, peanuts and drinks. Elizabeth would chide her children at each appearance, to little effect. Clearly this was a totally ridiculous situation – the children had basically taken the dinner party over from the adults.

Both Elizabeth and her host needed to act firmly as a team. 'Divide and conquer' is an effective measure in these circumstances. The children could have been split up and dispensed to different parts of the house to sleep. When children are separated, even into pairs, their capacity for disturbance is effectively reduced. If Elizabeth's children had refused to co-operate with this measure, it may well have been appropriate for her to leave. This is the best of two bad choices – stay and feel hassled by the children or leave and miss the dinner party. The second option has the advantage of teaching children that Elizabeth is willing to back up her talk with action. They will be less likely to misbehave next time they are out for a visit if they know that their mother is willing to take action. This is a case of short-term pain for long-term gain.

Outings

Here are the reactions of two different parents who, when confronted with awkward situations in public, managed calmly and effectively to avoid conflict and teach their children that their behaviour was unacceptable.

Tina took her six-year-old daughter to an aquarium to see some fish close up. The child initially delighted in the size and the shape of the exotic fish but she soon grew bored. She decided to play a game of hide-and-seek with her mother. She ran off and hid behind one of the fish tanks. When Tina approached her, the little girl would run off and hide in another place. Tina recognised the game that her daughter was playing and refused to be dragged into it. Instead, she ignored the child and continued looking at the fish. She knew that her daughter would not wander out of sight so she was not concerned about her safety. When it was time to leave she went towards her daughter. The little girl scooted off in another direction continuing her little game. Tina announced that she was leaving but the child refused to join her. Tina left the aquarium and waited for her daughter outside the entrance. The young girl did not disappoint her mother. She raced out of the aquarium in a flash when she thought that there may have been a chance of being left behind. Through her own behaviour Tina demonstrated that she was unimpressed with her daughter's game, which is unlikely to be played again.

Evelyn and Max took their two children to the cinema to watch a school-holiday movie. Five-year-old Ramon sat entranced by the movie while nine-year-old Tessa, who chose the film, fidgeted about in her seat with little regard for anyone else around her. She began hitting and kicking her little brother to get a reaction. Evelyn noticed this and gave Tessa a choice: 'Either you watch the movie or you and I can wait in the foyer.' Tessa continued annoying her brother, so during the interval Evelyn took her daughter out. She suggested that they return when Tessa was willing to behave properly. Tessa soon grew bored sitting in the foyer and asked to go back in. They did and Tessa quietly watched the movie.

MIND THE STEPS

Expect children to behave in socially acceptable ways when in public.

Prepare children thoroughly for outings by:

- explaining what they may be doing on the outing
- outlining behaviour expected of them
- involving them in planning if practical.

Avoid overreacting to misbehaviour in public.

If practical, take children home if they misbehave when on an outing. Alternatively, they can miss the next trip, if appropriate.

Sharing

The ability to share time, space and possessions needs to be encouraged in children from the earliest possible age. Sharing is an important element in forming friendships and is a prerequisite for starting school. Many children who have difficulty making friends don't have the ability to share. Watch two eighteen-month-old children at play and you will see that they play beside each other rather than with each other. As children mature they begin to interact more. Their games involve a great deal of communication and sharing. They may share a sandpit or co-operate to build a tower from construction material. Children who can't share, like soldiers protecting their hard-won pieces of ground, will defend their own space. They will be unwilling to allow others to use their toys, even when they are not playing with them.

Young children, who are egocentric, often have difficulty sharing with others. Sharing is a developmental process which can be enhanced by providing experiences that require sharing to occur. Children can learn the skills of sharing when situations are structured in such a way that joint participation is inevitable.

Often an only child has great difficulty playing with peers. Such children are sometimes unwilling to allow others to use their possessions and become angry when games do not proceed the way in which they wish. These children are not required to share at home, so sharing skills need to be nurtured by parents. It is important that an only child has contact with other children through play groups, kinders and visits with other children. An only child needs to develop the social skills required to function happily in the wider world.

Everyday family life provides many opportunities for children to learn the skills of sharing. Food, toys, television, parents' attention, bathrooms and games are not the domain of a particular family member. All involve co-operation and sharing if family life is to proceed with a minimum of conflict.

At times children have the right not to share their possessions. It is important to respect a child's wish not to share his belongings, at the same time pointing out the benefits of sharing. When friends are about to visit, ask a child to find the toys that other children can play with and put away those possessions that he doesn't wish to be used. Children often have favourite toys that they shouldn't be expected to share. However, it is reasonable to expect that a child should share some possessions with others.

Some children are tyrants when they deal with group possessions such as trampolines or computers. They refuse to allow other children to play with them. These toy hogs are experts at creating conflict – their tormented siblings or playmates invariably retaliate physically, verbally or by telling tales. Who can blame them?

Children who are unwilling to share group possessions should have the privilege of use withdrawn until they agree to respect the rights of others. In this way they can learn from first-hand experience the benefits of sharing and the discomfort that selfishness causes others.

Encouraging children to share

Parents can stimulate children to share by establishing a co-operative atmosphere at home. There are many everyday situations that can be used to foster co-operation and sharing. It is helpful to be aware of opportunities to teach children the skills of sharing.

Here are some ways in which you can promote sharing.

- When serving sandwiches, place them on a large plate for everyone to share rather than on individual plates.

- Allow children to help dish up a meal at the dining table instead of putting it on plates for them.
- Play group games with simple rules that all must abide by.
- Have a regular games time at home. There are many commercial games available which promote co-operation.
- Encourage children to play outside games which teach them to share and have fun together.
- Buy toys for the whole family to share, as well as individual toys.
- Promote a sense of generosity by encouraging children to swap toys with each other or to give them to friends.
- Share television time.
- Read stories to children as a group. Take it in turns to choose books.
- Plan family outings together with children.

Children need to have models to help shape their behaviour. Seeing their parents sharing with each other and with them has a significant influence on children. Don't forget to let your children see you sharing and co-operating with others.

MIND THE STEPS

Sharing is a vital social skill that is a prerequisite for forming friendships and attending school.

You may need to provide situations that require children to share time, space and objects.

Shopping

Maureen wished the ground would open up and swallow her. She was waiting at the checkout counter of the supermarket when her eight-year-old son came running down the nearest aisle pushing an empty trolley that he had found. 'Stop that, Jake!' she pleaded. At the same time her five-year-old daughter threw herself to the ground in a tantrum because her mother wouldn't buy her a treat. Alex, three, sat in the trolley throwing packets of food onto the floor. Maureen knew by their stares that the other shoppers weren't particularly sympathetic to her situation. 'Just get me out of here,' she thought to herself.

Shopping is a traumatic experience for many parents. Children often take advantage of parents in public places as they know that they feel quite vulnerable when children misbehave. They also know that parents will often give in to demands to avoid embarrassment. Temper tantrums are an effective form of blackmail in crowded places. Watch any child who is refused the lolly or a toy she wants. She will probably try whining persistently. If the parent does not wilt, then the child will bring in the heavy artillery – a tantrum. Because parents will do anything to avoid a scene in public, this generally has the desired effect.

Supermarkets seem to bring out the worst in children. They are open and spacious with shelves full of potential missiles and tantalising goodies. The trolleys are a treat in themselves. They are great substitutes for billycarts. Never mind that they can't be properly steered; this only adds to the fun. It is little wonder that a child once remarked to me, 'I love shopping with Mum. The super-market is better than a fun park.'

It is not reasonable that you should be subjected to unco-operative behaviour, whether it is in the privacy of your home or in a public place such as a supermarket. Children should be expected to behave as a situation requires. They must learn that they cannot always do as they wish and get what they want. This is part of life. If a situation requires that they wait quietly at the checkout counter, then that is what they should be expected to do. Of course, the expectation needs to be realistic. You are asking for trouble if you are entering your fifth clothes shop in search of an outfit and you expect the children to be perfect angels. This is an unreasonable expectation which is bound to lead to disaster.

Shopping does not have to be an horrendous experience for parents. With a little planning and common sense, shopping can be enjoyable as well as educational for children.

Children can contribute

Parents often believe that taking children to the super-market is a burden that they can do without. This is understandable – they have enough to do without the added concern of dealing with disruptive children. Children should be seen as an asset rather than a burden. It is far better to view children as helpers rather than as unwanted company. Children of all ages like to feel useful. They are less likely to misbehave when they believe that they can make a real contribution to the shopping trip.

Even preschool children know the products that you regularly buy. Ask any child to identify the breakfast cereal or the biscuits that you usually buy. They will do this easily. Use this product knowledge to your advantage. Give children simple tasks to do when shopping. Ask them to find the breakfast cereal, the biscuits or the jam. Children usually enjoy finding the food that they generally eat. They also enjoy choosing products as well. If you are concerned that they will choose expensive or unhealthy food, then you can limit their choice between two acceptable products.

Supermarkets are full of colourful items of all shapes and

sizes. It is easy for children to identify various brands and types of foods. They are great places to develop pre-reading skills and maths concepts. Consider this list of questions and directions that are applicable to any supermarket:

'Can you find me the jar with the red lid in this aisle, please?'

'Get the packet with the rooster on the front.'

'One of the packets begins with the same letter that your name begins with.'

'Pass me the biggest tub of ice-cream, please.'

'Can you get me three tubs of margarine, please?'

'I would like the peanut butter in the middle of the shelf. Look on the second shelf.'

'Which jar is the heaviest? Good, I'll buy that one.'

'Pass me that round tube over there.'

With a little thought and effort, a routine shopping trip can be turned into a valuable educational excursion. Young children can be kept busy in a useful way that benefits everyone.

As children mature and develop more complex skills they can assist in any number of ways. Consider these contributions they can make:

- Children can help to compile a shopping list. They enjoy being given the responsibility of listing the grocery items that they use. With assistance they can itemise a part of the list, such as the fruit, vegetables, meat or toiletry items.
- Some children enjoy planning and even cooking a meal. They can plan the food needed and take charge of buying those items.
- Children can be given the task of selecting a certain type of food or grocery item.
- Some children love to accompany their parents to the supermarket armed with a calculator. They can add the prices as you select items. This is a great maths activity

which teaches children about money, numbers, decimals and the importance of sticking to a budget.
- Some children are experts at selecting specials from supermarket catalogues.

There are many ways that children can help on shopping trips. When children are occupied in useful ways they are less likely to be disruptive.

When children misbehave

Ensure that your children fully understand the behaviour expected from them when in public places such as supermarkets and shops. This should not be explained at the top of your voice when they are screaming for lollies and you are busy fidgeting in your purse for money to pay the shop assistant. There is little point in talking to children when you are feeling hassled or angry. Your words will more than likely be interpreted as threats and may cause an escalation of misbehaviour. Discussions about appropriate behaviour should always occur when you are calm and the children are receptive to your ideas.

Avoid offering bribes or rewards for co-operation: 'If you are good I'll buy you an ice-cream when I've finished shopping.' This gives children the message that you think that they will only behave if they are given a reward. It displays little faith in children and ensures that they will think 'What is in this for me?' It's fine to finish the shopping with a treat or a fun activity, but it need not be contingent on being good. The treat should be considered part of the shopping trip.

It is pointless threatening, scolding or pleading with misbehaving children when shopping. Firm action is the most appropriate strategy. When children are so disruptive that the shopping becomes intolerable, they should be taken home immediately. Perhaps a friend or relative could mind the children while you continue shopping. This strategy is rarely used – parents find it inconvenient to leave a half-full trolley in the supermarket in order to take their children home – but it is worth considering. An hour or two of inconvenience is surely a small price to pay for the longer-term peace achieved by such action.

Consider Sharon's reaction to the misbehaviour of her four-year-old daughter, Lisa, in the supermarket. Lisa was pulling everything off the shelves that was within reach. She would scream when her mother tried to stop her. She created such a fuss that her mother felt like disowning her. Sharon invited her daughter to co-operate but Lisa didn't wish to. Sharon said, 'I see you are not willing to behave, so it is time to go home.' She left her half-filled trolley in a convenient spot and promptly left the supermarket with her daughter following, screaming in protest. She left the child with a friend and continued with her shopping. Next time she shopped she left her daughter with a friend, carefully explaining to Lisa that she was not willing to take an unco-operative child to the supermarket.

A week later, the child asked her mother if she could go shopping with her again. Sharon agreed to her request, as she assumed that Lisa was willing to behave responsibly. Lisa knew that her mother was not going to tolerate any misbehaviour. Sharon encouraged her to help with the shopping and Lisa actually began to enjoy the trips to the supermarket. She chose food from the shelves and counted out various items. As Lisa's contribution was valued, she found it was more beneficial to co-operate than to misbehave.

The following mother used consequences to teach her children that their behaviour was inappropriate.

Brenda, a single mother, took her three school-aged children to the supermarket one Saturday morning. They behaved so poorly that she returned home without purchasing anything. She had no one to leave them with but she was unwilling to take them back to the super-market, so she allowed them to experience the consequences of their misbehaviour. She did not scold or punish them. She recognised that the children would have to learn the hard way that their co-operation was essential.

They soon began to run short of groceries. By Wednesday Brenda's eldest child approached her. 'Please go shopping, Mum. We'll help you. I am sick of eating rice and spaghetti.' Brenda, who worked full-time as a secretary, reminded her son that Saturday was the only day that she could shop. When Saturday arrived, the children, who realised that their mother needed assistance, had organised the shopping list and beat Brenda to the car. They helped her in the supermarket and offered to unpack the groceries and stack them in the cupboards at home. The children had been taught a powerful lesson about responsibility by experiencing the consequences of their misbehaviour rather than the anger of an adult. Brenda maintained her self-respect by refusing to submit to the children's disruptive behaviour. She acted calmly, firmly and effectively.

As with all family activities shopping should be as enjoyable as possible. Many families conclude a shopping trip with a treat or an interesting activity. This shows appreciation for children's assistance and demonstrates the importance of give and take in family life.

MIND THE STEPS

Children generally behave in public in the manner they are trained at home.

Encourage children to help rather than hinder you when shopping.

With a little thought and preparation, a mundane shopping trip can be turned into a valuable educational experience for children.

When children misbehave, be prepared to abandon the shopping trip.

Shyness and Showing Off

Shyness and showing off are two totally different behaviours that have the same purpose or goal. They both gain children a great deal of attention from concerned parents. While shyness is passive, showing off is an extremely active and irritating type of behaviour. Both activities are influenced by parents' reactions. While showing off usually receives adverse reactions from parents, shy children can also keep parents both busy and concerned.

SHYNESS

Six-year-old Karl accompanied his class to the playground for a physical education lesson at school. When the teacher asked the children to join hands for a game, Karl remained on his own in a corner of the asphalt. Spying the child out of the corner of his eye, the teacher dutifully took Karl by the hand and implored him to join in with the others. After some prompting, Karl joined in with the rest of the class and thoroughly enjoyed the activities.

The purpose of Karl's shyness was revealed in the teacher's reaction. He came over and gave the child special attention. Thankfully for the teacher, he didn't have a class full of shy children. I wonder if his approach would have been the same if twenty-five children had stood on their own with fingers in their mouths when he issued the invitation to participate? He would have spent all his time coaxing instead of coaching. Karl was momentarily the centre of attention. He may have been a little anxious about joining in, but there were others, more than likely, who felt the same way. Karl learned that shyness has a dramatic effect on adults. They will generally go to great lengths to comfort shy children or include them in activities.

The physical education teacher could have said, 'I see that

Karl doesn't wish to join us today. That's all right', and directed his attention to the children who were ready and eager to play. Karl would have probably participated when he received no attention and realised that he was missing an enjoyable activity.

Many parents, like the physical education teacher, consider that shy children warrant special attention. This is a fallacy. It is easy to create a problem that is not there by paying unwarranted attention to a behaviour. Many children, like Karl, may lack confidence in many situations or require reassurance. Confidence and self-assurance develop when children face difficult situations on their own. Assisting or shielding shy children teaches them that they cannot face situations on their own. Children develop courage and self-esteem every time they conquer a fear or deal with a new situation on their own. In their desire to assist children, parents often rob them of opportunities to handle difficult situations by themselves.

At times children do not wish to talk to others or prefer to be alone. There is nothing unhealthy or sinister about this. You need to respect a child's right not to talk or join in. Some children are solitary by nature and prefer their own company. It is often unhelpful to force these children to talk or mix with others, as this will often drive them further away. By drawing attention to a behaviour it is easy to create a problem where one doesn't exist.

Heidi introduced her seven-year-old daughter to one of her friends. The child gave a polite greeting but indicated by looking down at the ground that she didn't wish to talk any more. She felt a little uncomfortable in the company of her mother's friend. The acquaintance said to her mother, 'She certainly is a shy lass, isn't she?' Heidi replied that she was not shy – she just didn't feel like talking today. She avoided attaching a label to her daughter and respected her wish not to talk.

Showing off

Carlo was really embarrassed by the behaviour of his son Alberto when the family was camping with friends. Eleven-year-old Alberto was the eldest child on the holiday and was determined to let everyone know this fact. When the families joined together at the beach or at mealtime, Alberto was rude, loud and generally obnoxious. He would interrupt others, tell smutty jokes and generally try to impress others with his cleverness. His behaviour naturally drew a great deal of undue attention to himself. By impressing others with his cleverness, he was trying to place himself above the other children.

Showing off, like shyness, reflects discouragement. A child who shows off wants to be seen as special. He also needs the approval of others to heighten his feelings of self-worth. Self-esteem cannot be gained at the expense of others – there will always be someone bigger or better to burst the bubble.

Children such as Alberto need a great deal of encouragement. This is often difficult to give when all you usually want to do is wring their necks. Carlo had great expectations for his eldest boy, who was a huge disappointment to him. Alberto was failing at school and he wasn't very good at sport. He also found it difficult to make friends. It is little wonder that he showed off in front of his father at every opportunity. 'Look Dad, notice me. I am clever you know!' was the message that the lad was giving. Carlo needed to accept his son for who he was and explore other ways of seeing his specialness.

Although children who brag or inflate their egos by showing off need encouragement, their behaviour need not be tolerated. They can be shown that their behaviour is unacceptable by your reactions. Let them know that you don't wish to be around them when their behaviour embarrasses you or others. Carlo could have explained his concerns about showing off to his son and indicated that he would not be invited to eat meals with the other families at the camp if his behaviour continued. Carlo would need to ensure that he put this consequence into action at the first opportunity, even if it inconvenienced himself. A combination of firmness and encouragement is a powerful influence on children's behaviour.

The danger of labels

The use of labels such as 'shy', 'show off', 'pest' and 'smart alec' should be avoided at all costs. When we label children they think of themselves in those terms. 'I know I am a shy girl because everyone tells me so,' thinks five-year-old Monica. Monica is not a shy girl. She displays behaviour that people interpret as being shy. It is necessary to separate the behaviour from the child. This sounds a little like splitting hairs but it is significant. It is easy to change behaviours; it is quite difficult to change people. Call a person who has just been released from gaol a criminal and you have little chance of rehabilitation. She is a person who committed a crime. Place labels on children and you are giving them a name to live up to.

Mind the steps

Shyness and showing off can gain children a great deal of attention.

Encourage shy children without drawing attention to their shyness.

Ignore showing-off behaviour but not the show-off – encourage these children.

Avoid placing labels on children, as they tend to become self-fulfilling prophecies.

Swearing

Parents shudder when they hear their children swear. 'Where did he hear that?' they ask themselves. Children learn language from those around them. Initially they learn language from parents. Toddlers are exposed to few role models, so it is relatively easy to influence their vocabularies and speech patterns. As their social circles widen, their exposure to behaviour and language grows beyond your control. They see and hear things in the schoolyard that you may not consider suitable. It can be scary to think that the innocent baby you held in your arms only a few years ago is now exposed to those things you once tried so hard to shelter her from.

Swearing needs to be considered as a form of language – albeit an unacceptable form. Children have heard it, so they use it. Just like any other speech habit, children feel as if they need to use it once they have heard it. Unfortunately, once obscenities have been heard they cannot be unlearned, although children can learn not to use them. Children need to learn the place of swearing within a social context. This is not to say that you condone it. Rather, it is an acceptance of the fact that your children, more than likely, will hear unacceptable language and they need to understand its use and purpose.

Children swear for many reasons and purposes. Young children learn that they will gain a terrific reaction from when they drop a clanger at the dinner table, particularly when there is company. Imagine the reaction of four-year-old Cara's parents when they heard her say, 'I saw a ★★★★ big cat at kinder today. It was ★★★★ huge.' This statement was at odds with their image of blonde, blue-eyed Cara. It brought an amusing reaction from her parents, or so Cara thought. Young children often enjoy experimenting with the use of swear words. They know that it is not correct to use them but they also know that you really do squirm when they swear. 'Now which words make them squirm and which words make them yell?' think children who have discovered this new toy.

Some children have worked out that the 'big' kids swear at school, so swearing is associated with worldliness, toughness or maturity. Children will often try to outdo each other. This is particularly the case with older primary-school boys, who have been known to turn the air blue with their utterances.

Some children learn that swearing is a great weapon to use against their parents. They know that parents are opposed to its use yet they continue to swear in the presence of elders. It is as if they are saying, 'I can swear and you can't stop me'. It is an expression of personal power, particularly when they know that their parents are sure to react strongly to their use of unacceptable language.

It is particularly distressing when children swear directly at parents. This is generally done in an effort to hurt, as a form of retaliation for a perceived injustice or when they do not get their own way. Consider how one mother felt when her nine-year-old son called her every name under the sun when she refused to give in to his demands for a new pair of fashion jeans. She felt extremely hurt that her ungrateful son was so unreasonable in his response. She recognised the purpose of the tirade and removed herself immediately from his presence. The child received no reaction from his mother so his scornful attack did not achieve its goal. He learned that swearing at his mother did not achieve anything – it merely forced her to leave him alone.

Don't overreact

It is best not to overreact when children swear. It is often helpful to look at the purpose of the swearing. When it is to gain attention, as in the case of children experimenting with language (and your response to swearing), let them know that you are unimpressed with that type of speech. Consider the mother whose five-year-old said, 'Excuse me, Mum, pass me that **** piece of paper.' Her mother did not move. The child repeated the request. Her mother replied: 'I do not like being spoken to like that. I do not wish to be around you when you talk like that.' The message needs to be made clear to children – you are unimpressed with swearing and you are willing to leave them alone when they swear. Children generally alter their behaviour when they don't receive the response that they want.

Similarly, children who swear to prove their toughness or to flex their muscles should be shown that you are unimpressed by such behaviour. Let them know that you have heard it all before and that you are not really shocked by it. One mother I know gave her eleven-year-old son, who was trying to show her how old he was, permission to swear as long as it was not in the presence of a family member. The boy soon realised that it was not much fun swearing at himself, so the bad language ceased, at least at home.

Another mother realised that she had no control over her son when he was with his friends outside the home, so she discussed the use of swearing with him. She pointed out that there were times to swear and times not to swear. There were places where swearing was more appropriate than others and there were people who did not wish to hear such language. She was one of those people. While not condoning the use of swearing, this mother accepted the fact that her son not only had been exposed to swearing but was quite conversant with its many forms. She let him know that she could not stop him from swearing but that she expected him to use language with discretion. By granting her son permission to swear within guidelines, she had removed bad language as a source of fighting at home. As with any forbidden fruit, it never tastes as sweet when we are allowed free access to it.

Other approaches

Sometimes it can be fun to make up alternative words to replace expletives. Children, like adults, can use bad language unintentionally or out of habit. It can sound terrible when a child who is concentrating on a game makes a mistake and immediately utters an obscenity. In all likelihood, this has been learned at home. Many parents I work with help their children to make up words that replace swearing. For instance, one mother related how her family had replaced swearing with names of different fruits. They had a fruit for every situation!

A commonly used approach is the penalty system. This involves all members of the family acting as watchdogs for the use of unacceptable language. When family members swear they are fined an agreed amount. One family I encountered used this effective approach in a way that benefited everyone. When anyone swore, no matter what the circumstance, that person was fined twenty cents. The money was placed in a money box that was opened once a month and was used during a family outing. The father complained at the completion of the first month that he had contributed enough for everyone to enjoy a meal out. The children delighted in their father's habit of swearing and were disappointed when he began to curb his excesses. Naturally, they were constantly on guard as to their own choice of language.

While children's swearing often brings a strong emotional response from parents, there is another type of language that children often use that potentially does far more harm – personal put-downs. A personal put-down is a negative comment about another person's appearance, gender, history or background. Children can be downright cruel with the callous remarks and taunts that they can make to each other. Make your home a 'put-down free zone'. Explain what put-downs are to children and let them know they can do a great deal of harm.

Personal put-downs violate a child's right to live and learn in a psychologically safe place and should not be tolerated. Put-downs call for quiet assertion and insistence that the language not be used in your environment. Your attitude of unacceptance will go a long way to teaching your children to leave this type of language out of their repertoire. Sometimes we can build up a tolerance for this type of language as we hear it so often in the media and within the community. But just because personal put-downs may be prevalent in the playground or in the community doesn't mean that it becomes part of your family's culture.

You are role models for children's behaviour and language. Examine your own choice of language to judge if it is an acceptable model for children. It's usual for children to approximate the language of their parents, although there may be many aberrations along the way.

MIND THE STEPS

Children swear for a number of reasons:

- to experiment with language
- to make themselves appear bigger or older than they are
- to gain attention
- to flex their muscles

Children need to learn that swearing is an unacceptable form of language in most situations.

It is best not to overreact when you hear children swear amongst their peers. Accept that you have little control over children when they are with their friends.

If a child swears at you, let her know that you do not wish to be around anyone who uses inappropriate language. Leave the child immediately.

Tantrums

The day at the zoo had been great. Moira, six, had really enjoyed seeing all the exotic animals for the first time. It was getting late and her parents had had enough for one day. 'It's time to go, dear,' her mother said. 'But Mum, I want to stay a little longer, please,' replied Moira. 'Time is getting on and the traffic will be heavy if we wait any longer,' her mother answered. 'Mum, it's not fair. I want to see the giraffes again.' 'No, Moira. We are going.'

With that, Moira flung herself on the ground, screaming and crying. Her parents, feeling embarrassed by the scene that Moira was creating, conceded and offered to take her to the giraffe enclosure one more time. Moira jumped up and cheerfully led the way to the giraffes.

Moira's temper tantrum achieved its purpose – she managed to win her own way. Temper tantrums can take many forms but they all have the same purpose – to gain the things that children want. Throwing a tantrum is a form of blackmail that is very effective in achieving a child's goal. 'Give me what I want and I'll stop making this embarrassing racket' is the message a tantrum thrower gives parents.

Children choose to throw a tantrum when they don't get their own way. They are not the victims of their emotions, as many people think. They use anger as a powerful weapon to defeat parents and teachers. So effective are tantrums that parents will often give in to children's demands to avoid creating a scene. Just the threat of a tantrum is usually enough for children to get their own way.

Children who are prone to emotional outbursts to defeat parents are generally in complete control of themselves. Watch a child who throws a tantrum when denied an ice-cream in a milk bar. She will carefully check for dangerous objects before she throws herself on the floor. She is not going to hurt herself. When her mother gives in to her blackmail she will stop her screaming and kicking immediately so that she can choose the flavour she wants. Temper tantrums, like all displays of emotion, have a goal. They are not thrown so that a child can exercise her lungs. The purpose is always to make parents give in to a child's demands.

Temper tantrums require an audience. Children always require at least one witness for a display of anger to be worthwhile. Of course, they know the bigger the audience, the greater the chance they will get their own way. So milk bars, supermarkets, trains and zoos are ideal locations for full-blown temper tantrums – although children are not averse to losing their tempers at home if they know that a parent will give in just to achieve some peace and quiet.

Recently, a mother complained that her seven-year-old daughter would scream at the top of her voice when she couldn't get what she wanted at home. The mother was confident that her daughter would grow out of the behaviour in time. It is true that the screaming may cease, but this is likely to be replaced by a more socially acceptable tantrum, such as sulking. Sulking is a quiet temper tantrum – less embarrassing, but just as disruptive as the noisy variety.

REMOVE THE AUDIENCE

Eleven-year-old Allan came home from school and asked if he could quit his tennis lessons because he didn't like his coach. His mother denied the request, saying that he should give it a little more time before deciding to stop. Allan went into a rage, accusing his mother of forcing him to do things that he didn't want to do. He slammed his schoolbag on the kitchen table. His mother was quite taken aback by his reaction and immediately left the house to give herself some breathing space. Her son followed her outside, as it was pointless shouting at the walls. Allan's mother said that she would talk with him when he was calm and went inside the house to be away from her son. He eventually calmed down and went to his bedroom and closed the door.

This mother showed that she was not willing to provide an audience for her son's temper tantrum. He regained his composure when he realised that his mother was not going to witness or bear the full brunt of his anger. After a considerable time his mother approached Allan and offered to discuss the issue of tennis lessons with him. She refrained from chiding him for his display of anger. This would be pointless, as Allan had already learned that such behaviour was ineffective in terms of achieving a result. They both agreed that he should give tennis another try and that the matter would be discussed again following the next lesson.

It is not so easy to escape a tantrum thrower in a public place. However, the same principle applies in public as in the home. In the case of Moira's tantrum at the zoo, her parents would have been better off moving away from their daughter. They could have kept an eye on her while the tantrum ran its course. When Moira realised that her anger was not achieving the desired result she would have calmed down eventually. At this point her parents only needed to say: 'I see you are ready to come home now.' There would have been no need to punish Moira for her behaviour. She would have learned at first hand that tantrums did not work with her parents.

I witnessed an effective response to a temper tantrum in my local newsagent's recently. A four-year-old boy wanted his mother to buy him a toy, which she refused to do. He immediately flung himself onto the ground right in the doorway of the shop, screaming. Unperturbed, his mother stepped over him and proceeded down the street. He scrambled to his feet and raced after her, shocked that she would consider leaving him.

This mother refused to be blackmailed by the misbehaviour of her son. She effectively deprived him of an audience through her apparent lack of concern for his tantrum. Often just reacting to children's behaviour in amusing or unexpected ways provides an effective counter to tantrums.

Don't give in

When you give into tantrums you encourage the behaviour to continue. You need to be firm and in many cases downright strong to avoid capitulating to behavioural blackmail. Often temper tantrums will increase in intensity before they cease. Rachel explained to her eldest son that television rights would be withdrawn for a day because television was the cause of too many disputes. Her son reacted angrily to this suggestion. His anger grew as he realised that his mother was taking little notice of him. He tried door slamming, to no effect. Eventually he allowed his anger to subside when he saw that it was having no impact on his mother. He resigned himself to an evening without the television.

You can't stop children from displaying their anger but you can control your own reactions. By remaining calm and refusing to give in to temper tantrums, you are sending a powerful message of your own: 'I will not be blackmailed by such behaviour. I shall respond positively to you when you behave calmly and rationally.'

MIND THE STEPS

A temper tantrum is a form of emotional blackmail that children use to get their own way.

When a child throws a tantrum it is important that you don't provide an audience for the performance. Remove yourself physically or in a psychological sense from a tantrum thrower.

Don't give in to tantrums – you will merely validate the behaviour in children's eyes.

Television Viewing

You're not watching the box again!' Nick bellowed to his children as he walked into the living room. 'You kids are always glued to that TV like zombies. No wonder homework never gets done. I bet you don't even know the name of the program that you're watching.'

Children's use of television concerns both parents and educators. Many children spend a great deal of their waking hours at home watching television. It often keeps children away from chores, homework and physical activity. And while there are many programs of considerable educational value for children, there are at least an equal number of programs that can best be described as time-fillers offering little in terms of informative or entertaining content.

The television set itself is not the problem, but rather the way it is used. It is too often used as a babysitter for children. It is easy to turn on the television to occupy children while parents are busy with other matters. The children soon become used to the 'third parent' watching over them and forget that there are many other ways that they can choose to keep themselves busy. Television occupies children and robs them of opportunities to occupy themselves.

Television is blamed for many of our social ills. While some of these criticisms may be unjustified, there is little doubt that too much television has adverse affects on children. Television viewing can encourage children to have short attention spans. Many programs are presented in short segments to accommodate advertising so that the viewer's attention is constantly being diverted from one thing to another. Television viewing does not promote conversation unless parents or teachers use it as a basis for discussion. Usually little conversation occurs between children or adults when the television is on. It invites children to be passive watchers rather than active participants. They are not often required to exercise their imaginations as they do when they read books. Children and parents often argue over the choice of programs to be watched. Used incorrectly, television can control a family. Many family routines are based around certain programs.

Television does have its good points. It is a valid form of relaxation, particularly for tired children after a hard day at school. Many programs are high in educational content. They are able to introduce children to a whole range of ideas and issues that they would not otherwise be exposed to. Research has shown that children who watch up to ten hours of television a week appear to do slightly better in school than children who watch none. However, more than ten hours of watching can lead to a decrease in performance at school.

Let television serve you

Television can be a useful asset to the family home as long as it is used wisely. It can easily become your master unless sensible rules and guidelines are established. Perhaps the most important television rule is that the usual position for the power switch is the 'off' one. In many homes the television remains on regardless of whether it is being watched or not. It should only be turned on when there is a particular program to be watched. When that program has finished then the set should be turned off. This discourages children from watching television just for the sake of it and encourages them to pursue other activities.

There are many rules to be adopted regarding television viewing. These will vary with different families. However, there are two rules that seem sensible and are applicable to every family. First, television should not be watched during mealtime. This is a time for the family to talk about the events of the day in a relatively quiet atmosphere. It provides a marvellous opportunity for conversation and a sharing of ideas as well as food.

Second, to enable families to pursue alternative forms of entertainment there should be at least one television-free night each week. Children are often surprised when they discover that there are actually other forms of entertainment. The family might play games, listen to or play music, or even share a book or a story on the television-free night. There is a whole range of activities available for families to amuse themselves when the television is turned off.

LIMITS

Children should not be allowed to watch unlimited amounts of television. A number of years ago I asked a group of ten-year-olds at a primary school to record the amount of television that they watched for a week. They were required to list the viewing times as well as the titles of the programs that they watched. I was shocked by both the amount of television viewed and the times that they were able to watch. The majority of the children watched at least two hours during week days and significantly more on weekends. The majority of children watched at least half an hour of television before coming to school. Very few limits apparently had been placed on these children regarding their viewing habits.

Television viewing can be limited in terms of hours watched each day or during the week. For instance, children could be limited to an hour per day on school days and two hours a day on weekends. Alternatively, they could be allowed to watch a set amount during the entire week with the amount varying each day. Once time limits are set, children are able to choose their programs subject to suitability within that framework. This weekly limit is much harder to control, as it is difficult to account for viewing over a longer period of time.

Consider how these two families dealt with the problem of setting limits and establishing procedures that made them the masters of the television set rather than its servants.

Geraldine's children were all television addicts until she decided it was time to change her family's viewing habits. The issue of television viewing was discussed by the whole family over a period of time. Geraldine led the discussions and made many suggestions to her children. Eventually they came up with a series of rules and limits that accommodated everyone, including Geraldine.

It was a high priority for Geraldine that her children become more critical of the programs that they chose. So her family chose the shows they were going to watch for the week from a television guide each Sunday. This encouraged them to be discriminating. She was amused at the discussions that occurred between her children as they chose their weekly programs. They would energetically debate the strengths and weaknesses of various programs in an effort to reach agreement about the choice of shows. The children had agreed that a limit of one hour per day was reasonable. They decided that Saturday would be a television-free day. This suited everyone, as they were hardly at home then anyway.

Geraldine and her husband took care to control their own viewing habits. They often discussed the quality of the programs that they intended to watch. Not wishing to set double standards, they also turned the television off when there was nothing that they wanted to watch.

Frank and Sharon's family were always in full control of their television set. It was turned off at dinner and not turned on again until the children were in bed. They had one day each week when the television remained off. Sharon took no chances and removed the aerial lead from its socket. When visitors were around, the television was generally turned off.

Frank and Sharon made an effort to offer stimulating alternatives to television. They joined with their children in playing board games and reading stories. They also videotaped many programs that the children wished to watch but were unable to due to their time limits. This taught the children to be discriminating in their choice of viewing. They also regularly discussed programs with the children to encourage them to be critical viewers rather than passive receptors.

Sharon was fairly liberal with her children about their choice of programs. She was aware that banning a show often made it appear much more desirable.

ARGUMENTS

When inevitable arguments occur over the choice of programs to be watched, the television should be turned off until the dispute is resolved. Often one child, usually the eldest, will dominate the choice of shows. This type of dispute is best handled in a conciliatory manner at a family meeting or during a group discussion. If frequent disregard for rules occurs or arguments persist, then the right to use the television should be withdrawn for a reasonable period of time.

If you want children to watch less television, you need to offer children stimulating alternatives so that they will voluntarily leave the television. The father in the first example who criticised his children for watching like zombies might have suggested that he would join them in a game outside.

Television exerts a powerful attraction on children, but there is no television invented that can kiss, cuddle or talk to a child like a parent.

MIND THE STEPS

Be in control of the television rather than the other way round.

Encourage children to exercise discretion when they choose the programs that they wish to view.

Establish sensible rules and limits for television viewing with the whole family.

Have a television-free day where alternative forms of entertainment are enjoyed.

Telling Tales

'Mum, Sam hit me, and I didn't do anything!'

'Dad, Gina hasn't done her homework and she's watching TV.'

'Melissa got into trouble today at school. She broke a window'.

'Sergey spilt the milk and he hasn't cleaned it up.'

Children often seem to take great delight in seeing their brothers and sisters on the receiving end of a punishment. This is particularly true in families where children compete with each other for parental approval. When a child draws parents' attention to a sibling's misbehaviour, she is really saying, 'I am better than my brother or sister. I wouldn't behave in such a way.' She is attempting to gain a sense of approval at her sibling's expense.

Children who regularly tell tales don't particularly want to put a stop to the behaviour which they are drawing to your attention. They generally just want you to know about the misbehaviour. Watch your children when one of them is being bellowed at or punished in some way. Will the others rush to the defence of the child who is being dealt with? Not on your life. They will be perfect angels, their virtuousness in sharp contrast to the behaviour of the 'bad' child. The 'good' children behave well, not because they want to make a contribution to the family but so they can appear better than the other child. They are being good at the expense of the misbehaving child. This is a competitive notion based on the wish to keep ahead of a brother or sister.

Tale telling is an attempt to draw you into children's disputes. You should refuse to be drawn into children's squabbles. If you respond to a tale told by a child, you rob the children of a valuable opportunity to settle their own disputes. Invariably, parents take sides when responding to a tale. This leads to a winner and a loser, a victor and a vanquished. The dispute will subside temporarily until the next opportunity to tell a tale presents itself. Responding to tales encourages sibling rivalry, as children become involved in a subtle game of one-upmanship. Getting even with the tell-tale can also become an obsession with some children.

Children of all ages are capable of resolving their own disputes. They can be given guidance but should not have their disputes settled by an adult. This implies that they are incapable of dealing with their own battles.

Pay little heed to tales

Parents should let children know that they are not interested in tales or stories about children's misbehaviour. A father was constantly besieged by petty tales, particularly from his nine-year-old daughter, who loved seeing her younger brother punished. He told her that he no longer wished to hear stories. Whenever she approached him with a tale he would tell her, 'You know I don't listen to tales' and he would leave her if she proceeded. She soon stopped the tales, as there was little point to them if her father didn't respond.

Persistent tell-tales

An excellent strategy for persistent tell-tales is to ask them to write down the tales they wish to tell. Let them know that you will only listen to stories about other children's misbehaviour if the complaints are made in writing. This has a profound effect on the incidence of tale telling. First, it ensures that only serious complaints are made, since children aren't generally too keen to take the trouble to write about tales. Second, they often cool down when writing and they realise that on reflection the misbehaviour they are reporting is rather trivial. So when children come to you with a tale, it is a good idea to direct them to the nearest piece of paper. This will test how keen they are to tell tales.

A mother at a parenting seminar told how she dealt with children's tales. When either of her two children came to her with a story about the other's misbehaviour she would ask both of them to go to their bedroom and agree to the tale being told. In reaching an agreement about the nature of the reported crime they would invariably resolve their differences.

When children have difficulty resolving disputes or have legitimate complaints about a sibling's behaviour, then they should be discussed by the entire family. You can provide valuable guidance in dealing with tales and disagreements during a family meeting, or at least at a time when the whole family can calmly resolve their differences through discussion.

MIND THE STEPS

Children generally tell tales about siblings' behaviour in an attempt to draw you into disputes.

Children are usually capable of resolving their own disputes.

Pay little heed to children's tales. Display your willingness to help children to resolve conflicts sensibly as a group and avoid taking sides as a result of listening to children's one-sided tales.

Tidiness

Children are not generally neat. There is a huge gap between children's concepts of tidiness and what adults consider to be neat. Many children are able to function easily when surrounded by mess, whereas adults tend to flounder.

Six-year-old Sam was busy drawing in the kitchen. She had spread paper, pencils and cardboard all over the table. She was easily able to locate the coloured pencils she wanted among all the clutter. When she finished her art she went to her room to obtain some construction material which she added to the mess on the kitchen table. Her mother was astounded that she could function amongst all the mess, but Sam was able to do so easily.

Untidiness, leaving toys around and forgetting to put away clothes can be annoying to many parents. In fact, the issue of tidiness is a source of conflict in many families, particularly where there are fussy parents. Although children are often unconcerned about mess, adults often see tidiness as a high priority in their homes. Children, then, must learn that mess and clutter affect others. In a family, the actions of one member often infringe on the well-being or rights of others. It is important that children learn to respect order, as its violation leads to discomfort for one or more of of the family.

Children need to learn that a certain amoung of tidiness is beneficial to them. For instance, it is easier to find toys and clothes when they are kept in drawers or stacked on shelves.

If you wish to stimulate tidiness in children, it is essential that you set a good example. A friend recently complained that his three children, who all had own bedrooms left their clothes on the floor, never made their beds and left food scraps in cupboards. He was expecting a cholera outbreak any minute! However, I had an opportunity to look in his own room and I could see little difference between it and his children's bedrooms that he so vividly described. Children need to have a good model to copy. It is pointless and unfair to expect children to be neat if you are not tidy yourselves. Children are very aware of double standards.

The matter of neatness and tidiness should be addressed by the entire family. Guidelines and procedures should be decided upon so that children and parents are aware of their responsibilities. Decide which areas are children's responsibility to keep tidy, which areas belong to the whole family and which areas are for you only. Cleaning-up procedures should also be clearly outlined. You should communicate to youngsters your expectations about tidiness. When agreement has been reached about neatness, you should not constantly remind children about their tasks. Children learn best about order and tidiness when they experience the discomfort of disorder and untidiness.

Common areas

There are many areas in a house that are commonly used by all the family. Living rooms, family rooms, bathrooms and kitchens are places to which everyone has access. Establish areas for playing, studying and quiet activity. Children should know where they can play with toys and where they can't. For instance, establish that bath toys are permitted in the bathroom but not cricket bats and balls. Simple rules about tidiness in various areas should be generated. The following rules for common areas were suggested by a participant at a parenting program.

- Toys must be put them away by those who used them.
- Toys must be cleared away before a new game is started.
- All children's things are to be cleaned away before dinner.
- Clothes are to be left in bedrooms, not in living areas.
- Food is to be eaten while sitting down.

These procedures evolved over a period of time. They are commonsense rules that serve this family very well. The children helped to formulate them and generally stick to them as they feel that they own the rules. They weren't imposed on them by their parents.

Discuss with children reasonable consequences for untidiness. Toys left in common areas should be confiscated for a period of time. If children have the right to play in family areas, they have the responsibility to clean up after them. Some children may need some assistance but usually they're quite capable of cleaning away their toys. Many parents place toys which are left lying around in a deposit box, which the children are allowed to empty once a week.

Clothes left lying around in living areas can be placed in a clothes box. They remain in the box until children get them out. This often causes considerable inconvenience to children, particularly if a favourite piece of clothing remains unwashed. An effective variation of this method is the hide-and-seek game. Clothes thrown on the floor or left in family areas are hidden in an obscure place. Children are informed about the hidden items and may look for them. Children find this fun at first but it soon grows tedious, particularly when they are in a hurry.

If children are continually messy in a commonly used room, they should lose the right to use the area. For instance, one family constantly left food scraps in the television room. Their mother suggested that food could not be eaten in there for a week. She withdrew the right to eat in that room to teach her children respect for order. The same consequence applied to the adults.

Your expectations of children's tidiness should be realistic. A mother I know was so fussy about mess that her four-year-old son ceased to play with his construction toys. He claimed that he spent more time cleaning up than playing with his toys.

BEDROOM TIDINESS

Some bedrooms look like a tornado has struck and others are quite orderly. There appears to be no evidence that girls keep tidier rooms than boys. Both sexes are equally capable of keeping rooms messy. Many parents become engaged in running battles with youngsters over the cleanliness of bedrooms. Children should be responsible for the state of their own rooms. Bedrooms are their sanctuaries.

Young children need considerable daily assistance to maintain their rooms in an orderly fashion. They should assist in making their beds, putting clothes away and keeping floors clear of junk. In this way they can develop the skills needed to maintain their own rooms. Giving them small tasks, such as arranging teddies on beds and putting shoes away, stimulates independence.

As their skills develop you can give children more responsibility for their own rooms. Give them the choice to keep their bedroom tidy or allow them to be disorganised. Children can be stimulated into keeping bedrooms tidy if they feel the consequences of untidiness. These three examples demonstrate how consequences can be used to induce a sense of order and illustrate the benefits of keeping bedrooms tidy.

Monica refused to enter the shared bedroom of her nine- and eleven-year-old boys because it was too untidy. She allowed them to keep their room as they wished but she explained that she was unwilling to go into rooms that resembled a war zone. She left their clean clothes folded outside the room for the boys to put away and she would not read them a story in bed. Instead, she indicated that she was willing to read to them on the couch. The boys responded positively to this approach when they found they were inconvenienced by her actions. Monica didn't tell the boys what to do; she told them how she would react to an untidy room.

John, ten, raced into the kitchen and said to his mother: 'I can't find my footy boots and the bus will be here in five minutes.' She replied: 'I wouldn't know where to start looking.' John learned that it is difficult to find things in an untidy room.

Sonia's family agreed that bedrooms were children's, to keep as they wished. They agreed that it was reasonable to clean rooms before visitors arrived. Eight-year-old Damon asked if his friend Peter could come over to play. Sonia replied: 'Sure, but do you think he can play in your room in the state it is in?' 'No,' Damon said grudgingly. The choice was clear to Damon – keep the room messy and play with Peter elsewhere or clean it up and use it.

Twelve-year-old Eva didn't have any clean school uniforms. She had left them all in a pile beside her bed. She complained to her mother that she had nothing clean to wear to school. Her mother replied: 'I only wash clothes put in the dirty washing pile in the laundry. You know what to do about it.'

A regular weekend overhaul of bedrooms is often welcomed by many children. At times rooms can become so messy that children are simply overwhelmed with clutter – they don't know where to start to tidy up. Together with your children you can tidy rooms, discussing different ways of organising toys, clothes and various knick-knacks. This should be a pleasant sharing activity rather than an opportunity for an adult to criticise a child's untidy ways.

Shared rooms

Sharing bedrooms often presents problems when one child is neat and the other is untidy. You can be easily drawn into temptation to interfere in the children's affairs. They may be assisted to establish some procedures which they both agree to. Help them to work through the dispute rather than resolve it for them.

MIND THE STEPS

Children are not generally as tidy around the house as adults. They can, however, learn that a certain amount of neatness is beneficial to them. They must also realise that you may require different standards of tidiness.

Establish common cleanliness procedures for different areas of the house and use consequences to maintain a respect for order.

Ensure that you set a reasonable standard of tidiness for children to follow.

Whining

Eve struggled in the front door after a day at work. She had just picked up her three children from two different child minders. Simon, eight, was minded by a friend after school, while four-year-old twins Emily and Sasha spent the day in a creche. As soon as Eve placed her bag down she was besieged by requests. 'Mum, can I have a drink?' asked Sasha. 'I'm hungry,' chimed in Emily. 'Ah Mum, my stomach hurts,' Simon added. 'What's for dinner?' Emily said, reminding her mother that she was hungry. 'Mum, I'm thirsty' ...

Like Chinese water torture, constant whining works slowly and persistently. Each whinge and whine is like another drop of water on the victim's forehead. 'Mum' ... drip ... 'It's not fair!' drip ... 'You never do anything for me' ... drip ... 'I've got a headache' ... drip ... 'Muuuum!' drip ... 'All right kids. I give in! Have what you want. Just give me some peace!' moaned Eve.

Whining is a common way for young children to gain parents' attention or get their own way. It is a very effective tactic because it is difficult to ignore. Whining children typically develop a tone of voice that sounds like a wounded animal crying. Children often whinge when they are tired, but everyone else shouldn't have to suffer because of their lack of sleep. There are many approaches you can use when faced with whining children.

Don't give in

You should not give in to children's unacceptable behaviour as this only encourages them to continue. Children are usually well aware of those behaviours that work in terms of getting their own way. While it is easy to vie in to a child's whining, this is really reinforcing that way of acting. Peace and quiet will be achieved in the short term but the whining will recur at another time. Children maintain the behaviours that achieve their goal and discard those that have no effect on parents.

Whining children should be ignored. Some parents have the ability to tune out from annoying behaviours. They are a breen, though – not many people can remain in the vicinity of a fully-fledged whiner without capitulating. If you are in danger of losing your temper or caving in, then it is best to get as far away from the child as possible. This may mean going into a bedroom and shutting the door, or leaving the house for a while. Whingeing seems somehow easier to bear outside.

Sometimes it is impossible to put space between you and a whinger, particularly when you are engaged in a task that you can't leave. One mother I know invested in a stereo headset and wore it when her children whined or made unfair demands on her. Her children were infuriated when their whingeing fell on extremely deaf ears. They particularly disliked it when she would sing out loud to a tune on the radio while they were in full cry. 'How dare Mum be happy when I'm whining. It's not fair.'

Sometimes older children engage in the odd spot of whingeing. Usually it is sufficient to make them aware that they are whining. 'Melissa, you are talking to me in a horrible tone of voice.' This brings the behaviour to their attention and leaves them with the option of changing.

A successful strategy used by many parents is to let children know that you are only willing to do anything if asked properly. In this way you are not telling children what to do, rather you are informing them of your behaviour. This is a powerful way of achieving a behavioural change. Six-year-old Melanie whined to her father, 'Dad, I want a drink.' Her father replied: 'Melanie, I only get drinks for people who use manners and speak properly.' The onus was on Melanie to change her behaviour if she wanted to elicit her father's assistance. She learned that the only way to obtain help was to use manners and a reasonable tone of voice.

Do the unexpected

Children are the actors and parents are the reactors. Parents often respond to misbehaviours in predictable ways that invariably ensure that they continue. To avoid knee-jerk reactions to misbehaviours, it is sometimes effective to do the unexpected when children misbehave. For instance, a mother told me of her nine-year-old son's total dismay at her unpredictable response to a bout of his whingeing. After listening to him whine about the food, the weather and whatever else he could think of, she replied, 'Thanks Peter, that was great. I really enjoy it when you whine at me. Come and sit down and whinge about a few more things.' She sat down and pulled out a chair for her son who looked at her as if she had just arrived from Mars. 'That's not how mothers are supposed to act,' he told her and went off to his room, scratching his head.

Children are quite happy to offload all their complaints onto parents, but watch them run if you do the same. When a child whinges to you, try giving him the same treatment. 'I'm sorry to hear about your sore leg, Matthew, but my back is aching and I've been on my feet all day. I think I'm coming down with a cold as I'm getting a nasty throat. My neck is a bit stiff and ...' Keep it up until your child retreats to another part of the house to escape a whingeing parent. It is nice for a change!

Whining is an irritating misbehaviour which children use to gain attention or get their own way. It is essential that you do not cave in to demands made by whingeing children. If the behaviour does not achieve its goal it will cease in time –

children will not engage in any activity that does not serve a purpose. Whining will stop if you don't give in for the sake of peace and quiet.

MIND THE STEPS

Recognise that children whine to gain attention or their own way. React to whining in a way that defeats the purpose of the behaviour.

Respond to your child's whining in unexpected ways, such as telling him of your own aches and pains. This often defeats the purpose of whingeing.

PUBERTY AND BEYOND

What's a section on puberty and adolescence doing in a book on three to twelve year olds, you might ask. The whole ethos of this book has been to encourage parents to think about the issues and concerns their children might face as they grow so that if or when they occur, parents can respond positively and confidently.

It's never too early to think about the fact that your children will not be children forever; to have your eye on the big picture and to see your role as parent as one in which everything you do throughout their childhood will help them grow to become healthy and happy adults. It is fitting then to end this book with some advice on the kinds of things you and your child will face during what will be the most dramatic transition you'll experience together.

Puberty, the stage when children make the transition to adolescence can be a difficult time. Not quite children and not yet adolescents they are caught in a kind of limbo. It can be a sad and scary time for young people. Many look back at their childhood and realise that they can never really act the same way yet they look ahead and realise that adolescence will present them with its own peculiar challenges.

The onset of their child's puberty can come as quite a shock for many parents who have been enjoying the relative ease of middle childhood. Many parents suddenly discover that they have a son for whom everything 'sucks' or that their formerly very communicative daughter becomes sullen or morose. Parents often discover that their authority is challenged seriously for the first time and that the opinions of their children's friends carry more weight than their own considered views.

Children are reaching adolescence earlier than ever. The World Health Organisation has estimated that in Western Countries puberty begins about three months earlier every ten years. In Australia many girls have begun menstruation well before their thirteenth birthday, with 95% having begun breast development by that age. Boys begin puberty about eighteen months later than girls with many showing pubic hair development at the age of twelve although many will not, which is perfectly normal too.

Puberty is a stage of immense body changes. The body grows at a faster rate than at any time except in the womb. Male and female sex hormones set off different development in both boys and girls. Girls are often far more mature and 'worldly' than boys at this stage who can feel gawky, gangly and very awkward. Bodily changes are more evident for girls and are accompanied by huge mood swings, which can be disconcerting for parents. Testosterone, the male hormone also affects mood swings in boys but it usually leads to increased energy and activity. Boys' appetites are legendary around puberty increasing to account for growth spurts and bursts of energy. These increases in appetite are just a precursor to the insatiable appetites of boys in full-blown adolescence. Both girls and boys usually need more sleep during puberty than in previous years and they have a need for greater privacy so they spend more and more time in bedrooms, locked in bathrooms or arguing with younger siblings about personal space. This can also become a point of frustration for younger siblings who just can't figure out why they are being left out of the picture by their big brother or sister or why they are unwilling to play the same games as they always have.

A CRUEL AGE

Children in the pre-teen age group can be cruel to each other. Girls, in particular, can exclude other children from their social groups on the slightest pretext. Becoming more image conscious some pre-teens will align themselves with peers who follow certain fashions or admire certain music groups. Girls at this age tend to form exclusive friendship groups or have best friends whereas boys form larger friendship groups usually according to interest such as sport. It doesn't help to be different or step apart from the crowd during this stage. Early maturing girls and late maturing boys seem to be the two groups most likely to experience social difficulties associated with pre-teens' intolerance of difference.

Pre-teens often engage in new experiences and like to experiment and find things out for themselves. This is a stage when young people will often try their first cigarette or alcoholic drink. Parents often become very alarmed when they discover such behaviours but in many cases it is simply a matter of trying new experiences and doesn't mean that those behaviours will continue.

Window of opportunity for parents

It may be stating the blindingly obvious but puberty is a great time to work your relationship with your child – especially if it is a little shaky. Relationships are based on a foundation of trust. Shared interests, encouragement and a sense of mutual regard are the building blocks of parent-child relationships. Sometimes fathers in particular leave it too late to spend time with their children and they try to build relationships during adolescence, which presents huge challenges. Girls can leave their fathers out in the cold and boys sometimes like to challenge their fathers and enter a battle of wits with them. It is easier to navigate through the difficulties and challenges of adolescence if you have developed a strong relationship through the earlier years. During puberty it is crucial that you work at keeping the lines of communication open.

SECONDARY SCHOOL

Unfortunately the physical and emotional changes of puberty are accompanied by the transition to secondary school, which places its own demands on young people. Being at the bottom of the school pecking order where they are unsure of the playground rules and school procedures is just one adjustment to make. They have many subject teachers, which can be disconcerting when they are used to forming a relationship with just one teacher. Changing classrooms for each subject, reading a timetable, altering eating habits and carrying a load of books around is difficult enough without the added task of meeting and making new friends. Some kids take these experiences in their stride but it is natural to experience some difficulty making the transition from primary to secondary school. It is no coincidence that a number of research projects indicate that children's learning levels out in Year 7, presumably as the social task of readjustment takes precedence over academic performance.

This period can be unsettling, so parents need to be understanding of their child's circumstances, supportive and prepared to listen if they are having difficulties. It also helps to take a positive attitude during this time. Kids can think that this unsettled time will last forever, so help them understand that they will readjust and soon get used to their new school. Talk up the positive aspects of secondary school such as the new subjects they are studying or the new sporting or interest activities that they can undertake.

Children's early attempts at making new friends at secondary school can sometimes be distressing for parents. During the early days of secondary school children just want to fit in with the crowd so they can form friendships with the most unlikely children or those whom their parents may disapprove of. It often takes kids a couple of attempts to form their friendships groups so relax if your child at first becomes friendly with someone whom you think is unsuitable. Children after a few attempts will eventually find a peer group that suits them and meets their particular social needs.

Information about their development

Children need information about what happens to their bodies and also their emotions during puberty. They will often tell their parents that they know everything that there is to know about sexuality but in actual fact they often know very little. Boys as well as girls need to be prepared for the physical and emotional changes they will experience. In many ways boys are often more ill-prepared for puberty than girls. Menstruation is obviously a momentous event that signals major changes for girls. Most girls these days are given information prior to their first period and a great deal of information during the early phases as they learn to cope. But because there is no obvious event that effects boys, they are often not given the information they require. Puberty for boys begins when their testes enlarge and the first signs of pubic hair appear. They need to be told by a loving caring adult about the changes that they will experience both physically, hormonally and socially.

Renegotiate responsibilities

Consider giving pre-teens new responsibilities that challenge them at home rather than more of the same jobs they have always done. Give them some prestige and an opportunity to stretch themselves with challenging responsibilities such as cooking an evening meal, shopping or even doing their own washing and ironing. Resist telling them what to do all the time but let them work out their own systems and allow them to learn from their experiences. If you have to wait half an hour for a meal because their timing is out or a child forgets to buy the milk they will learn from the experience. Real delegation means that parents have to stand back a little and allow young people to figure things out for themselves. Pre-teens really need to be allowed to use their resourcefulness and initiative in the relatively safe environment of home.

MAKE SURE YOUR HOUSE IS TEEN-FRIENDLY

You know you have a teenager in the house when they want to spend more time with their peers than they do with their parents. During puberty children will begin to do things with their friends that they used to want to do with their parents, which can be a little hurtful. However it is a sign that children are ready to break away and want some independence. It is a good idea at this stage to make sure your house is peer-friendly so that your child feels that he or she can bring their friends into your home. In this way you can get to know his or her peers and will know where they are – at least some of the time.

Some ideas to make your home teen-friendly:

- Your children's friends are welcome at any reasonable time of the day.
- Phone calls from young people are given a friendly welcome.
- Talk to your children's friends. Take an interest in what they are doing without prying.
- If possible, make an area of the house available where they can chat, listen to music or watch television.
- Keep plenty of food handy. Pre-pubescent and adolescent boys like to eat and eat. Their appetites may keep you poor but at least you know where they are.

TALK ABOUT REAL-LIFE ISSUES

Young people these days face a range of issues that we didn't face at their age. Alcohol, drugs, depression and suicide are just some of the issues that young people are conversant with. So make sure that you discuss these real-life issues with children as they move into adolescence. Establish an openness and a willingness to discuss such issues so that children can feel comfortable talking with you. Resist the temptation to lecture or be too moralistic about behaviours. Adolescents are on a fairly serious voyage of discovery and often want a sounding board for their experiences and their views. At this stage it is your willingness to talk and discuss some of life's tough issues that is vital rather than the information you can provide.

ADOLESCENCE

Adolescents have a poor public image. If you were to take notice of some media coverage of young people you couldn't help but think that most teenagers are drug-crazed, sexually rampant gorillas intent on creating mayhem. Take note that the majority of kids make it through adolescence unscathed, although they will invariably give their parents and teachers a few headaches along the way.

It helps for parents to know what is normal and what's not. Following is a list of ten common problems, behaviours or issues that many parents of adolescents encounter.

1. **My teenager thinks about three things – sex, sex and sex.** Anyone who can remember their own adolescence would realise that sex and sexuality is a pretty big issue for this age group.

   Don't be surprised if your son sticks pictures of scantily clad females all over his bedroom wall or your daughter displays posters of males from the entertainment industry. Both sexes are obsessed with body image. While many teenage boys spend time building up their pecs, over 50% of teenage girls diet at some stage.

Younger adolescents like to talk about sex and tell each other and their parents grubby jokes. Much of a teenager's talk about sex is just that – talk. It is in the later adolescent years when kids will actually try to put into practise what they only fantasised about in earlier years.

2. **I can't live with the mood swings.** Sometimes the smallest thing can trigger a noisy emotional outburst from a teenager. The slightest remark about their appearance or even a harmless joke can send teenagers stomping off to their bedrooms shouting 'leave me alone'. Often there is no real reason for bad moods. When asked what's wrong they may answer truthfully, 'Nothing' or 'I don't know'. Frustratingly for adults many teens will resist any attempts to cheer them up giving the impression that they actually enjoy their bad mood.

   Hormones can be partially blamed for the mood swings but more than likely they are influenced by a combination of factors. Teenagers are experiencing an enormous number of physical, social and psychological changes all at once, which can be confusing. It is helpful if they have somewhere such as a bedroom to retreat to rather than inflict their mood on others.

   But while moodiness seems to be normal, if it continues, then it may be a sign that something is really troubling them and that help is needed.

3. **My teenager no longer wants to be part of the family.** Teenagers, particularly the eldest, often don't want to join in with the rest of the family activities. 'It's childish', 'It's kids stuff' are words often on their lips.

   It can come as quite a shock when an adolescent refuses to participate in family activities particularly birthdays or gatherings that involve grandparents and broader family. Sometimes the only way to entice a teenager to join everyone on an outing or even a holiday is to allow them to take a friend. One of the challenges of adolescence is to gain a sense of individual identity so some opting out of mainstream family events is to be expected. But while it's sensible to be flexible and allow your teen to opt out of some activities you'll need to be firm that other family events such as birthdays are non-negotiable.

In wanting the rights of an adult but only taking on the responsibilities of a child some teens stop helping out around the house at this time too. Parents need to gently but firmly point out that rights and responsibilities are linked and even though there may be heaps happening in their lives a little help is still required around the house.

4. **The peer group rules.** A significant authority shift occurs when children become teenagers. The opinion of peers suddenly carries far more weight than yours. In early adolescence physical appearance becomes important which is influenced by acceptability in the eyes of peers. Wearing unfashionable footwear or sporting the wrong type of hairstyle can mean instant ostracism from a peer group; wearing an acceptable label on their clothing or even having the right parts of their bodies pierced can be a very big deal to them.

   Membership of a peer group often becomes an obsession during middle adolescence as young people identify with particular forms of music, icons and even lifestyles. It is ironic that in their search to be individuals adolescents go to great lengths to resemble each other.

   But things haven't changed much. I recall spending most of my sixteenth year dressed in the uniform of a surfer – ugh boots, flannelette shirts with button up collars, long blond hair and Neil Young music were de rigueur. The fact that I had never actually seen a wave let alone surfed one was irrelevant. The important aspect was that I felt that I belonged to a group.

Peer groups help adolescents bridge the gap as they separate from their family and develop their own opinions and learn to stand on their own two feet. But while most peer groups are relatively harmless, acceptance to some groups is linked to participation in dangerous or illegal behaviours. If you're concerned that your child might be getting involved with the wrong crowd, it's important not to panic and start interrogating him or her – they'll only clam up. Keep those lines of communication open and you've got a better chance that your teen will come to you if they feel out of their depth or if they do get themselves into trouble.

5. **Parents know nothing and are complete dags.** The young child who may have looked up to his or her parents as wise and possessing some savvy as an adolescent reminds them about how little they actually know. Teen-agers commonly think that theirs is the first generation to reach puberty. 'You just don't understand. You don't know what its like ...' is a type of anthem that blocks parents' attempts at making themselves heard.

   Fathers often suffer from the Clark Kent syndrome when their sons reach full-blown adolescence. Young boys invariably put their fathers on a pedestal holding them in some superman-type awe. However, when they reach fifteen or sixteen they go to great lengths to prove that their fathers like Clark Kent are human and fallible.

   This fall from grace can be hurtful for many parents – especially when your teenager insists on being dropped off three blocks from any function or walks ten paces behind if you are in public together. But don't worry, their rejection of you will not last forever.

6. **My teenager is in trouble at school and shows little interest in schoolwork.** With so much going on in kids' lives it is a rare individual who can keep his or her nose clean throughout secondary school. Often problems at school occur around Year 8 or 9 when the novelty of secondary school wears off and detentions, the occasional truancy and skipped homework become a badge of honour for some kids. Children who have learning difficulties often get by in primary school but will give up or display a lack of interest in all things educational in secondary school rather than appear inadequate or stupid in front of their peers.

   While some problems may just blow over parents may need some assistance when kids mess up or display little interest in school. The best course of action is to work together with your child's school to find the source of the problems and formulate some type of plan to get your adolescent back on track.
7. **I know my teenager drinks alcohol.** The legal age for drinking maybe eighteen but the reality of adolescent alcohol consumption is quite different. Recent Australian research shows that over one third of fifteen-year-olds drink regularly (not just experimenting). Those teenagers who drink do so at weekends and will often binge on alcohol becoming excessively drunk. The harm minimisation approach that has been adopted by Australian health and educational professionals encourages those who work with and raise teens to teach them to drink sensibly and responsibly. Alcohol is a pervasive part of our culture so teens need to be encouraged and taught to drink safely and in a socially acceptable way.
8. **My teenager is smoking.** Many kids will have choked on their first cigarette or raided their parents' liquor cabinet

before they reach adolescence. Twelve or thirteen is a time for experimentation in many behaviours that belong to the adult world. But often one sip of spirits or a few puffs of a cigarette are enough to satisfy their curiosity – for a while at least.

Despite the health promotion campaigns teenagers are still lighting up – approximately 30% of fifteen- and sixteen-year-olds smoking regularly. Research indicates that the longer a teenager puts off deciding to smoke the less likely he or she is of taking up the habit.

Despite the fact that it is illegal to sell cigarettes to children and that smoking is harmful, expensive and not too bright, smoking remains a matter of personal choice. Although it might seem there's little you can do to stop it, you might try to point out to your teen that the average smoker spends around $4000 on cigarettes over two years – enough for that first car or overseas trip your teen will soon be dreaming about.

9. **My teenager spends long periods in his or her bedroom.** It is common for a teenager to spend long periods in his or her bedroom doing very little – perhaps, playing music or just 'mucking around'. This can be extremely disconcerting if you believe that kids should be productive and always making the best use of their time. But time alone is not necessarily time wasted. Adolescence is a confusing time so young people often need to be alone to reflect, to daydream and draw on their inner resources.
10. **My teenager always wants more money.** It is the universal law of adolescence that teenagers never have enough of the folding stuff. Many moody teens will suddenly become communicative and extremely obliging when they put the sting on their parents for some hard-earned cash. Does this approach sound familiar? 'Mum, do

you want some help? By the way can you please loan me $10? I am meeting my friends down at the hamburger place.' Astute observers will notice that teenagers will always round the amount up to the nearest ten when they want money and they never give back change.

Rather than continually increasing the pocket money or forking out for every whim, encourage your teen to take on a part-time job. Not only will this provide some extra cash but it may teach him or her some valuable job skills, as well as how to manage their money.

Parenting adolescents is a little like a roller coaster ride. When you get on you know there are thrills ahead but you never quite know what is around the next corner. It can be disconcerting knowing that much of the ride is out of your control but you need to hang on for dear life because you also know that you can't get off once you have started. But the ride does end and you will look back on the highs and lows, the twists and turns and realise that you have just been on the ride of your life – and you survived!

Good luck, keep your eyes open and enjoy the ride!

RESOURCES

For assistance with specific issues and problems try your local council. Most councils offer a range of options for parents, including resources on parenting, and can also put you in touch with other helpful associations. Your child's school or pre school should have access to a list of resources available in your local area too.

Following are some websites and books you may also find useful.

On the Web

www.Parentingideas.com.au
This is my site and it contains free articles and on-line parenting programs.

www.Essentialbaby.com.au
Ideas, chatrooms and advice about raising young children.

www.Boxplanet.com.au
Good Australian general family site for information about family issues.

www.Parenthoodweb.com
Comprehensive site with advice, articles, Question & Answer, range of ages.

www.Parenting.org
Good site for help and general information.

www.Parenting.sa.gov.au
Quality information about a range of ages and issues.

BOOKS

Balson, Maurice, *Becoming Better Parents*, ACER, Melbourne, 1981

Biddulph, Steve, *Raising Boys*, Finch Publishing, Sydney, 1997

Burns, E. Timothy, From Risk to Resilience, Marco Polo, Dallas, 1996

Colorosso, Barbara, *Kids Are Worth It!* Lothian, Melbourne, 1995

Court, John, *The Puberty Game,* HarperCollins, Melbourne, 1997

Darvill, Wendy and Powell, Kelsey, *The Puberty Book,* Newleaf, Dublin, 2001

Dreikurs, Rudolf, *Children: The Challenge,* E.P. Dutton, New York, 1987

Faber, A & Mazlish, E, *How to Talk to Kids so Kids Will Listen & Listen so Kids Will Talk,* Avon Books, New York, 1980

Goleman, Daniel, *Emotional Intelligence*, Bantam, New York, 1995

Gottman, John, *The Heart of Parenting,* Bloomsbury, London, 1997

Hardiman, Michael, *Healing Life's Hurts*, Newleaf, Dublin, 2001

Humphreys, Tony, *Self-esteem: The Key to Your Child's Future*, Newleaf, Dublin, 2002

Ó Donnchadha, Réamonn, *The Confident Child*, Newleaf, Dublin, 2000

Pollack, William, *Real Boys,* Scribe Publications, Australia, 1998

Rodd, Jillian, *Understanding Young Children,* Allen & Unwin, Australia, 1996

Schmidt Neven, Ruth, *Emotional Milestones,* ACER, Australia, 1996

Seligman, Martin, *The Optimistic Child,* Random House, Australia, 1995

Sulloway, Frank, *Born to Rebel,* Abacus, London, 1996